Emerging Voices:
Women in Contemporary Irish Society

by

Pat O'Connor

For
Sheila – in sadness
Stella – in gratitude
Emma, Suz, Mags, Claire and Lizzie – in hope

Emerging Voices:
Women in Contemporary Irish Society

by

Pat O'Connor

First published 1998
by the Institute of Public Administration,
57–61 Lansdowne Road,
Dublin, Ireland

British Library Cataloguing in Publication Data

ISBN 1 872002 74 9

Cover design by Butler Claffey Design, Dún Laoghaire

Typeset by Typeform Repro
Printed by Smurfit Print, Dublin

Author

PAT O'CONNOR is Professor of Sociology and Social Policy at the University of Limerick. She has been a teacher and researcher for almost thirty years. Before taking up her present position, she was director of the MA in Women's Studies at the University of Limerick. She has worked at the ESRI, Dublin; the University of London; the National Institute for Social Work, London; and Waterford Institute of Technology.

Professor O'Connor has published widely on women's issues. In 1992 her *Friendship Between Women* was nominated by *Choice* as an outstanding academic book. She has published extensively in British and American sociology journals on friendship, mother/daughter relationships and sister/sister relationships. She has also published articles in the *Economic and Social Review* on women in rural tourism. Her most recent publication is *Barriers to Women's Promotion in the Health Boards*, published in 1994.

Acknowledgments

My debts of gratitude are many and varied. They are owed firstly to Tony McNamara for his patience in enabling me to take the time to complete and revise the manuscript. Jim O'Donnell (IPA) and John Jackson (TCD) contracted the work and I am indebted to them and to Sylvia Walby (University of Leeds), Graham Allan (University of Southampton), and two anonymous readers for perceptive comments and helpful advice.

I owe a special debt of gratitude to the women of the 60s, 70s, 80s and 90s who made it possible to speak and write about the position of women in Irish society. The 90s have seen an increasing number of such voices emerging – focusing on different themes and issues. Nevertheless, a focus on women still appears problematical – an idea captured by Susan Liddy in the title of a recent conference and one which she has been gracious enough to let me use.

I am grateful to the students and staff at the University of Limerick who have deepened my understanding of the position of women in Irish society in more ways than they can imagine. The University Research Achievement Award gave me the space to finalise the manuscript and in this context I would like to thank Professors Stuart Hampshire (DR), Geraldine Sheridan (ADR), Eddie Moxon Browne (previous ADR), Colin Townsend (DH) and Nick Rees (HOD). Stella Reeves has yet again undertaken the arduous task of proof reading with her customary efficiency and good humour while Carmel Gould, Sandra O'Shea, Grace Anderson, Sharon Cleary and Sharon O'Donnell helped at various times with the typing of the preliminary drafts, etc. The Library staff at the University of Limerick have been extraordinarily helpful: without them no academic work would be possible.

Finally, I would like to thank the many people who in their very different ways have given me the courage to finish the text, especially Stella and Tommy Reeves, Marian McNamara, Denis Doherty, Chris Whelan, Deirdre O'Toole, Graham Allan, Noel Whelan, Peggy and Patrick Caffrey, Edward Walsh, Bernadette Whelan, Michael Shanahan, Claire O'Connor – and of course, Emma, Suz, Mags, Claire and Lizzie.

Contents

1

Understanding the Position of Women in Contemporary Ireland

Introduction

ANY discussion of changes in the position of women in Irish society over the past thirty years tends to elicit two views: that it has changed completely, and that it has not changed at all. It is easy to find evidence for both statements. Those endorsing the first view draw attention to the fact that, for example, since the early 1970s, different wage scales for men and women have been abolished; the 'marriage bar', obliging women to retire on marriage from a variety of jobs in the public service, has been lifted; inequalities based on gender have been substantially eliminated from the social welfare system; legal entitlement to maternity leave, without the possibility of dismissal, has been established; divorce has been introduced and extra-marital births have increased dramatically, both in absolute terms and as a proportion of total births.

On the other hand it can be argued that many elements in the lives of Irish women have not changed. Irish women are still under-represented in the political system, at the higher echelons of the economic system and in the institutional church structure. Like other European women, their average wage is lower than men's; they are usually huddled into a small range of paid occupations, predominantly service ones; and they typically carry the main responsibility for domestic and child care activities. In addition, and in contrast to their European counterparts, the participation of Irish married women in the labour force, although it has increased dramatically over the past twenty years, is still lower than the European average; issues surrounding sexuality, especially abortion, are highly emotive, and the ideology of the family is still firmly embedded in the Irish Constitution.

Continuities and changes in the position of women in Irish society need to be located in a wider social and cultural context. This too is a complex reality, despite the fact that the total population is very small indeed (3.6 million in 1996) and the labour force even smaller (1.5 million in 1996). Up to the late 1980s the economic situation was 'one of crisis – the most obvious manifestations of which were mass unemployment, emigration, a massive public debt and sluggish economic growth' (O'Connell, 1996). Gross Domestic Product (GDP) is generally viewed as an indicator of a country's economic well-being. At 3.1 per cent Ireland's GDP was among the lowest in Europe from the early 1970s to the late 1980s (Hearn, 1995). At the end of the 1980s Breen *et al* (1990:209) concluded that

> Despite the enormously bloated role of the state as an economic intermediary, it has been monumentally unsuccessful either in ensuring sustained economic growth or in moderating inegalitarian tendencies . . .

Yet in the 1990s, the Irish economy experienced a period of remarkable growth. In 1995, real growth in GDP, at over 10 per cent, was the fastest in the industrialised world. It has slowed down somewhat since then but nevertheless it is expected that the economy will continue to grow at around 6 per cent (The Economist Intelligence Unit, 1997). Hearn (1995) argued that the use of GDP as a measure of economic well-being has been misleading since it ignored both the outflows of repatriated profits to transnational corporations and the interest paid by the Irish government on the national debt. He suggested that Gross National Product (GNP) would be a more accurate measure of real economic well-being. In 1993 Irish GNP was 15 per cent below the GDP level, so our economic well-being, using this measure, was less satisfactory.

Nevertheless the increase in employment in Ireland in the mid 1990s was the highest in the EU and led to the identification of Ireland as the Celtic Tiger. O'Connell (1996:2) noted that this 'sudden transformation – from sick man of Europe to European tiger – appears to have misconstrued the gender of the animal'. Between 1971 and 1996, 90 per cent of the growth in employment was in women's employment (Central Statistics Office, 1997), a pattern which although extreme is not atypical, as evidenced by the feminisation of the wider European labour market (see Chapter 7).

Ireland became a member of the European Community in 1973, and although it is difficult to distinguish between the effects of such membership and other national and international developments, it has clearly impacted on Irish society at many levels. At a very practical level, over the 1973-95 period, direct EU funding to Ireland amounted to IR£21,000 million; and over that period Irish per capita GDP rose from 58 per cent of the European Community average in 1973 to 87 per cent in 1996 (Department of Foreign Affairs, 1996). It is widely accepted that, legally and politically, membership of the EU has impacted positively on the position of women in Irish society, although it is clear that many of the changes occurring in the position of women in Irish society are also occurring in a wider European context.

The approach adopted in this book will recognise the usefulness but also the limitations of cross-national comparisons. The complex nature of an Irish cultural and social reality is evident from the fact that the overwhelming majority (96 per cent) of the population have a religious affiliation – overwhelmingly Catholic (Hornsby-Smith and Whelan, 1994). Furthermore this has been reflected in a high level of weekly church attendance (81 per cent: Hornsby-Smith and Whelan, 1994). A recent MRBI (1998) study suggested that church attendance was falling dramatically, with only 58 per cent of Catholics attending mass weekly or more often. Nevertheless, this figure was still considerably higher than the European average (30 per cent). Ireland has experienced a dramatic decline in the acceptance of the authority of the institutional church and state. This indeed was reflected in the MRBI (1998) study insofar as just over three quarters of the respondents thought that recent scandals involving Bishop Casey and Fr Brendan Smyth had damaged church authority a lot. Mahon (1995) suggested that the European perception of Ireland as a predominantly patriarchal society emerged because of its 'traditional stance' on reproductive rights and the low participation of women in the labour force. In this context the 'peculiarities' of Ireland, insofar as they exist, are said to arise from the dominance of the church and from state employment policies which inhibited women's participation in paid employment. The influence of the Roman Catholic Church, culturally and socially, is still considerable in Ireland and, in collaboration with the state, it has continued to foster a particular definition of the position of woman.

Nevertheless in Ireland as in other European countries, policies concerned with equality in the broad area of employment opportunity have been developed and at least rhetorical endorsement has been given to the issue of the representation of women at the higher echelons of power in the Civil Service, the Oireachtas and the wider arena of paid employment. The presence of women in the public arena has been legitimated by the EU, on the basis of a need for social solidarity and for a more broadly based democracy. Yet women continue to be seen, effectively, as 'outlaws' – people who are 'different', 'suspect', 'not like us', people whose loyalty to 'the system' is problematic and who cannot and should not be trusted to occupy the higher echelons of public power. In Ireland the ambiguous status of women in the public arena militates against arguing in terms of social rights other than those which derive from their relationship with an individual man. The idea of such rights, long taken for granted in social democracies such as Sweden, or in Eastern bloc countries such as Slovenia, and which underpins the EU concept of social cohesion and citizenship, is very much at odds with our concept of woman.

In Ireland, as in other Western European countries, there has been a dramatic decline in the rate of marriage and an increasing awareness of the extent to which the concept of 'family' has been and can be used to exploit and/or nullify the needs of women and children. There has been a growing recognition of the 'darker' side of family life. The majority of Irish married women, particularly those in their forties and older, are in an economically vulnerable position as compared with married women in other parts of Western Europe. Furthermore, Ireland still has a cultural system which is dominated by what O'Carroll (1991:70) calls an absolutist, non-representational style in which:

> Discourse is virtual rather than real in that it is assumed that the traditional part may represent and decide on behalf of all.

Nevertheless in a post-modern world (Derrida, 1978; Irigaray, 1985, 1993) the very concept of 'woman' can be seen as problematic, and it is necessary to justify this focus before proceeding any further.

Why women?

The focus of this book is specifically on women. The perspective being adopted is a social constructionist one. Implicit in it is the idea that at this point in time, women in Irish society have a culturally and structurally identifiable position. Women in Ireland, regardless of their age, life stage, ascribed class position and participation in paid employment, are surrounded by structural and cultural cues which define their lives. These cues refer not only to their position in the economic, political, religious and domestic arenas, but also presuppose their positive experience of responsibility for child care, and the 'naturalness' of subsuming their identities in families and/or in other caring relationships. They assume their relative disinterest in the 'normal' male trappings of individuality, viz. economic independence, individual autonomy, money and power. In many ways the social and cultural implications of biological femaleness in Ireland are similar to those experienced by their European counterparts. These very continuities highlight the fact that as Walby (1992:3) has noted:

> gender relations could potentially take an infinite number of forms; in actuality there are some widely repeated features.

There is no suggestion in this text that all women in Irish society experience their position in a similar way. Indeed it is increasingly clear that women, even those in similar social, legal and cultural situations may experience their situation quite differently, e.g. some seeing full-time housewifery as fulfilling, with others seeing it as exploitative. In Alcoff's terms (1988:435), it is suggested that to be a woman is to occupy:

> a position within a moving historical context and to be able to choose what we make of this position and how we alter this context.

The very concept 'woman' has begun to be deconstructed (Irigaray, 1985; 1993), a perspective which can be seen as implicitly undermining the validity of any attempt to provide structural explanations. However, as Giddens (1992:114) has argued:

> There is absolutely no reason why, on the level of logic, acknowledgement of the context-dependent nature of language dissolves continuity of identity.

Implicit in such a perspective is the idea that one could envisage a society where the social and cultural correlates of being a woman were no more significant than hair colour or shoe size. Thus, as Weeks (1989:207) has argued, it is possible to acknowledge that 'identity is not inborn, pregiven or natural', while at the same time recognising that, at a certain point in time, a particular identity may have an important social, cultural and indeed psychological reality. Weeks (1989:204) has gone on to provocatively suggest that the salience of sex/gender as an identity today may well provide an important insight into tensions in the wider social and political context:

> In times of heightened industrial conflict we might emphasise our class positions – as working-class or middle-class – and make fundamental political decisions on that basis. In periods of racial conflict and intensified racism, our loyalties, as black or white, might well come to the fore.

It is logically possible that, by focusing on women, gender may be elevated to an even greater position of importance. Such a tension, which at this point in time appears inevitable, has been recognised by Vance (1989:29):

> Defending women or advancing their interest (in equal pay, abortion rights, or child care, for example) emphasises their status as a special group with a unique collective interest, distinct from men, thus replacing and perhaps reinforcing the gender dichotomy crucial to the system of gender oppression.

It is recognised that by focusing on women, similarities between the experiences of men and women may be obscured. Nevertheless, such a focus seems appropriate in view of the fact that the issue of gender has generally been ignored in core texts (e.g. Breen *et al*, 1990; Goldthorpe and Whelan, 1992). Hence, there is obviously a need for further work comparing and contrasting the experiences of men and women in Irish society. Such a task lies beyond the scope of this text, which centres women within the discussion and explores their experiences. The position of women in Northern Ireland likewise is not included here, since such a discussion would necessitate a far more extended and more complex discussion of church and state. There is obviously a need to compare and contrast particular aspects of women's experiences, North and South. Again, however, such a task lies beyond the scope of this book.

Increasingly, it has been recognised that attempts to understand the position of women in a particular society need to be located within an understanding of that society and of the differential importance of, and accommodations between, its various institutional structures, particularly as they affect the position and experiences of women in various situations and/or at various life stages. Hence the focus in the book on women in contemporary Irish society. Implicit in the analysis is a concept of patriarchy; a concern with discourses; with other practices and processes involved in patriarchal control and with the facilitators of social and cultural change. These concepts underpin the perspective adopted here. They are outlined in the remainder of this chapter.

The concept of patriarchy

Patriarchy has been variously defined and differentially weighted in models dealing with the position of women in society. At its simplest, it simply refers to male control. It implicitly raises issues about older men's control over younger men and/or heterosexual men's control over homosexual men (Walby, 1989). However, from a woman's point of view, the concept of patriarchy implies that 'there is a system of social structures and practices in which men dominate, oppress and exploit women' (Walby, 1990). Some theorists, e.g. Hartmann (1981), have been particularly concerned with patriarchy at a material level. However others, e.g. Walby (1990:4) have suggested that:

> Gender relations are seen as importantly constituted by discourses of masculinity and femininity which are not immediately reducible to the economic relations of capitalism.

Ideas about what it is to be a woman, common-sense assumptions about women and their place, all reflect this ideological reality.

Implicit in this book is the idea that the experiences of women in Irish society can be illuminated by locating them within the context of a description which illustrates the patriarchal nature of this society. Among both men and women in Ireland, there appears to be a good deal of cultural unease surrounding the concept of patriarchy, the suggestion being that although it may have existed in the past, this is no longer the case. Among sociologists, the concept is sometimes seen as being tendentious or as purporting to explain an aspect of social reality by simply describing it (Pollert, 1996). The concept itself is popularly seen as implying hostility to individual men; as suggesting that all men are 'bad' and/or that all men consciously want to exploit or oppress women. It is seen as socially provocative in view of the psychological and economic dependence of married women (particularly those who are not in paid employment) on their husbands. It is criticised for obscuring the existence of divisions between women on class, age, racial background or religious lines. However, as Gaffney (1991b) suggests, such responses, together with denials of inequality, demands to 'tell me what to do', male feelings of hurt and outrage, and appeals to 'pull together, as we are all in this together', are all methods of resistance, designed to render patriarchy invisible.

The concept of patriarchy is useful since it highlights certain important and frequently ignored realities in Irish life. It is important to note that patriarchy is not of course peculiar to Ireland. The nature or form of male control will vary at different times and in different societies. The shape it assumes in Ireland is influenced by our particular historical, economic, legal, political and social structures. Nevertheless, many of its characteristics and processes are similar to those occurring in other European countries.

For Hartmann the position of women is one of inequality and subordination. In a widely quoted definition, she refers to patriarchy as 'a set of social relations between men which have a material base and which though hierarchical, establish or create interdependence and solidarity among men that enable them to dominate women' (1981:14). This definition draws attention to the fact that it is men who own and/or control resources such as land and other kinds of wealth and who are more likely to be in well paid jobs and in positions of legal, economic or political power. Even today in Ireland men make up approximately 95 per cent of those in senior positions in the civil service, the local authorities, the health boards, etc (see Chapter 8). This situation of course is not peculiar to Ireland. Indeed it has been noted that, 'In no society today do women enjoy the same opportunities as men' (United Nations, 1995:29).

Hartmann's definition recognises that not all men are in similar positions of power. Indeed it specifically suggests that there is a pecking order among men. However, it goes on to suggest that although not all men benefit equally from what one might call the 'aristocracy of maleness', they all benefit to some degree simply because they are men. Hartmann does not outline the processes involved in the perpetuation of this male privilege. However, the definition suggests that male solidarity is important – that men are encouraged to feel loyalty to each other, as individual men, and as part of an institutional elite which is predominantly composed of men at its higher levels.

Implicit in Hartmann's definition is the idea that such solidarity is an important element in maintaining the position of men relative to women in society. At an informal level, such ties might be associated with an unwillingness to challenge certain kinds of behaviour towards women and children; at a legal level they might be reflected in a lack of enthusiasm for passing or enforcing laws which seem to punish what could be seen as 'trivial' sorts of behaviour that 'only' affect women or children. The existence of bonds of solidarity between men, through which they perpetuate male privilege, has been neglected as an academic topic; O'Reilly's (1992) account of networking among right-wing, anti-abortion groups is the most systematic attempt to map their existence within Irish society.

Hartmann argues that the key elements in the material reality of patriarchy include men's control over women's labour power, as reflected in expecting women to provide personal service work (housework, child care etc); attaching lower value to women's work in the paid employment area and creating and maintaining paid employment structures which reflect these assumptions. However, the concept of patriarchy is also seen as implying a certain relationship between men's occupancy of positions and a contextual definition of male interests. Implicit in this is the idea that those who have power have the ability to create ideologies which effectively obscure the extent to which the structures they control further their own interests. This phenomenon has long been recognised by sociologists, though they have been concerned with its implications in a class rather than a gender perspective (Lockwood, 1964). Implicit in this is the idea of a 'male agenda', albeit one that will vary at particular times, in particular contexts and in particular societies. Implicit also is the idea that where male interests differ, the male agenda will reflect the interests of 'dominant males' – whether these are defined in terms of class, race or sexual orientation.

Of course men may not be conscious of their interests or see them as peculiarly 'male'. Rather, such interests may appear to them to be the 'obvious' ways to increase employment, create economic growth, etc. Similarly, at a very different level, an all-male committee might see seed potatoes, rather than a child care facility for tourists, as an obvious area for rural tourism initiatives (O'Connor, 1995a). Implicit in this is the notion that these ideas reflect and reinforce a gendered reality and so constitute a kind of gendered myopia. Thus, at a national level, it was taken for granted in Ireland up to the late 1980s that the way to create employment was by encouraging industry and maintaining agriculture, rather than by encouraging the service sector. The fact that the majority of women were employed in the service sector and that the feminisation of the services sector in general, and the labour force in particular, was a widespread European phenomenon was somehow seen as irrelevant. Although such gendered myopia reflects and reinforces a gendered social and cultural reality, individuals, both men and women, depending on their experiences, may be able to transcend such realities. Thus, quite clearly, the concept of male interests is not rooted in biological essentialism.

The systemic character of patriarchy is implicit in Walby's definition, viz.. that 'patriarchy is a system of social structures and practices in which men dominate, oppress or exploit women' (1990:20). A man who consciously does not want to do this is in a similar sort of position to that occupied by whites who were opposed to apartheid in the old South Africa. Such men benefit reluctantly and unwittingly from a system that they are trying at the same time to erode. Men in this position can feel angry about the use of the concept patriarchy, and see it – wrongly – as an attack on men like themselves, who are trying to change things. Such an attitude, although understandable, is as unhelpful as pleas by the middle classes to abandon the concept of class because some of those in the middle class are working towards a more equal society.

The concept of patriarchy is not in itself sufficient to explain the position of women; it needs to be located in a wider context. Some theorists such as Hartmann (1981) and Young (1981) focused on capitalism in conjunction with patriarchy, seeing these systems as analytically distinct but empirically interactive. Hartmann (1994:572) suggested that, in fact, the system that exists is 'patriarchal, capitalist, white supremacist'. Others such as Walby (1990) suggested that patriarchy was affected by the form of capitalism operating within a particular society at a particular moment in time. Walby suggested that the rise of capitalism led to the development of 'a new form of patriarchy' but not to any alteration in its basic structures or in the degree of exploitation. In contrast to those who have distinguished, at least analytically, between capitalism and patriarchy, Walby argued that in contemporary Britain, a patriarchal system of social relations was 'in articulation with capitalism and with racism' (1990:2). In this way she avoided the difficulties which arise when an attempt is made to depict capitalism and patriarchy as analytically separate, even if interrelated, systems.

Walby (1990) suggested that it was possible to distinguish two forms of patriarchy, viz. private and public patriarchy. At its simplest, she suggested, the crucial factor in this distinction was whether women were excluded from the economic system (private patriarchy) or segregated within it (public patriarchy). She argued that the dominant site of private patriarchy was in household production, and that the focus in this context was on individual men; that public patriarchy was based principally in public sites, i.e. paid employment and the state, and thus that the focus was on men who were employers or part of the state apparatus. She argued that in private patriarchy, individual men benefited from what she called 'the appropriation of women's labour' (1990:24). Building on Hartmann's insights, it seems plausible to suggest that solidarity between men would be strongest in this context. In relation to public patriarchy, Walby suggested that here there was a more 'collective appropriation' in the sense that employers and/or the state benefited. In this situation one might suggest that class allegiances would weaken men's solidarity with one another. However, on particular issues, e.g. violence, class interests might not be relevant and male solidarity might continue to reinforce 'the aristocracy of maleness'.

Walby (1990:180) recognised that the economic system might operate more or less on its own (as in contemporary USA), in combination with the state (as in Western Europe) or more or less controlled by the state (as in Eastern Europe before the collapse of Communism). Furthermore she suggested that the form of patriarchy found in any particular society was affected by the existence of the women's movement. She argued that, where capitalism existed, but without a feminist movement, private patriarchy persisted. This meant, for example, that women, although working in factories, remained subject to the patriarchal control of their fathers. With the emergence of the women's movement this form of control weakened, being replaced in time by what she called public patriarchy.

She suggested that in nineteenth-century Britain, the main site of women's oppression was in the household, whereas in twentieth-century Britain, the main site involved paid employment and/or the state. The position of Ireland today in this schema is ambiguous. On the one hand, male privilege and authority within the household still tends to be supported by the state and the church. Within a society where the majority of married women are not in paid employment it is difficult to ignore the importance of private patriarchy. On the other hand these latter patterns are changing (see Chapter 7). Indeed, Mahon (1987 and 1995) has argued that in terms of Walby's model, Ireland is now moving from private to public patriarchy.

Walby (1990:20) started from a position which saw patriarchy 'as a system of social relations'. At a less abstract level, she suggested (1990:2) that it consisted of six structures, viz. the patriarchal mode of production in the household; patriarchal relations in paid work; patriarchal relations in the state; male violence; patriarchal relations in sexuality and patriarchal relations in cultural institutions. Walby's model thus identified a number of relatively autonomous structures, i.e. violence, sexuality and culture, so as to capture, as she saw it, the variation which existed in gender relationships across Western society. In this way she avoided the unidimensionality implicit in models which have focused on a single site. Her inclusion of the state as an alternative key site of public patriarchy is very much in tune with contemporary thinking.

In each case Walby was concerned with the actual practices which ultimately created and/or reflected these structures. She described violence as a social structure and suggested that the social practices in this area included rape, marital violence, sexual harassment in the workplace and child sexual abuse. She highlighted the way in which these structures varied over time. For example, in terms of sexuality the main focus by middle-class husbands and fathers in nineteenth-century UK was on the direct control of women's purity, whereas in the twentieth century these structures had weakened although the sexual double standard was still a reality.

Walby's work (1989, 1990) thus moved away from a universalistic, and implicitly essentialist, definition of patriarchy. However, she has been criticised for her lack of attention to agency, i.e. the individual's choice or action (Pollert, 1996). This criticism has been echoed by others. It has been argued (Cooper, 1989:21-22) that the concept of patriarchy, like other structural concepts:

> does not carry any notion of how women might act to transform their situation as a sex . . . Patriarchy suggests a fatalistic submission which allows no space for the complexities of women's defiance.

Such criticism is valid and is a constant source of tension in structural approaches. Barrett (1992:216) has been among those who have recognised that:

> Debates about ideology and subjectivity have shown that we need a better conception of agency and identity than has been available in either (anti-humanist) post structuralist thought or its (humanist) modernist predecessors.

Pollert (1996:643) has also been critical of Walby's systemic view of patriarchy because, as she sees it, 'there is no intrinsic motor or dynamic within "patriarchy" which can explain its self perpetuation'. In this context she suggested that gender relations are a 'constitutive part' of class relations. Thus, although she recognised the reality of gender at one level, she felt that 'a gendered historical materialist' theory was needed. However, Pollert (1996:655) recognised that patriarchy as a concept was useful 'in the limited sense of a short cut for describing male dominance'. She suggested that it described phenomena rather than explained them; and that it ignored issues related to day-to-day practices and processes. In the next section an attempt will be made to highlight some of the practices and processes through which patriarchy is maintained: this, rather than the way in which patriarchy was originally created, being the focus of this book.

Practices and processes involved in patriarchal control

Connell (1995a) suggested that although we think of gender as a property of individuals (male/female) it is necessary to go beyond this, and to think of it as a property of institutions. He sees gender as

> a fundamental feature of the capitalist system: arguably as fundamental as class divisions. Socialist theory cannot any longer evade the fact that capitalism is run mainly by and to the benefit of men (1995a:104).

He suggested that the practices and processes in various societies may be more/less mapped by gender. He argued that gender relations were present in all institutions and that although they might not be the most important, they were a major structure in most institutions. He saw gender relations as having to do with three key issues, viz. the division of labour (who does what; what work is seen as valuable and to what extent this is related to its paid/unpaid character); the structure of authority, control and coercion (viz. who has legitimate authority to formulate ideas, to define morality, to set agendas; who has legitimate access to positional power or to resources, and ultimately the legitimate right to use force; who actually does exert control and ultimately use force); and what he calls cathexis (viz. the affective relationships – the 'structure of attachments' between men and women – with their implications as regards our definitions of desire, sexuality etc). Implicit in his work is the idea that the practices and processes of patriarchal control exist at each of these levels. He suggested that it was not sufficient to change the division of labour or even of power – but that it was necessary to re-envision the affectionate and sexual relationships between men and women.

It is argued (drawing on Connell's ideas) that a variety of practices, which we take for granted, reflect and reinforce patriarchal control. To date most attention has been paid to identifying them within the area of paid employment; although increasingly it has been recognised that they are part of the bureaucratic structures of the state. Some of these processes will be explored in the next section. At an even more fundamental level, such processes underlie the very way in which work is defined. Within an increasingly commodified society, the unpaid nature of work within the home, and the perception of it as 'not really work', implicitly devalues it. It also increases women's economic dependence on men – and even potentially affects their own evaluation of themselves and of their contribution to the family and to society.

The cultural depiction of men as the appropriate authority figures, and of 'male' educational and occupational choices as more valuable than 'female' ones is similarly a subtle manifestation of patriarchal control. Among young women the persistence of sexual double standards and the culturally created difficulty of treading a line between being too sexually available and not sufficiently sexually available are important elements in patriarchal control. Similarly the depiction of male violence, rape, sexual harassment, child sexual abuse, marital violence or pornography as 'not that serious' erodes women's sense of their own bodily integrity and ultimately their sense of their own value. These too are elements in the processes through which such control is exerted.

Paid employment

At the most general level within the area of paid employment the practices and processes involved in patriarchal control are ways of minimising direct competition between men and women. Walby has been particularly concerned with 'segregation' and 'exclusion':

> The exclusion strategy is aimed at totally preventing women's access to an area of employment, or indeed to all paid employment; segregation is a weaker strategy aimed at separating women's work from men's work and at grading the former beneath the latter for purposes of remuneration and status (1990:53).

Witz's (1992) concepts of exclusionary and demarcatory closure are similar, and are seen as being used by one group, e.g. men, to define other groups, e.g. women, as 'ineligible'. At its most extreme, an exclusionary strategy excludes all women explicitly because they are women. In its more subtle manifestation, an exclusionary strategy effectively excludes women by precluding them from access to resources, skills, knowledge, etc. Once criteria have been specified, however, there is a possibility that individual women will meet them. Of course, because of the nature of such criteria, it is highly likely that only a minority of women will do so, and that they will be seen as 'tokens' whose main loyalties are towards men rather than women; who effectively become 'honorary males', who may well continue to enforce the gendered collectivist criteria of exclusion as the price of their own inclusion.

A demarcatory strategy is concerned with creating and controlling boundaries between occupations. Witz (1992) gives examples of the strategies used by the medical profession in relation to radiographers, chiropodists and physiotherapists. She notes that resistance to such demarcatory strategies could involve an attempt to use such exclusionary strategies against others, e.g. making a certain level or type of formal education a prerequisite for employment in the area and seeking state recognition for these educational criteria. Such strategies are apparent in nursing and primary teaching where until very recently the accreditation was provided by denominational training colleges and nursing schools underpinned by state recognition. Witz (1992:203) also touched on the extent to which 'internal demarcatory strategies' might occur within particular professions. These are attempts by males to demarcate female and male spheres within an occupation by putting forward an equivalence between the skills or qualities required in these areas and concepts of masculinity and femininity. These sorts of processes can be easily identified in the teaching area: primary teaching being seen as a 'caring' and appropriate female activity; while teaching in University with its 'knowledge creation' character has been defined as an appropriate male activity. Indeed Hearn (1982) suggested that professionalisation was a process through which men – either in particular professions and/or in the state – exerted patriarchal control over experiences which women had controlled in the private sphere.

The processes involved may be even more fundamental. For example, the labour that women undertake – whether inside or outside the home – may not be viewed as work but as 'natural', something that women do. These evaluations may be reflected in the conception of the nature of the skills involved in a task and their perceived value (Tancred, 1995). The labour that men undertake appears then in a rather different light. Differences in the definition of work have implications as regards men and women's economic independence since men's work is much more likely than women's to be paid and to be viewed as skilled (United Nations, 1995). For example, the skills involved in cleaning or air hostess work, social work, etc. may be 'invisible' and viewed as simply characteristic of women, who typically occupy these positions. The perception of these skills as 'natural' is used simultaneously to define these jobs as low skilled, as suitable for women and as low paid.

The very structuring of female dominated careers, such as nursing, reflects their predominantly female nature. For example, the ratio of senior to junior posts in nursing has been shown to be less than in male dominated areas (O'Connor, 1996a). Similarly, their remoteness from those decision-making structures which allocate resources ensures that their work is under-resourced. These practices affect women's ability to financially support themselves and to have access to power structures whether in the economic or political arenas.

Witz and Savage (1992:6) called attention to 'the gendered process internal to the bureaucratic process of the state' as an important element in understanding why women are not moving upwards within the management and administrative structures of the state bureaucracy across societies which vary widely in their economic and social structures. Halford (1992:172) recognised that once we move away from Weber's depiction of those in the hierarchy as 'depersonalised automatons', and

> we accept that staff bring their personal interests into organisations, and that these shape the way they discharge their functions, we must also accept that gendered perceptions, practices and attitudes will be present too.

These bureaucratic structures are thus shaped by individual and collective male interests, prejudices and fears (Witz and Savage, 1992:234):

> What feminists are confronted with is not a state that represents 'men's interests' as against women's, but government conducted as if men's interests are the only ones that exist.

The task then becomes one of not simply attempting to ensure that women are represented at senior level (as Kanter, 1993 has argued) but also raising questions about the characteristics of those who are included, as well as those who are excluded, from senior positions in those structures (Davies, 1992). Even more fundamentally, as Davies (1992 and 1995) and Witz and Savage (1992) have argued, it is necessary to raise the issue of the extent to which gender is embedded in the manner in which work is organised on a day-to-day basis and in authority structures whether these are part of the public or private sector.

In Ireland, the state has implicitly and explicitly endorsed full-time paid employment as the norm. As an employer, it effectively penalised those who opted for job sharing by reducing their increments. In 1997 the European Court of Justice ruled that this was indirect discrimination (Honan, 1997). It is difficult to avoid the conclusion that implicit in this practice was the (male) organisational message that insofar as women 'specify their difference', they will be excluded from the 'normal' (male) career paths (Cockburn, 1991:219):

> You may find a place as long as you simulate the norm and hide your difference. We will know you are different and continue ultimately to treat

you as different, but if you yourself specify your difference, your claim to equality will be nil.

At a fundamental level, the laws and practices of the state in dealing with women as individuals, as opposed to being their husband's dependant or their children's mother, sets a critical tone in terms of undermining or perpetuating individual male control over women. The practices and policies of the state are also important in affecting the demand side of the labour market, e.g. in stimulating the service sector, where women are predominantly employed, as opposed to the industrial sectors where they are under-represented. Ideas about the most 'viable' sectors or occupations as regards employment creation may be gendered, and may reflect gendered assumptions about what constitutes work. The state's preoccupation with the creation of employment in the agricultural and industrial sectors rather than the services sector prior to the 1990s can be seen as reflecting this kind of gendered myopia.

Individually or collectively, by exerting power 'on behalf of women', men's own self-interest is obscured. Increasingly, however, within an industrialised society, the appropriateness of this sort of position is being questioned not only in a gender context, but in the context of race and disability. This ability to 'act for' or on behalf of women is intimately related to a concept of masculinity which suggests that 'greatness' can be achieved by men through representing women's interests,

> In pursuit of a cause, the struggle for power is ennobled and becomes worthy. The man with the cause is the hero, the leader, the one who can achieve true greatness (Davies, 1995:32).

Indeed, within a society where men are seen as more credible authority figures and are valued more highly, the continuance of this practice can be justified on pragmatic grounds, although it simply perpetuates the situation.

Corcoran *et al* (1995) among others have noted that usually employment structures are based on the assumed existence of a male employee, and that these trends are exacerbated in areas of predominantly male employment. Since the early 1970s (Oakley, 1972) it has been recognised that although social practices build on culturally and socially constructed difference in a way which makes them appear 'natural' and inevitable, these practices do not simply reflect biological difference. For example, it is popularly believed that the participation of women in paid employment is affected by the presence of children. However, contrary to the popular depiction of this as reflecting the incompatibility of paid employment and motherhood, such participation varies very considerably across the EU, depending on the role played by the state as regards state funded childcare, taxation, and social welfare.

The embedding of gender in organisations is reflected in persistent patterns of gender segregation, as well as in the reproduction of the gendered identity of occupations. Kanter early argued that gender entered the picture in affecting the characteristic images of those occupying particular roles. She suggested that managers were generally seen as having 'male' characteristics. This led her to conclude that:

> while organisations were being defined as sex-neutral machines, masculine principles were dominating their authority structures (1977:46).

This is not necessarily an intentional, or even conscious procedure. Rather, the gendered character of jobs and the processes which maintain them can be seen as a part of a taken-for-granted reality. However, Connell (1995b:231) has challenged the idea that the perpetuation of male power is accidental:

> presuming that there had been some cosmic accident in which bodies as penises happened to land in positions of power to recruit their friends with penises to replace them ever after.

Increasingly the practices and processes which reflect patriarchal control within organisations have been recognised. Organisational cultures characterised by male prejudice, so-called 'humorous' comments and, at the extreme, sexual harassment have all been identified as social practices which make it difficult for women to gain access to the top of occupational hierarchies (O'Connor, 1995b and 1996a; Rosenberg *et al*, 1993). Equally, it has been recognised that organisational procedures, including the predominantly male composition of interview boards, gender differentiated access to training, and lack of access to high profile tasks provide opportunities to effectively perpetuate the position of men within organisations. In a situation where areas of predominantly female employment are effectively starved of resources, women are forced into a coping style of management, their assent to the low resourcing of their areas being effectively maintained by what can only be described as intimidation (O'Connor, 1996a).

One might expect that economic structures within a capitalist economy would promote women, regardless of gender, if this was in the interests of greater efficiency. Hedstrom (1991) and Laumann (1991) noted that the majority of firms have not done so even where on a 'purely profit basis, one might expect them to do so'. Implicit in this is the idea that capitalism cannot be seen as gender neutral but that it is interwoven with the patriarchal self-interest of individual men or groups of men.

Wage differentials between men and women which are widespread in Ireland and more generally in Western society reflect and reinforce patriarchal control mechanisms. Even in Sweden, when at particular points in time, and in particular sectors, such as banking in the 1980s, managers acquired greater discretion to set individual weekly wages over and above those agreed collectively (e.g. deciding the point on the scale at which employees entered; when they should be promoted; and how merit payments should be distributed), the net effect was to increase the wage differential (Acker, 1991). Acker, like Rubery *et al* (1993) and Whitehouse (1992) concluded that wage differentials are likely to be minimised by wages being collectively negotiated. It is impossible to say why it should be so, although Pollert's (1996:654) observation that 'male dominance feeds on itself in terms of vested interests defending the status quo' is provocative.

Sexual violence

There is a paucity of evidence concerning sexual double standards and the way in which ideas about sexual reputation affect young women's behaviour. However, it seems at least plausible to suggest that such phenomena, together with sexual harassment and other forms of sexual violence, are mechanisms through which patriarchal control is exerted. Marital violence and rape have long been seen as important elements in controlling women, both individually and collectively, while the popular depiction of them as 'not really serious' further erodes women's sense of their own value as women.

It is clear that patriarchal control becomes a reality through a wide variety of practices which will be illustrated in subsequent chapters. It is important to note that frequently the practices are so taken for granted that the element of control is not even perceived. Indeed this reflects the ideological reality of such control.

Ideology, discourses and the structures maintaining them

Abbott and Wallace (1990:6-7) define ideology as:

> a pattern of ideas (common sense knowledge) both factual and evaluative which purport to explain and legitimate the social structure and culture of a

social group or society and which serves to justify social actions which are in accordance with that pattern of ideas.

This definition is useful insofar as it highlights the taken-for-granted nature of ideologies. It also highlights the way in which ideas both explain and legitimate social action. These are key elements in understanding the part that ideology plays in effectively closing off possible options or alternative courses of action by making them literally 'unthinkable'. A recognition of the competing nature of ideologies in an increasingly fragmented post-modern world has evoked the use of the word 'discourse'. A discourse is a collection of related statements which 'makes sense' of the nature of experiences and which creates identities. Competing discourses in a sense constitute ideological 'micro-worlds'.

The concept of discourse has become particularly associated with Foucault (1979 and 1980). He started from a position which saw power and knowledge/truth as very closely associated. He suggested that various powerful groups put forward what he called competing discourses, e.g. in relation to sexuality. Such discourses incorporated a particular view of sexuality, as well as rules about who could speak authoritatively about it, what the appropriate assumptions were etc. For Foucault knowledge involves a power to define others – a discourse embodies knowledge and so embodies power. The problem then, as he saw it, was not changing people's consciousness, but changing the political, economic, and other institutional structures which were involved in the production of these 'truths' (Rabinow, 1991).

Foucault suggested that institutional structures such as the church and the medical profession created and embodied discourses, which in turn perpetuated their control over these areas and the legitimacy of their attempts to define then and to speak authoritatively about them. For him the process through which discourses were created and the way in which power was exercised was critical in beginning to think about the 'who' of power (Barrett, 1991). He identified the confessional and the panopticon (a kind of physical structure used in prisons which exposed the inmates to the controlling gaze of the prison staff) as ways in which power is exercised, and which provided a clear insight into who had power in these situations.

For Foucault 'truth' was relative and yet he perceived the production of competing truths as a core activity of modern capitalist society: 'We must produce truth as we produce wealth' (1979:93). For Foucault these competing versions of reality remained in an uneasy state of tension. He was pessimistic about the possible emergence of a 'better' social order.

However, he was optimistic about an individual's power to resist. As he saw it, people were never totally contained by the prevailing ideas, beliefs or views about the nature of reality. Indeed the very relativity of these ideas discouraged such containment, leading him to conclude that 'where there is power, there is resistance' (1979:95).

Gramsci (see Forgacs, 1988) on the other hand used the concept of ideological hegemony to capture the idea that the ruling class used their economic and political power, as well as the educational system, religion, etc to produce, and maintain the consent of, the various strata in society. Although Gramsci saw the different classes as having opposing interests, he did not interpret power as simply constituting the overt exercise of coercion or force. Rather he suggested that power was used in a subtle way to create, and maintain the consent of, those subordinated to it. Those who had power shaped individual consciousness through the establishment of what he called ideological hegemony.

Neither Gramsci nor Foucault were specifically concerned with gender. However, their ideas can provide a framework within which the discourses involving women can be located. Within a patriarchal society fundamental ideas about the nature and value of womanhood are seen as part of the mechanisms of patriarchal control. Within the dominant discourse concepts of womanhood continue to revolve around caring, familism, reproduction, love, sexual attraction and gendered paid employment, preferably in a 'little job' which is part-time, low paid, and undertaken for the 'good of the family'. Resistance thus effectively involves a re-evaluation and a re-invention of concepts of womanhood, and indeed of manhood.

Furthermore, these definitions are generated and maintained by social structures such as the church, the state, and the economic system. Particularly in times of structural and cultural upheaval, various discourses are at least potentially available. Of course, they will be differently available to different women, at different life stages, in different social classes. Furthermore, the structures which reflect and/or reinforce the dominant discourse are not monolithic. For example, particular parts of the church structure, or particular state policies, might reinforce some aspect of the dominant discourse of womanhood; others may subtly challenge or erode it. These contradictions indeed are seen as part of the way in which change occurs.

Connell (1995a:215) argued that it was because men wished to be men, within a society and culture where being a man involved the subordination of women, that patriarchy was perpetuated:

> The subordination of women and the marginalisation of homosexual and effeminate men are sustained neither by choice nor by the mechanical reproduction of a social system, but by the commitments implicit in conventional and hegemonic masculinity and the strategies pursued in an attempt to realise them.

Only a minority of men, he argued, will practise masculinity in the hegemonic form, i.e. actively subordinating women. However, the majority of men gain an advantage from the subordination of women, i.e. in terms of honour, prestige and the right to command. They also gain a material dividend (Connell 1995b:82). He described this as complicit masculinity (1995b) and earlier as conventional masculinity (1995a). In this case, the enjoyment of power is dependent on it being 'given to them [men] by an external force, by nature or convention or even by women themselves rather than by an active subordination going on here and now' (1995a:215). In this case women's subordination is obscured. Connell suggested that men thus have a vested interest in maintaining the status quo. Gender is not simply a social reality but becomes part of our idea of ourselves as men and women. This is captured in the idea of 'consensual control' (O'Connor, 1995a). In particular circumstances women may 'assume' that their interests will be looked after, that they are in fact the same as 'everyone else's' interests (O'Connor, 1995a). These assumptions too can be seen as part of the ideological reality of patriarchal control.

Underlying these processes and practices lies the whole question of women's value relative to men within a society where the institutional structures are overwhelmingly controlled by men. There was a time when this was seen as an unproblematic issue. Nowadays in Irish society, it is difficult to imagine statements being openly made about the relative value of male and female children. In this context, the higher positive evaluation of 'male' subjects and career choices within the educational and occupational areas is provocative. Walby (1990:104) has suggested that:

> The keys to the patriarchal relations in culture are the differentiation of the discourses of femininities and masculinities and the valuation of masculinity above those of femininity.

Implicit in it is a devaluing of women relative to men – an idea which was first flagged by De Beauvoir (1972/49) in her discussion of woman as 'the Other', essentially an object to a male subjective reality. Indeed, one might go further and suggest that it is a fear of 'difference' which lies behind the structural realities of violence and the privileging of heterosexuality which is a characteristic of patriarchy. Within a system characterised by private patriarchy the higher evaluation of maleness can be concealed by ideas about difference. However, as one moves towards public patriarchy, issues related to the relative value of men and women come into sharper focus, particularly in the presence of an active women's movement (unless of course they are concealed by attempts to deny the extent of women's disadvantage and its relationship to discrimination). It will be argued (in Chapter 3) that there is an emerging discourse of womanhood – at least partly shaped by the women's movement – which revolves around an as yet inchoate discourse of personhood.

A decline in confidence in the institutional structures of European society, including the church, the educational system, the legal system, parliament, trade unions etc, has been clearly documented in cross-national studies, while the very collapse of communism and the rise of ethnic conflict in Europe has shown the extent of disenchantment with established legitimating ideologies. Similarly, the rise and popularity of 'protest movements' of various kinds, including ecology, human rights, anti-nuclear and anti-apartheid movements, as well as the women's movement, has clearly highlighted the widespread disenchantment with traditional political agendas (Barker *et al*, 1992). The extent of at least verbal support for such protest movements in Ireland is very considerable, with, for example, 85 per cent of an Irish sample endorsing support for the women's movement: (Barker *et al*, 1992:15). The fragmentation of the taken-for-granted discourse about womanhood, and the increasing challenge to the legitimacy of the dominant patriarchal discourses, can be set in this wider context.

Social and cultural change: individual resistance

It is widely accepted that however powerful the processes and practices of patriarchal control, and however tightly woven the ideological parameters of women's lives, the possibility of social and cultural change or individual resistance cannot be eliminated. It is extremely difficult to identify specific explanations for such phenomena. For example, it is difficult to definitively explain the rise in the participation of married women in paid employment, the fall in marital fertility, or the dramatic rise in births to lone parents in Ireland. Furthermore since these trends have occurred in a number of European countries at slightly different times over the past twenty-five years it is clear that the phenomena involved may be international, although the specific patterns that emerge, or their timing, may reflect a particular historically specific social and cultural milieu. To see them as indicative of a weakening of the processes and practices of patriarchal control can be problematic – reflecting an obscuring of the distinction between explanation and description (Pollert, 1996).

This book is not putting forward a model of change. Its ambitions are much more modest. It simply attempts to describe the changes and continuities in the lives of Irish women, and to locate these within the wider structural and cultural parameters of Irish society. Connell's notion (1995a) of crisis tendencies provide a potentially useful way of understanding changes in the position of women in Irish society. In particular his idea of a crisis of institutionalisation seems useful. He sees this as involving a 'weakening of the ability of the institutional order of family-plus-state to sustain the legitimacy of men's power'. He suggests that the long-term political source of this is 'generalisable claims to equality' as the basis for the state's legitimacy (1995:159, 160). He suggests that it is this which led states to invest in women's education; to introduce no fault divorce; to fund refuges; and to introduce legal changes which allowed married women to hold property in their own right. These changes, he suggests, directly or indirectly weakened the bases of male power within the family, and generally increased the vulnerability of male power to the challenges posed by the availability of the contraceptive pill, by secularisation, and by the fragmenting of the dominant discourses in a post-modern society.

Connell (1995) identified other crisis tendencies, including what he called a crisis of sexuality, and a crisis of interest formation. He saw the first as reflecting the fact that heterosexuality was 'not a natural fact but a state of play in a field of power and cathexis' (1995a:161). This could be destabilised – leading to a commodified and alienated sexuality which was corrosive of reciprocity at a personal level. The crisis of interest formation he saw as arising in a situation where the social bases for the definition of women's interests were not always or entirely the family. For example, women who worked together might have shared interests as employees, which in particular situations transcended or obscured their interests as wives or mothers. It is not clear to what extent these crises are important in Irish society.

However, implicit in this book is the idea that there are what Connell called 'crisis tendencies' within Irish society at both a structural and cultural level. Within the Irish context the most obvious structural source of these crisis tendencies is the changing relationship between church and state. There are other tensions, e.g. those between the current social and cultural construction of heterosexuality, which stresses men's economic position as a key element in masculinity, and the economic opportunities for women generated by an increasingly service-oriented economic system where there is growing demand for 'flexible' labour. There are tensions too arising from the state's need for inclusiveness as a basis for its own legitimacy and the patriarchal nature of Irish public life, where the 'normal' situation is for men to represent women's interests.

At a less complex level, it is obvious that the nature of institutions is such that while particular elements reinforce patriarchal control, other elements disrupt such control. The reality of this sort of situation and the way in which it may affect action has been captured by Benton (1981:181) who has suggested that:

> A woman who has been socially constituted as a member of a family and identifies with her position and role within that family may also, through contact with feminist ideas and organisations, come to acquire partially, or even wholly, conflicting identifications, and so come to deploy a new conception of her interest, which under at least some circumstances, may issue in courses of action inconsistent with her identity as a member of a family.

Such patterns are particularly likely to occur where changes have taken place in 'collective consciousness', and this is likely to be associated with the emergence of a women's movement (Staggenborg, 1991). Of course the existence of such a movement in itself reflects certain structural and cultural possibilities. However, its presence accentuates them, both at an individual and collective level.

In this context it seems useful to focus not only on the organisational structures which can be seen as key elements in the Irish women's movement but also on the ways in which individuals and groups have worked within the institutional parameters of Irish society to bring about change, and on the ways in which more radical individuals and groups have challenged or extended the discourse and hence created a larger 'space' within which the more reformist elements could operate. Furthermore, it seems important to recognise that there may be what Faith (1994) called 'a choreographed demonstration of co-operation' but one which watches for openings or allies to mount a challenge to the status quo. This book looks particularly at the way in which 'ordinary' women, by changing their own behaviour, have affected the shape of Irish society.

The perspective adopted

This book is concerned with trying to understand the position of women in contemporary Irish society, drawing in a speculative and insightful way on a wide range of Irish sociological material. It is particularly concerned with describing the relationship of women with two of the main institutional structures which impinge on their lives, viz. the world of family and the world of paid employment, and with locating these within the structural and ideological parameters within which Irish women live and make their choices. Additionally, since it is recognised that the experiences of younger and older women are very different, this difference will be highlighted.

It is suggested that the main elements which need to be included in a structural model, to 'make sense' of women's position in Irish society, are the economic system, the state, the church, the social and cultural construction of the institution of heterosexuality, and the women's movement. The inclusion of some of these elements is theoretically unproblematic. Thus, typically, capitalism and/or patriarchy have been used to explain the position of women in society (Hartmann, 1981; Young, 1981; Jaggar, 1988). At its very simplest, capitalism can simply be defined as a particular kind of economic system which is concerned with the pursuit of profit. British and American authors generally assume that industrialisation is part and parcel of the creation of a capitalist economy, with mature capitalism being assumed to exist in such societies. However, in Ireland, the situation is somewhat complicated insofar as some would argue that if Ireland had an industrial revolution it occurred after 1958. The implications of this difference in the form of capitalism here and, for example, in the UK have not really begun to be discussed. What is agreed, however, is that with the First Programme for Economic Development in 1958, the state committed itself to a programme which relied heavily on the attraction of foreign manufacturing investment to Ireland (Lee, 1989; Breen *et al*, 1990). Hearn has suggested that at least until the 1980s the arguments were between those who saw Ireland as going through a process of economic and cultural modernisation, so as to become more like other 'developed' countries in Europe and North America; and those who saw it more in terms of an international dependency model, with Ireland being compared to industrialising countries in Latin America and Asia whose economic possibilities were very dependent on transnational corporations which were highly mobile and completely outside state control.

In any case, issues related to the role of the state in affecting women's access to employment have been seen as having equal, if not more importance, than the economic system in affecting the position of women in Irish society. Yet, it is only in the past ten years that theoretical work has focused on the state as a key player in shaping the position of women (Connell, 1994). In Walby's (1990) model, the state is a key element in the public arena. However, it is clear that in Ireland, the state has tended to confine women to the familial arena.

A further dynamic for change has arisen from the fact that the authority of the nation state itself is under pressure from above and below. In Ireland European directives and regulations have steadily (since the Treaty of Rome) enhanced the possibilities and opportunities available to women in general, even though these have been particularly relevant to women in the labour force. This influence seems likely to continue in the face of the EU's concern with social cohesion and citizenship, and women's perceived wariness about the European Union (Eurobarometer, 1996). In this context the commitment to gender auditing EU funds constitutes, at the very least, a symbolic affirmation of the value of women and their status within society.

In Walby's model the institutional church is simply one of the cultural institutions. Within Ireland, the institutional church is a social and cultural reality. Even today, its influence on various aspects of social life, such as the educational system, is very considerable. Much of the dynamic for change in Irish society at this point in time, can be understood as arising from a tension between church and state. Thus it is argued that, culturally and structurally, the church is a very important element in understanding the position of women in Irish society.

The social and cultural construction of heterosexuality is another element which is considered to be important in understanding the position of women in Irish society. It is obvious that at its narrowest heterosexuality refers to the purely physical aspects of male/female relationships. However, it can also refer to the way in which relationships between men and women are socially and culturally constructed. Implicit in it is the idea that the relationships of men and women with each other occur within a context where, as Connell (1995b:230) has put it, 'a patriarchal gender order constitutes difference as dominance, as unavoidably hierarchical'. This 'gender order', he suggests, 'involves social relations as well as broad cultural themes' (1995b:231-232). Implicit in it is the idea that the 'normal' relationship between men and women is one of dominance – whether as lovers, spouses, or simply as men and women. This social and cultural construction underpins fundamental assumptions about the differential value of men and women, ideas about the 'normality' of the division of labour within the home and of the appropriateness of male power and authority. This idea 'is so deeply embedded in culture, institutions and body-reflexive practices that it functions as a limit to the rights based politics of reform' (Connell, 1995b:232). Walby (1990) has included some of these elements in her model by referring to private patriarchy in the household, to violence, sexuality and culture. It seems more useful to follow the thinking of Connell, himself a male heterosexual, by seeing these various phenomena as affecting the way in which relationships between men and women are constructed.

These four structures – the economic system, the state, the church, the social and cultural construction of heterosexuality – differ in many ways. However, in Irish society, as indeed in most other European societies, men are, in effect, in powerful positions within each of them. In the institutional Roman Catholic Church, at some level, the subordination of women is a key element. The state and the economy can be seen as potentially more contested sites, although in fact, given cultural definitions of worth, division of labour and resources, it is difficult to imagine women's interests being consistently central to such structures. In the case of the current social and cultural construction of heterosexuality, it is clear that although hegemonic masculinity is comfortable with overt dominance, the key element in conventional masculinity is the assumption that women's subordination is 'natural', inevitable, 'what women want' – that indeed it is, at a very fundamental level, an expression of sexual difference.

In this context, it obviously makes sense to include the women's movement as a rather different kind of element in the model. Faith (1994) has suggested that the key element is 'resistance to invisibility and silencing' and that this resistance is articulated 'through the women's movement and through individual actions, including refusals and separations'. Here it is similarly argued that the women's movement is a form of resistance to the patriarchal context generated by the dominant structures in Irish society. The inclusion of this element however poses difficulties insofar as in Ireland, as indeed in other Western societies, there is an inevitable looseness about the concept of a movement although a number of attempts have been made to map its various stages (Connolly, 1996 and 1997; Mahon, 1995; Smyth, 1988 and 1993). These will be briefly referred to in the next chapter. In subsequent chapters an attempt is made, within the limits of the data available, to look at the way in which 'ordinary' women have constructed their lives within what are effectively patriarchal institutional structures, taking into account the influence of the women's movement on the structural and cultural reality of those institutions.

The central focus of the book is on the interrelationship between the family and work. It is perhaps inevitable that in Ireland at this point in time ideas about agency and subjectivity fit more 'naturally' within a discussion of the sense women make of their lives within the family than in the world of paid employment. However, it is by no means clear that this is inevitably so.

Within each of the major institutional structures the taken-for-granted nature of male authority is being steadily eroded. Indeed it is widely accepted that as a part of a post-modern world, dominant discourses are fracturing. In Ireland, the process has been accelerated by a series of revelations concerning the abuse of male power within these institutional structures (see O'Connor, 1995c). Within this context, the appropriateness of defining the common good in terms of male interest has become visibly problematic. The importance of these tensions and the opportunities they create are accentuated by the fact that Ireland's structural and cultural reality was monolithic at least up to the 1960s (Breen *et al*, 1990). Thus, the weakening of each of these overall structures is, as it were, being compounded by the diversity of fronts on which it is occurring.

Within Irish society, the strength of familial intergenerational relationships between women themselves has created further possibilities in relation to change. The experiences and options of women in their twenties in Ireland are very similar to the European average. They are very different to those of Irish women in their forties and older, whose experiences in turn are very different from the European average (Walby, 1996). Yet these two groups of women are not infrequently mothers and daughters, whose ideas and attitudes impact closely on each other. Indeed it can be suggested that it is the acceptance by mothers of, for example, lone parenthood which poses one of the most fundamental challenges to the position of working class men in society.

Summary

This chapter has been concerned with indicating the kinds of concepts which underpin the approach adopted in the book. The chapter briefly justifies its focus on women. It suggests that the concept of patriarchy is

a key element in understanding the experiences of women in Irish
society. It is recognised that it is necessary to go beyond identifying this
to explore the practices and processes through which it becomes a
reality; the discourses which legitimate and/or obscure these practices;
and the crisis tendencies which facilitate social and cultural change. It is
suggested that the position and experiences of women in Irish society
can be understood by being located in the context of the economic
system, the state, the institutional church, the social and cultural
construction of heterosexuality, and the women's movement. There is a
certain arbitrariness in choosing these as key structural elements within
which the lives of Irish women can be located and understood. Different
elements might well be important in other societies. These do however
seem to provide a useful context within which the important events
which have impacted on Irish women's lives in the past twenty-five years
can be located. They are briefly described in Chapter 2.

Since it is suggested that the meaning of women's lives is also
constructed within ideologically dominant discourses, the key themes
which are available to them within an Irish context will be explored in
Chapter 3. Chapter 4 explores the changing social and cultural realities
of work and family in Ireland – including the increasingly contested
nature of work, and the reality of lone parenthood. Chapter 5 focuses on
what is often seen as the 'ideal' situation for Irish women, viz. working
full-time in the home. Women in this situation are predominantly older
women. Chapter 6 specifically focuses on the situation of young
women. It suggests that their experiences and achievements effectively
take the male as the norm. Chapters 7 and 8 look more closely at the
arena of paid employment, at the increasing presence of women,
particularly married women, in this arena and the factors which have
been identified to explain variation in this. It will be shown that men's
wages are higher than women's and that women predominate among
the low paid. The benefit to women of such participation in paid
employment is double edged, since it reflects and reinforces the low
economic value of their work. Chapter 8 looks specifically at the extent
to which women have come to occupy positions of authority and/or
prestige within the system. It will be shown that although women
constitute the majority of those in professional services in Ireland, they
constitute only a minority of those in management positions in the
private or public sector. Thus their challenge to men's control within
these structures can be seen as limited in the sense that they are side-
lined into positions of 'expertise' as opposed to 'authority' (Savage,

`1992:147). However, within a society where there is an increasing reliance on expertise as the basis of authority, this strategy may be less effective than it might otherwise be. The final chapter briefly summarises the changes which have occurred in the place occupied by women in Irish society and speculates about some of the choices that confront us as a society if Ireland is indeed to become a country where women may find their own space in both structural and cultural terms.

=========== 2 ===========

Locating Women within Irish Society

Introduction

IT has been suggested in Chapter 1 that women's family and (paid) work-related experiences need to be located within a wider context. It was recognised that the specific elements which might be included would vary between different societies and at different periods of time. However, it was suggested that in an Irish context the most important elements are the economic system, the state, the institutional church, the cultural and social construction of heterosexuality, and the women's movement. In this chapter women's relationship with these aspects of Irish life will be explored. In each case, an attempt will be made to describe the current position of women within these structures and to indicate how that position has changed over the past twenty-five years.

Women and the economic system

Explanations for the position of women in a particular society frequently refer to the economic system. In some cases the reference is implicit: for example, the notion that as a society modernises the position of women inevitably improves. In other cases the economic system becomes a focus for those who are concerned with the erection of explanatory models and/or with a more social and culturally specific explanation of the position of women (e.g. Walby, 1990; Mahon, 1994). In this section the main focus is firstly on international reports which have included references to the economic position of women; secondly, a brief reference is made to changes in the position of women in the Irish labour force; thirdly, there follows an outline of how the position of women in the labour force has been affected by the state and the trade unions (a more detailed discussion of the position of women in the labour force is to be found in Chapters 7 and 8).

Optimistic assessments of the implications of economic growth for women are increasingly seen as problematic. It is now recognised that economic resources may be used very differently in different countries, on behalf of the health, well-being and empowerment of individual citizens in general, and of women in particular (United Nations, 1995). Three measures have been used to facilitate international comparisons of these dimensions, viz. a human development index (HDI) which takes into account life expectancy, education and income; a gender development index (GDI) which takes into account the same basic characteristics, but specifically measures the inequalities between men and women; and the gender empowerment measure (GEM) which focuses on the extent to which women participate in the (public) economic and political life, by looking at their share of managerial and professional jobs, their share of parliamentary seats and their income earning power.

The United Nations Report (1995:75) clearly showed that, in industrialised and developing countries, 'gender equality does not depend on the income level of a society'. Gender equality may or may not be given priority at any particular level of economic well-being. Clearly, it is given this priority in Scandinavian countries such as Sweden, Norway, Denmark (see Table 2.1). The HDI values minus the GDI values are positive in these countries. In Ireland the difference is negative – clearly showing that greater priority is given to the creation of economic well-being than to its translation into improving the situation of women as assessed on the GDI index. In the Human Development Report, Ireland was nineteenth on the HDI index, and thirtieth on the GDI index (see Table 2.1).

It is clear that some countries, for example Portugal, which are far more economically disadvantaged than Ireland (HDI rank, thirty-sixth and nineteenth respectively) have given greater priority to gender related issues (GDI rank twenty-fifth and thirtieth respectively). However, other countries, for example Spain, which have a higher score than Ireland on the human development index (HDI) have attached an even lower priority to gender related issues. It is also clear that the prioritising of gender related issues is by no means peculiar to what we can regard as typically capitalist countries. In fact, there is some evidence to suggest that the opposite is true. The Czech Republic, Slovakia, Poland and Hungary are ranked higher than Ireland on the gender development index.

TABLE 2.1
RANKING OF SELECTED COUNTRIES ON HUMAN DEVELOPMENT INDEX (HDI); GENDER DEVELOPMENT INDEX (GDI), AND GENDER EMPOWERMENT MEASURE (GEM) IN 1992

Country	HDI Rank	Value	GDI Rank	Value	HDI[1] minus GDI[2]	GEM
Belgium	12	.926	18	.852	-7	21
Denmark	16	.920	4	.904	10	4
France	8	.931	7	.898	0	31
Germany	15	.921	–	–	–	–
Greece	22	.907	27	.825	-8	67
Ireland	19	.916	30	.813	-13	24
Italy	20	.912	14	.861	4	10
Luxembourg	27	.893	35	.790	-12	13
Netherlands	4	.936	20	.851	-16	7
Norway	7	.933	3	.911	3	2
Portugal	36	.874	25	.832	5	30
Spain	9	.930	34	.795	-26	26
Sweden	10	.929	1	.919	8	1
USA	2	.938	5	.901	-3	8
UK	18	.916	13	.862	3	19

1 GDI is available for only 130 countries; a new HDI ranking has been done so as to allow comparisons.
2 A positive difference between a country's HDI and GDI ranks indicates that it performs better on gender equality than on average achievement alone (UN Report, 1995:77).

    The Scandinavian countries and particularly Sweden are ranked at the top of both the GDI and GEM indices. The rankings of some countries may differ on GDI and GEM (e.g. GEM is lower than GDI in the case of Greece; is higher than GDI in the case of the Netherlands and Ireland, and is practically equivalent to GDI in the case of Sweden and Denmark). These trends reflect the extent to which the position of women in the public arena is treated as more or less important than gender issues in general. Table 2.1 demonstrates that in Ireland the position of women in the public arena was slightly more favourable than one would expect in terms of the general prioritising of gender issues.

    The UN Report also noted that, although considerable variation existed as regards the position of women in industrialised and developing countries, 'no society treats its women as well as its men' (UN 1995:75). The GDI values of all countries improved between 1970 and 1992, although they improved more in developing countries than in industrialised countries (i.e. 62 per cent change versus 28 per cent change: UN Report, 1995:78).

Ireland's percentage change in the value of GDI was broadly similar to that of average industrialised countries, but our position in the overall ranking deteriorated slightly between 1970 and 1992 (see Table 2.2). In contrast, Scandinavian countries such as Norway and Sweden, and Southern European countries such as Portugal and Greece, improved their rank position over that period.

The UN Report clearly demonstrates that the position of women in a particular country was not related in any simple way to the level of economic development in that country. Broadly based theoretical ideas about convergence, modernisation and economic determinism are challenged by the statistical trends of the Report. The Report also suggested that the position of women was not related to the type of economic system operating in these countries (i.e. capitalist as opposed to socialist). Implicit in these trends is the idea that gender prioritising by political systems is crucial; and that this prioritising can occur in countries as diverse as Sweden, Portugal, Greece and the Czech Republic.

TABLE 2.2

POSITION OF SELECTED COUNTRIES ON THE GENDER
DEVELOPMENT INDEX IN 1970 AND IN 1992[1]

Country	Percentage change in value	Rank in 1970 minus rank in 1992[2]
Belgium	22%	-4
Denmark	19%	0
France	21%	-2
Germany	–	–
Greece	45%	4
Ireland	32%	-3
Italy	32%	2
Luxembourg	17%	-8
Netherlands	21%	-7
Norway	27%	4
Portugal	66%	12
Spain	32%	-4
Sweden	20%	2
USA	11%	-4
UK	25%	0

[1] UN Report, 1995: 80.

[2] HDI and GDI values have been recalculated for the universe of 79 countries on which information is available at both times. A positive difference in rank means an improvement from 1970 to 1992.

Women in the Irish labour force

The participation of women in paid employment in Ireland increased very substantially between 1971 and 1996 (by 212,000 as compared with a growth of 23,000 in male employment; CSO, 1997). Thus, as is clear from Table 2.3, when one focused specifically on those at work, using principal economic status, the proportion of women at work increased from 27 per cent in 1971 to 35 per cent in 1996 (while the proportion of men decreased from 76 per cent to 59 per cent). Using the more inclusive ILO definition of employment (focusing on actual activity in the previous week) by 1996, 41.1 per cent of Irish women aged 15 years and over were in the labour force, as compared with an EU average of 45.3 per cent: the highest participation rates being in the Scandinavian countries (Denmark, 59 per cent; Sweden, 57 per cent; Finland, 55 per cent) and the lowest in the Mediterranean countries (Italy, 35 per cent; Spain 36 per cent and Greece, 37 per cent: Eurostat, 1997).

TABLE 2.3
WOMEN AND MEN BY PRINCIPAL STATUS 1971-1996
(% AND N=000s)

Women aged 15 or over	1971 %(N)	1981 %(N)	1996 %(N)
At work	27% (276)	27% (329)	35% (488)
Unemployed	1% (14)	2% (29.5)	4% (52)
Students	7% (67)	9% (103)	13% (182)
Home Duties	62% (635)	55% (661.5)	41% (573)
Retired/Other	4% (36)	7% (82.5)	8% (107)
TOTAL	101% (1028)	100% (1205.5)	101% (1402)
Men aged 15 or over			
At work	76% (774)	68% (809)	59% (797)
Unemployed	6% (62)	9% (104)	10% (138)
Students	7% (70)	8% (97)	13% (176)
Home Duties	1% (3.5)	– (1)	1% (9)
Retired/Other	11% (111)	15% (183)	18% (234)
TOTAL	100% (1020)	100% (1194)	101% (1354)

CSO, 1997

This pattern reflected a dramatic increase in Irish married women in paid employment over this period, rising from 7.5 per cent in 1971 to 36.6 per cent in 1996. Thus, as is clear from Table 2.4, the number of married women at work increased, i.e. from 38,300 in 1971 to 241,400 in 1996, using principal economic status (CSO, 1997:29). This increase is typically linked to higher educational levels; a declining birth rate; a rising level of individualisation (Kennedy, 1989); capitalism's demand for a cheap labour force, and Irish women's willingness to provide that kind of labour (see Chapters 7 and 8). The low level relative to Europe is explained in terms of the role of the Catholic Church, as reflected in the educational system; in the legal context; in social attitudes to contraception; in the number of children; in the absence of state funded child care; in the relationship between women's wages, child care costs and taxation (Callan and Farrell, 1991; Mahon, 1987, 1994). Indeed Pyle was even more inclusive in her explanation and referred to a variety of other social institutions including 'household, firm, educational, and religious systems, unions and the military' (1990:134).

TABLE 2.4
WOMEN AT WORK 1971-1996, USING PRINCIPAL ECONOMIC
STATUS

	Single	Married	Other	Total
1971	212,600	38,300	24,600	275,600
1981	211,000	102,600	15,600	329,200
1991	191,700	173,800	20,800	386,300
1996	216,200	241,400	30,500	488,000

CSO, 1997:1

However, it is important to note that the participation of young Irish married women in paid employment varies little from that of their European counterparts. The biggest difference between the average Irish pattern and the average EU pattern is found among women in their 40s and 50s. Thus 63 per cent of Irish married women aged 25-34 years were in the labour force as compared with 37 per cent of those aged 45-54 (Labour Force Survey, 1996 [CSO, 1997:55]). It will be argued later that this reflects a combination of factors. However, it is important to note that in Ireland as in many West European countries, women from the 1930s onwards were subject to a marriage bar, which forced women in public sector employment to leave paid employment on marriage. In

Ireland the marriage bar was lifted in 1957 for primary school teachers, but not until 1973 for other public sector employees (e.g. civil servants, secondary school teachers). Although the marriage bar was not legally enforced in many other areas of paid employment, (e.g. the banks), up to 1973 there was a clear expectation that women would retire on marriage and this was institutionalised through the marriage gratuity (i.e. a lump sum paid to women on their marriage and subsequent retirement); through separate and higher pay scales for married men, and through related tax and social welfare arrangements.

Influence of the state and the trade unions

Breen *et al* highlighted the importance of the state as a direct creator of employment – noting that it has been directly involved in 'the creation of numerous places in the more advantaged employee categories within the public sector itself' (1990:93). It is estimated that in the 1970s, 85,000 jobs were created in the public sector (Breen *et al*, 1990:148). To a considerable extent these jobs were in the health, education and social welfare areas (typical areas of women's employment), and in the clerical and administrative arm of the state (at its lower levels also predominantly female areas of employment). Thus, inadvertently as it were, the state contributed to the creation of a substantial number of lower professional and clerical job opportunities for women. Ironically, it was much less successful in generating employment opportunities in the manufacturing and agricultural sectors – sectors to which it was ideologically committed, since these were areas of predominantly male employment.

Right across Europe the expansion of public sector employment has generated a demand for female labour, mostly in the health and related welfare areas (Smyth, 1997; O'Connell, 1996). This was strongest in Sweden where in 1994, because of its developed welfare state, over 40 per cent of total employment and over 60 per cent of women's employment was in the public sector. In Ireland, in 1994, over 25 per cent of all employment and 40 per cent of women's employment was in these areas (Bulletin on Women and Employment in the EU, 1996, 9:2).

O'Connell (1996) noted that, in Ireland, over the 1961-91 period, the overall proportion of employees in upper middle class occupations increased from under 10 per cent in 1961 to over 22 per cent in 1991. The increase occurred among both men and women – the proportion of women in such occupations rising from 15 per cent in 1961 to 28 per cent in 1991. Similar, though less dramatic, trends occurred among lower middle class employees so that by 1991 more than three quarters of the women at work were middle class employees as compared with approximately two fifths of the men. However, within the upper middle class the proportion of men in the higher professional category almost doubled while the proportion of women declined by about one third (O'Connell, 1996).

Maruani (1992:1) stressed that the increase in the presence of women in the labour force

> does not mean that women have won occupational equality ... Discrimination and segregation continue to reign.

Equal pay does not exist in any EU country (Maruani, 1992:51). In Ireland, as indeed right across the EU, women earn less than men (the differential varying, overall, from 14 to 40 per cent; Ireland being at the high end of that continuum). Furthermore, for the most part, the gap has narrowed only slightly in recent years. There is no evidence to suggest that the differences are in decline across Europe (Acker, 1988). Indeed at different periods since the 1970s, the gap between the wages of men and women has widened in a number of countries (e.g. in Denmark between 1977 and 1985). The United Nations (1995) noted that although the data was incomplete and not always comparable, in both industrial and developing countries, 'women's wages, on average, are considerably lower than men's' (1995:36), and that 'the average female wage is only three quarters of the male wage in the non-agricultural sector' (1995:4). Indeed women's hourly earnings in manufacturing industries in Ireland were still only 74 per cent of men's in 1996 (see Chapter 7).

Maruani suggested that this reflected a number of processes, viz. the concentration of women into a small number of (poorly paid) predominantly female sectors; the systematic failure to reward women's skills; structural and individual processes surrounding the payment of bonuses/increments and the greater difficulties women had in moving up the occupational hierarchy. In Ireland (and across the EU as a whole) women are concentrated into the health, education and domestic service areas. Only recently has reference been made to the extent to which Irish society, through its definition of what constitutes 'skill' and 'expertise', attaches little value to female skills whether in the paid employment or domestic arenas (Lynch and McLaughlin, 1995). There is no systematic information on bonuses or on promotion, but what evidence there is suggests that, despite the feminisation of the labour force, unequal pay and horizontal and vertical segregation remain a reality in Ireland and across Europe.

In Scandinavian countries there is a much lower differential between the earnings of men and women than in Ireland. This has been attributed to centralised wage negotiations and a commitment to limiting wage dispersion, strategies which have proved more effective than legislation in affecting the wage differential (Callan and Wren, 1994; Lester, 1997). Thus while Ireland and the UK theoretically have better legislative protection than, for example, Denmark, the wage gap is lower in the latter (Bergusson and Dickens, 1996). The idea of a national minimum wage (which is currently attracting support in the UK and Ireland) is advantageous to women since they are likely to be among the low paid. However, it is interesting that the CORI proposal (Clark and Healy, 1997) suggesting a basic income for every adult, and so representing the complete ending of the male breadwinner system, was greeted with derision by senior civil servants.

Whitehouse (1992) found that across the OECD countries the size of the (hourly) wage differential between men and women was affected by the existence of collective bargaining, while there was no clear evidence as regards the effect of legislative measures. She recognised that in some cases the capacity of the unions to regulate the labour market hindered the influx of women into paid employment. This pattern can be seen in Ireland where, at least up to the late 1980s, the unions were mainly concerned with the creation of full-time 'male' jobs in manufacturing industries. Whitehouse argues however that union involvement need not necessarily result in such patterns. In Sweden, for example, union control over the conditions associated with part-time work (predominantly done by women) was such that employers had to look for other ways of achieving flexibility, apart from creating low security, poorly paid, part-time jobs.

In Ireland, equal pay legislation in the 1970s was not campaigned for by the unions. In fact the unions negotiated on the basis of a male-female wage differential. They seem to have been caught between patriarchal self interest and an ideological commitment to gender equality. Until the mid 1980s they saw women's under-representation as reflecting 'social conditioning, family responsibilities, lack of confidence and experience, and apathy' (Cunningham, 1994:43). These explanations were in fact identical to those offered by personnel managers in the mid 1980s to explain the absence of women from management positions (McCarthy, 1986). In the 1980s there ensued what Cunningham (1994:40) called an intense struggle for power between 'the traditional male-dominated forces of the trade union movement and the newly arrived women activists'. At that stage, approximately two thirds of all female and male workers were members of trade unions, but only 4 per cent of full-time officials, and only approximately one in ten of those on the various trade union decision-making bodies, were women.

In response in this situation, the Irish Congress of Trade Unions (1993) adopted a number of equality programmes, in 1982, 1987 and 1992 and agreed to monitor on an annual basis the participation of women at senior levels of the trade union movement. However, women's access to positions of power within the union structure has remained less than satisfactory. Although the participation of women at shop steward/workplace representative and branch level improved, in 1992 only 17 per cent of those on the Executive Council of the Irish Congress of Trade Unions were women. This representation is less than half of what it would be if women were to be represented on the Executive Council in proportion to their membership.

It is in the interests of the Irish Congress of Trade Unions to ensure that equality is implemented within its ranks, and it is officially committed to this. Currently, just under half of all female employees are members of trade unions, 75 per cent of all unions have women's committees or equality committees, 59 per cent have sections on women/equality at their conference agendas, and 85 per cent employ an equality officer/official (ICTU, 1993). Nevertheless, power at the top echelons remains predominantly concentrated in male hands.

These patterns nicely illustrate the 'difficulty' that power holders have in actually sharing power – even when ideologically committed to doing so. However, the trade union experience also suggests that positive or affirmative action, and structures to facilitate this, can bring about change. For example, women's representation at the Delegate Conference more than doubled between 1987-91 (i.e. from 11.5 per cent to 27.5 per cent) after unions were required to include women delegates in proportion to their membership of the union. Nominations of women by the Irish Congress of Trade Unions to boards of outside bodies increased from 2 per cent in 1979, to 32 per cent in 1991. The proportion of full-time trade union officials who were women also doubled over a five year period, although it was still only 17 per cent in 1991 (Cunningham, 1994).

The persistence of predominantly male controlled structures within the unions has inevitably meant that the ability and willingness of the unions to challenge the patriarchal structures of Irish life has been limited. Indeed market forces, the expansion of the state apparatus, and the increasing importance of the service sector have played a greater part in facilitating the participation of women in paid employment than have those structures (such as the trade unions) which claim to be concerned with equality.

Women and the state

Peillon (1995:358) suggested that the state was

> the institution which exercises central power . . . associated with such attributes as centralisation of power, territorial sovereignty, a monopoly of the legitimate use of force.

It is typically seen as including not only the Houses of the Oireachtas but also a

> set of institutions supported by public finance and run by appointed staff. This would include the civil service, judiciary, police, army and state-run enterprises (O'Dowd, 1991:97).

This section examines the direct and indirect indicators of the representation of women in these structures. In the latter case, attention will be focused briefly on a number of specific aspects, viz. the state as the provider of a legal framework, the state as a controller of women's bodies, the state as a redistributor of resources, and the gendered nature of state employment policies.

Representation of women in state structures

The pattern in Ireland as regards the representation of women in the upper and lower houses of the National Parliament is virtually identical to the average European pattern across the EU member countries (i.e. 12% versus 12.3% respectively). This is a very recent development. Throughout the EU there is a huge range of variation in representation and this variation bears no clear relationship to a country's stage of economic development (Rapid Reports, 1993:11). The proportion of women who are involved at each level varies considerably in different countries (for example 6-39 per cent as members of Parliament and 9-35 per cent as Ministers: see Table 2.5). Hence essentialist arguments concerning the apolitical nature of women seem rather suspect.

  The Scandinavian countries generally have the highest representation of women at each level. The pattern in Ireland (with women making up

17 per cent of local council members; 12 per cent of the Parliament and 16 per cent of Ministers) is considerably less (see Table 2.5). In Ireland numbers rose slightly in 1996 with women constituting 14 per cent of the Oireachtas membership, holding 13 per cent of the Cabinet Ministries and 25 per cent of Junior Ministries. Nevertheless, it was still very much lower than in Norway – a country similar to Ireland in many ways – where women made up 39 per cent of the Parliamentary membership and 35 per cent of the Ministries (see Table 2.5).

TABLE 2.5
PROPORTION OF WOMEN AT MUNICIPAL OR EQUIVALENT
PARLIAMENTARY AND MINISTERIAL LEVEL OF THE STATE[1]

Country	Local Council	Mayors	Parliamentary (incl. Upper and Lower Houses)	Ministerial
Belgium	14%	4%	10%	11%
Denmark	28%	10%	33%	29%
France	17%	5%	6%	7%
Germany	20%	n/a	20%	16%
Greece	9%	2%	6%	5%
Spain	13%	5%	15%	14%
Ireland	17%	12%	12%	16%
Italy	10%	4%	13%	12%
Luxembourg	10%	10%	20%	9%
Netherlands	22%	12%	29%	31%
Portugal	10%	2%	9%	10%
UK	25%	n/a	7%	9%
Norway	28%	23%	39%	35%
Sweden	34%	n/a	34%	30%

[1] UN, 1995:60

Women are also significantly under-represented at the higher echelons of the non-representative areas of the state, such as the civil service (Rudd, 1982, Mahon, 1987, 1991; Randall and Smyth, 1987; Second Commission on the Status of Women, 1993). Despite the fact that there has been a popular view that men and women are 'different', there was no concern other than in the women's movement (Scannell, 1988) about the low level of representation of women in these institutions. It was assumed that women's interests were subsumed in men's and that they would be adequately represented by them. The credibility of this position has been increasingly challenged.

At a theoretical level there has been a move away from viewing the state as either inherently patriarchal (MacKinnon 1987), inherently capitalist (Barrett, 1992), or as both patriarchal and capitalist (Walby, 1990). The focus is less on the state as a structure, one coherent 'object', and more on the state as a site where power is contested, and where various alliances are formed (Foucault, 1980). This perspective allows one to make sense of the fact that various parts of the state apparatus may simultaneously act in different ways as regards the promotion or frustration of women's interests, though, typically, male interests provide the main focus of the state's activity. Peillon (1995) has argued that the state has its own project or vision – and that in Ireland this has been forged in the context of the major forces in Irish society (e.g. property owners). He has suggested that state activity in the area of redistribution reveals these biases so that all property-owning classes lose very little and 'more frequently gain by relating to the state' (1995:360). A similar conclusion was reached by O'Connell and Rottman (1992) and by Breen *et al* who noted that the state had been 'monumentally unsuccessful in moderating inegalitarian tendencies in the class structure' (1990:209).

Peillon (1995) has highlighted the attempt to deal with the plurality of interests in Irish society through a corporatist process. This attempt is most explicit in the area of national wage agreements, in which, since the 1970s, the social partners (i.e. the trade unions, employer/business and agricultural/farming interests) have been involved in negotiations with the state. It has been argued that the resulting structures are unstable and weak (Hardiman, 1992; Breen *et al*, 1990). Yet as noted by Peillon (1995) they have been remarkably persistent. However, they do not equalise power between groups. Two of the three social partners are property owners and they are overwhelmingly men. Hence, perhaps inevitably, particular issues are likely to be seen as priorities.

Peillon has argued that in this context the state's policies have favoured capital investment and 'satisfy the needs of the capitalist class' (1995: 361). For example, although non-agricultural self employment declined consistently from 1926 to 1961, it rose after that. By 1989 one in twenty men in non-agricultural work was an employer, and an additional one in twelve was self employed – a pattern that constitutes 'a strikingly high percentage by European standards' (O'Connell and Rottman, 1992: 217). O'Connell and Rottman saw these patterns as related to the policies of the state in the area of tax incentives, adaptation grants, etc. It is possible to see such trends as having a gender dimension, since women are highly unlikely to have the resources to be employers or self employed (MacDevitt, 1996).

The creation of the National Economic and Social Forum (with an equal representation of men and women) to contribute 'to the formation of a national consensus on social and economic matters' (NESF, 1996:55) was an attempt to create a more inclusive structure. NESF includes not only the social partners but also a third strand which consists of women's organisations, the unemployed, the disadvantaged, environmental interests, academics, elderly, youth and people with disabilities. Although women comprise 50 per cent of NESF, only a minority (i.e. 3 out of 25) specifically represent women's interests. NESF is simply a consultative forum, with no power and limited funding. Its success in challenging established priorities remains to be seen.

The state has, almost inadvertently, influenced the position of women in Irish society through its development of a mass communications system. The role of the state in this area can be seen as part of its outward-looking policies from the late 1950s onwards. Irish society up to that time had been heavily censored. Public opinion had been shaped by the Roman Catholic Church and by other organisations emphasising a familial, non-individualistic, servicing, a-sexual concept of woman (Peillon, 1988). However, with the introduction of TV, very different images became available. Equally importantly, perhaps, the Irish media began to employ left-wing dissidents who challenged accepted opinions. From the 1980s onwards, Ireland became increasingly penetrated by a huge array of British, mainland European and American programmes, and the very diversity of these influences undermined the 'natural' inevitability of women's position in society (Kelly and Rolston, 1995). However, change has not always been in one direction:

> Within the space of thirty years, the farming media had transformed utterly their portrayal of women. As the traditional areas of female production developed into commercial enterprises, the media redefined the role of the farm woman, relocated her within the home and denied her involvement in the apparently male domain of the farm (Duggan, 1987:67-68).

The state, in its attempts to distance itself from the Roman Catholic Church, to ally itself with Europe, to develop a modern mass communications system, inadvertently contributed to changing the position of women in Irish society. However, only with the election of Mary Robinson as President of Ireland in 1990 did the recognition of women as a 'force' to be incorporated into what Peillon (1982) calls the 'project' of the state become explicit. It is not clear, however, if this 'incorporation' will involve the commitment of substantial resources to a gendered agenda.

The state as a provider of a legal framework

The Second Commission on the Status of Women (1993: 26) noted that: 'Equality for women in spheres other than work does not have any underpinning in the Constitution, the basic law of our country'. In part, this arises because in the Constitution women are seen in the context of the family (e.g. Article 41.2):

1. In particular the state recognises that by her life within the home, woman gives to the state the support without which the common good cannot be achieved.

2. The state shall, therefore, endeavour to ensure that mothers shall not be obliged by economic necessity to engage in labour to the neglect of their duties within the home.

A Constitutional Review Body (1996) has produced a detailed report recommending substantial changes in the Constitution. It is not clear however to what extent, if at all, such changes will be implemented. It has been widely argued (Mahon, 1987:56) that the articles in the Constitution relating to women are patriarchal, or at least paternalistic, and that since they are not underpinned by taxation or social welfare policy, they are 'aspirational rather than practical in effect' (Second Commission on the Status of Women, 1993:71).

Although ideologically the state endorses the desirability of women's full-time work within the home, it has been very slow indeed to create a legal framework which would protect their position. Legislation to provide for joint ownership of the family home in those situations where the wife is not in paid employment (the situation of the majority of Irish married women) was found to be unconstitutional in 1994. The state has overwhelmingly been unwilling to initiate criminal proceedings against a father in cases of familial incest (McKeown and Gilligan, 1991). The ideological basis underlying such unwillingness is arguably the legitimacy of the father's authority as head of the household. The investigation into the Kilkenny incest case (Wood, 1993), however, has gone some way to opening up the question of the nature and extent of parental and marital authority, and the appropriate limits of family privacy. The state implicitly but firmly indicated that its support (e.g. in the 1991 Social Welfare Act) is ultimately for family life, whether this is established on the implicit basis of love and/or cohabitation, or on the basis of a union consecrated by church and state. The low level of funding given to the voluntary and community activities of women (Mulvey, 1991) and the high level of refusals in the case of applications for the Carer's Allowance, further suggest that statements concerning the social value of women's unpaid work are rhetorical. The one positive step which has been taken in this area has been in the old age (contributory) pensions regulations (1994), which allows for credits towards a contributory pension when, for example, a woman is caring for children under 6 years old (Fourth Report of Fourth Joint Oireachtas Committee, 1996:20-21).

The mid 1980s were also characterised by the defeat of the first referendum on divorce. The legislation which was proposed was in effect a 'no-fault divorce' allowing for divorce after five years of marital breakdown. Opinion polls showed that, initially, three fifths of the population were in favour of changing the legislation, but with 63 per cent of the electorate voting in the first divorce referendum (1986), two out of three rejected it. For some this reversal of opinion reflected the influence of the Catholic Church and the central role of the family in the lives of Irish Catholic women. However, as Mahon (1995) has noted, this vote was also influenced by the fact that the majority of Irish married women were economically dependent (a position which the state had not safeguarded prior to the introduction of the 1986 referendum). During the late 1980s and early 1990s, a series of legislative changes were initiated to deal with this situation. In addition the legal age of marriage was raised from 16 years in the 1972 Marriages Act to 18 years in the 1994 Family Law Act.

In 1995, a second referendum was held to amend the Constitution so as to allow for the introduction of divorce. All the main political parties and the Church of Ireland supported a yes vote. This amendment was passed, although by a tiny minority (i.e. 9,114 votes: 50.3 per cent of those who voted). Girvin (1996) suggested that the closeness of the vote reflected the continued existence of a morally conservative vote. There was indirect support for this in an MRBI poll undertaken three weeks before the referendum when those intending to vote no appeared to be doing so for reasons that

> could be loosely identified with the Catholic Church: destruction of family life; easy option, marriage is for life, against religion/catholic; would not solve problem (Girvin, 1996: 178).

For the first time both those in favour and those opposed to divorce addressed the issue of whether divorce was good or bad for women, although this was not a key issue in the campaign. Divorce is now available in Ireland when spouses have lived apart from each other for periods amounting to at least four years during the previous five years, where there is no reasonable prospect of reconciliation between the spouses, and where provision has been or will be made for the spouse, any children and any other person prescribed by law.

Over the past twenty-five years, the legal and constitutional framework provided by the state as regards the position of women in Irish society has come under a great deal of scrutiny. Initially, this arose in the context of entry to the European Community in 1973. As signatories of the Treaty of Rome, Ireland became bound by a series of directives relating to equal pay and equal treatment in the area of access to employment, vocational training, and social security (Fourth Report of the Fourth Joint Committee, 1996). Pressure for legal change was most effective when it came from outside Ireland, followed up by individual legal action and/or group pressure within Ireland (Mahon, 1987). Over the past twenty-five years, the state has provided important legal protections for women who were or had been in paid employment, through the enactment of laws such as the Anti-Discrimination (Pay) Act, 1974; the Employment Equality Act, 1977; the Maternity (Protection of Employees) Act, 1981 and the Maternity Protection Act, 1995.

It has been argued that the introduction of EC directives was at the insistence of France who already had legislation, and who did not wish to be at an international disadvantage within an economically integrated Europe (McGauran, 1996). Ireland's compliance with the EC directives on pay was prompt. Ireland was in fact ahead of the Netherlands, Belgium and Denmark, insofar as certain aspects of equal pay laws in those countries had to be amended to bring them into line with the EC directive in 1980/1981 (Women of Europe, 1987). However, because of the way in which the Employment Equality Act (1977) was drafted in Ireland, up to now it has been almost impossible to establish the existence of indirect discrimination since 'the Irish courts and tribunals have generally applied the law of indirect discrimination in a way that exposes subtle and institutionalised forms of sex discrimination' (Fourth Report of the Fourth Joint Committee on Women's Rights, 1996:13). The Nathan v Bailey Gibson case drawing on the Equal Treatment Directive, and case law from the European Court of Justice established for the first time that it was sufficient to show that a practice bore more heavily on one sex than another to constitute indirect discrimination and so nullified 'the impossible requirements of section 2 (c)' (Honan, 1997:12). It is salutary to note that such indirect discrimination continues to be seen as unproblematic by particular sections of the state. For example, the restriction of the state-funded FÁS Action Programme for Women to people on the Live Register has been defended although it 'suggests indirect discrimination in access to vocational training, contrary to the Equal Treatment Directive and the Employment Equality Act' (Fourth Report of the Fourth Joint Committee, 1996:22). Indirect discrimination has become so embedded in state practices and procedures that it is not even noticed.

More recently the Employment Equality Act and the Equal Status Act (1997) were passed by the Oireachtas but referred by the President to the Supreme Court for an assessment of their constitutionality. None of the sections which were found to be unconstitutional were specifically concerned with gender (Equality Act 1997: 15, 16, 35 and 63, 3). It is questionable to what extent either of these Acts is concerned with actively promoting gender equality. Certain kinds of positive action are allowed, but not required, in the Employment Equality Act. Furthermore, although Lester (1997) has noted that contract compliance, which has been widely used in Northern Ireland to combat discrimination, constitutes one of the most effective ways of combating discrimination (and one which is compatible with EU law), no interest has been evinced in introducing it in Ireland.

Crompton (1995) noted that only the Scandinavian states appear to be really committed to gender equality. Liff and Wajcman (1996) suggest that such a commitment involves transcending the debates about women's 'sameness' or 'difference'. It involves, they suggest, starting from a recognition that women are disadvantaged in the paid employment arena, and recognising that this arena is constructed in such a way that a full-time 'male' worker is seen as the preferred option. In this respect, the 1991 Worker Protection (Regular Part-time Employees) Act in Ireland is an interesting innovation insofar as it extends to such employees much the same labour law protection enjoyed by full-time workers, provided they work at least 8 hours per week (Conroy Jackson, 1996). It may be seen as reflecting the possibility that the state may not always act in a simple gendered way, in the broad area of equal opportunities.

The persistence of occupational segregation here, as elsewhere in Europe, has made further progress difficult and dependent on tackling the issue of the evaluation of women's work (Fourth Report of the Fourth Joint Committee on Women's Rights, 1996). This issue was initially identified as crucial in the European Community's Third Action Programme (1991-94). In 1996, in an attempt to tackle the problem, a Code of Practice was adopted at EU level on Equal Pay for Work of Equal Value. It aims to eliminate discrimination in job classification and job evaluation schemes (European Commission, 1997:10). However, it is not a legally binding instrument. There is also a proposal to include a reference to 'equal work of equal value' in the Amsterdam Treaty. It remains to be seen what effect, if any, such initiatives will have. The European Court of Justice has provided one possible lever by ruling that where a *prima facie* case of sex discrimination exists (e.g. the differential salaries of predominantly female and predominantly male professionals: Enderby versus Frenchay Health Authorities: Clarke, 1995), it is up to the employer to show that there are objective reasons for this over and above those related to the collective bargaining process (Fourth Report of the Fourth Joint Committee, 1996:8).

Despite the perceived importance of the mother in the care of children, the current statutory entitlement to 14 weeks paid maternity leave is not particularly generous by comparison with other countries in the EU (OECD, 1990). In addition, and reflecting its stereotypical assumptions about male and female roles in the family, Ireland, along with the UK and Luxembourg, is one of the few EU countries which does not yet provide a parental leave entitlement (although legislation on this has been introduced to comply with the 1995 EU Directive). Ireland has indeed one of the least developed systems of non-stigmatising state-subsidised child care in the EU to help mothers with their responsibilities as regards child care (Gilligan, 1991; O'Connor and Shortall, 1996; Second Commission on the Status of Women, 1993; European Commission Network on Child Care, 1996). This indicates the state's perspective that child care is a family responsibility, in fact a mother's responsibility, which it is unwilling to share. Indeed the threat of the removal of children who are seen as 'at risk' acts as an effective deterrent to any requests for help from the state, although there is ample evidence of the disproportionate admission to care of children whose parent(s) are unable to purchase child care. This raises issues about the role of the state in facilitating working class parents in their parenting roles: issues which to date have evoked little interest (O'Connor, 1992a). There is some indication that, with encouragement from Europe, this pattern may be starting to change. Thus, an allocation of £2.5 million has been made to child care programmes, to assist parents in disadvantaged areas to avail of opportunities for education and training (Department of Justice, Equality and Law Reform, 1998).

The state and control over women's bodies

Contraception and abortion illustrate the many attempts made by the Irish state to maintain control over women's bodies. The struggle for changes in the area of contraception, spanning almost 25 years, illustrates the slowness with which change can be expected to occur and the important part played by the women's movement in bringing about that change. It is widely recognised that from the late 1960s onwards, despite the 1935 Criminal Law (Amendment) Act which prohibited the sale, advertising or importation of contraceptives, and despite the Roman Catholic Church's view of 'artificial' contraception as being morally wrong, very considerable use was made of the contraceptive pill as a cycle regulator.

In 1979, legislative change was introduced to regularise the situation somewhat, i.e. to allow condoms to be available on medical prescription for 'bona-fide family planning purposes'. This development was hailed as an 'Irish solution to an Irish problem', but it was clearly unworkable and inappropriate. It was followed by the 1985 Family Planning Act (Barry, 1992) where contraceptives were legalised for those over 18 years. AIDS, in the final analysis, provided a useful cover for defining contraception as a 'public health' issue and condoms were made available in vending machines in 1993 (without official notice of this been given to the Hierarchy: Nic Ghiolla Phádraig, 1995). In 1995 the Minister for Health issued guidelines indicating to Health Boards that they had a responsibility to ensure that an accessible and comprehensive family planning service was provided by themselves and/or other service providers (Dept. of Health, 1995). It is questionable to what extent this exists. Thus Wiley and Merriman (1996) found that only half of their sample thought that family planning advice was available in their area, with over 80 per cent assessing the information that was available to them as inadequate.

The role of the state in reflecting and reinforcing the status of women as child bearers came into sharp focus in two referenda on abortion, in 1983 and 1992 (see Smyth, 1992a and b). As noted by Mahon (1995) Riddick (1993) and Smyth (1992a) abortion was illegal in Ireland under the 1861 Offences against the Person Act. Under pressure from right-wing groups (e.g. the 'Pro-Life' Group) an attempt was made to copperfasten its illegality by drafting an amendment to the Constitution. This amendment was carried in 1983, with 66 per cent voting in favour of it, although the overall turnout was only approximately 50 per cent (Mahon, 1995). Thus Article 40.3.3 was inserted into the Constitution, viz. 'The State acknowledges the right to life of the unborn, and with due regard for the equal right to life of the mother, guarantees in its laws to respect, and as far as practicable, by its laws to defend and vindicate that right'. This led to a series of court cases, referenda and catharses in public opinion and ultimately was interpreted by the Supreme Court as having in fact established a right to abortion in certain circumstances (Riddick, 1993; Mahon, 1995; Connolly, 1997).

Fine-Davis (1988) and Whelan and Fahey (1994) showed that the phrasing of the amendment obscured a wide degree of support for abortion under certain circumstances (for example, in the case of rape, incest or where the mother's health was at risk from the pregnancy). Indeed, in the 1990 European Values Study, 80 per cent of Irish women under 35 years approved of abortion when the mother's health was at risk. The conditional nature of attitudes to abortion also emerged when the Attorney General took out an injunction in 1992 to restrain a pregnant 14 year old girl ('X') who had been raped from travelling to England, with the support and consent of her parents, for an abortion. In the face of public dismay following this action, the Government (paradoxically) encouraged the girl's family to appeal to the Supreme Court and undertook to pay legal expenses (Smyth, 1992a). Subsequent legal developments indicated that the Constitutional Amendment on abortion had provided for the right to abortion when the life, as opposed to the health, of the mother was at risk. The Government has yet to introduce legislation to clarify the circumstances in which legal abortion may be carried out in Ireland. It is widely accepted that this will not be forthcoming in the foreseeable future (Riddick, 1993).

Paralleling such developments, referenda were held in 1992 as regards the legality of the distribution of information concerning the names and addresses of abortion clinics in England and as regards women's right to travel to England for lawful services including abortion (see Mahon, 1995; Riddick, 1993). Both of these referenda were passed. There is thus both a constitutionally guaranteed, and in EU terms a legal right to information about such services, and a right to travel abroad to obtain them. The very necessity for such referenda and the legal action surrounding the 'X' case vividly highlighted the perceived appropriateness of the state's role in relation to women's bodies.

The dominant discourses, both in the first and second abortion referenda, were medical and legal, with moral issues largely revolving around those related to 'ensoulment', rather than those related to a woman's bodily integrity, the nature of respect for her life, her status as a moral being or the limits of her personal autonomy. The Women's Right to Choose Campaign, founded in 1980, did attempt to put forward a woman centred discourse, but this was obscured in the actual campaign in the early 1980s. Conroy Jackson (1986) has argued that the dilution of a woman centred discourse arose because of the need to create alliances with conservative groups and 'power blocs' whose agendas were not centrally concerned with women – issues to which we return in the context of a discussion of the women's movement.

The state as a redistributor of resources

The Irish state has played an important role in the pursuit of social objectives and in the creation of structures which modify the impact of brute market forces. Acker (1988:478) noted the appropriateness of moving away from an exclusive focus on economic production within a societal context where 'classes are structured through relations of distribution as well as relations of production'.

At a national policy level Peillon (1982) argued that in the First, Second and Third Programmes for development, the orientation was basically economic, even though in the latter two, economic objectives were underpinned by social ones. Social expenditure did grow more rapidly than other areas of expenditure in the early 1980s. Breen *et al* however found that the state has perpetuated privilege with 'the cost of rising public social expenditure being disproportionately borne by the less well-to-do', thereby supporting a class structure based on the ownership of property and substantial class inequalities (1990:215).

A 'class audit' has never been attached to social policies, and it was only in the 1993 Programme for Government (under pressure from a similar requirement at EU level) that the notion of a 'gender audit' was endorsed. However, mid way through the second round of the structural funds, and despite its commitment to equality for women, people in poverty, people with disabilities and minority ethnic groups, less than 30 per cent of EU funds in Ireland were targeted at these groups. Furthermore, in contrast to other countries, there was no national annual report on the operation of the structural funds and little effort was made to implement the recommendations of the European Social Fund Evaluation Unit as regards gender auditing.

The Evaluation Report on Women's Training Programmes (Dept of Enterprise and Employment, 1994) noted:

> Currently, there is no forum for discussing women's participation in ESF co-financed training measures. The aspiration to increase women's participation is contained in the National Plan, but the monitoring of procedures which are designed to achieve this aim need further consideration.

It also noted that, although most of the agencies in receipt of ESF funds had an equal opportunities statement policy:

> Any meaningful attempt to address the considerable gender segregation that exists would require a commitment to positive action strategies (1994, Summary: 2).

Such developments have not been forthcoming. Indeed women made up less than 20 per cent of the membership of the national monitoring committee, and even less on the regional monitoring committees. These monitoring committees have a key role to play in the allocation of extra funds (amounting to 78 million ECUs in the second round of the structural funds). Thus, despite the prioritising of equality by the European Commission, funds have not been allocated appropriately in the light of this objective. As noted by Community Workers Co-operative and the Northern Ireland Council for Voluntary Action (1995:81):

> In their present form and role the monitoring committees do not and will not contribute effectively to the monitoring of equal opportunities or equality outcomes for women . . .

In the area of social welfare, it is fair to say that the state structures have shown an extraordinary inability to grasp even the most rudimentary notion of equality. Perhaps the most obvious example of this was the introduction by the state of 'compensatory payments' for married men between 1986-92, as part of its 1978-95 attempt to implement the EU Directive on equal treatment for men and women in social security (Fourth Report of the Fourth Joint Oireachtas Committee, 1996). Under this directive the practice of paying married women lower rates of benefit than men, for shorter periods of time, and not paying them unemployment assistance, was deemed to be discriminatory. Prior to this and arguably reflecting the state's underpinning of a male breadwinner model, married men could claim for their wives as dependants, regardless of what these women were earning. Equal payments for various kinds of benefits were introduced over the 1984-86 period. In introducing such payments, the state directed that married men could no longer claim for their wives as dependants, unless those wives were earning less than £50 per week. The state in an attempt to buffer the effect of this reduction in the income of married men, introduced compensatory payments in November 1986, and these were not discontinued until 1992. These payments, up to £20 pw, were paid to married men only, and were judged to be discriminatory in the European Court in 1995 – the case having been taken in 1987. Their introduction for married men, and not for married women, vividly illustrates the extent to which indirect discrimination has become so embedded in state practice that it is literally not even perceived.

Daly (1989) argued that the core values of the social welfare system do fundamentally affect women. She suggested that there were two central elements in that system, viz. the idea that women should be financially supported by men, and the idea that the traditional position of the male breadwinner in the family should be protected. These ideas are reflected in the existence of 'women's payments' derived from their past relationship with a man; and in the notion of adult dependent payments for those who are still living with a man.

Social welfare of course does allow women to live as lone parents. However, it can trap them in a cycle of poverty from which it is very difficult to escape. Millar *et al* (1992) noted that in the early 1990s Ireland had the lowest rate of economic activity for lone parents in the EC. Indeed, this was partly why the One Parent Family Payment was introduced. From 1997 onwards, lone parents, whether separated, divorced, widowed or never married, can earn up to £6000 pa (1997 monies) and retain their full lone parent payment. This (implicit) perception of lone parents as autonomous women towards whom the state has a responsibility, as regards facilitating their participation in paid employment, is very unusual within the Irish social welfare system. It can be seen as, at least partly, a pragmatic solution to what was regarded as the problem of the long-term economic dependency amongst lone parents. Paradoxically, this has meant that their situation is effectively better than that of married women.

Where women are married, the state implicitly and explicitly attempts to maintain their economic dependence on their husband. Indeed taxation policy, since the Murphy case in 1980 (Mahon: 1995), has reflected and reinforced the idea that what is of benefit to married men

is by a process of osmosis also of benefit to women and children. Double
allowances and taxation bands are, as Mahon noted, allocated to a
married couple, regardless of whether or not the wife is in paid
employment. This means that it is 'a marital rather than a child or
woman oriented policy' (Mahon, 1993:5). Furthermore, unless couples
specify otherwise, double tax allowances and tax bands are given to the
husband automatically if the couple married before 1993-94, and to the
highest earner (who is likely to be the husband) if they married after that
(Second Monitoring Committee, 1996). In practice then the primary
beneficiaries are married men who normally have their take-home pay
increased by the allowance. Only one additional tax concession is given
to a couple where both are in paid employment (valued at £800 pa:
1994), thereby effectively ensuring that in a situation where the wife is at
medium or low income levels, it simply will not benefit her economically
to return to paid employment. The 'deterrent' effect of the income tax
policy is further exacerbated by the fact that the bulk of the allowances
are credited to the main earner (typically the husband), while culturally
the wife is expected to cover child care costs from her wages (Callan,
1994; Mahon, 1994). In this situation the apparent net economic benefit
to the wife from participation in paid employment is further reduced.
This discourages married women from participating in paid employment
except in situations where they are either very high or very low wage
earners. Thus apparently innocuous arrangements as regards tax
assessment create a context which implicitly discourages the
participation of married women in paid employment, and implicitly
reinforces the position of the male breadwinner.

The gendered nature of state employment policies

Until very recently, the whole question of the influence of gendered
thinking on Irish employment policy was little discussed by sociologists.
O'Donovan and Curtin (1991) found no explicit evidence of gender bias
in the First (1958) and Second (1964) Programme for Economic
Expansion. They did note that the Second Programme initiated a wide
range of training programmes with state agencies in an attempt to deal
with the need for occupational mobility. However, although women
predominated in the industries which were in decline at that time, and in
the new foreign firms which were envisaged as replacement sources of
employment, industrial training places were overwhelmingly occupied
by men (Wickham, 1982). The equation of male with skilled work and
female with unskilled work did appear in the Third Programme for

Economic and Social Development, together with an explicit statement that: 'Projects with a high proportion of male labour are specially desirable' (1969:98).

In the 1960s and 1970s, the state directly and indirectly influenced the gender composition of the work forces of foreign firms. Wickham (1982) and Pyle (1990) argued that foreign firms entering Ireland in the 1960s and 1970s preferred female workers because of their lower wages. Pyle (1990) highlighted the tension between the brief of the Industrial Development Authority (IDA) to create employment in the late 1960s, 1970s and early 1980s, and its desire to preserve 'the male dominated structure of society' (1990:83). In 1970-71 the IDA's Annual Report specified that 75 per cent of the jobs created in the manufacturing area should be for men. Even up to the mid 1970s this policy continued to be officially endorsed, 'as an industrial objective which may override the imperatives of commercial profitability' (Industrial Development Authority Annual Report 1973-77 see Pyle, 1990:79). This policy had a direct effect on the kinds of foreign enquiries that were followed up, and on the proportion of women employed in foreign grant-aided manufacturing firms at least up to 1975.

Pyle indicated that whereas this preference for 'male' manufacturing industries had to be modified from the mid 1970s where foreign grant-aided industry was concerned, it continued to be the preferred option in the domestic grant-aided sector. Thus, although the percentage of the foreign grant-aided work force which was female rose in the 1975-83 period, the percentage of the domestic grant-aided work force which was female fell steadily from 1973 to 1983 (Pyle, 1990: 82, Fig. 4.3). Pyle also noted that there was evidence at an informal level that the IDA, even in the mid 1980s, was committed to the attraction of multinational companies who would provide 'male' manufacturing jobs, and industries which had a 'high male labour content'. Furthermore, it continued to offer more favourable conditions to companies employing predominantly male rather than female employees (Pyle, 1990:84-85). Indeed, this strategy was part of the reason why the electronics industry was less feminised in Ireland than in other developing countries (see Wickham and Murray, 1987; and Pyle 1990:85).

Based on their examination of national policies as well as regional policies in the Mid-West, O'Donovan and Curtin concluded that the state had upheld an ideology which viewed women's economic opportunities 'as secondary to that of men' (1991:230). Such explicit statements concerning gender bias are almost inconceivable today, even

though they act as a nice backdrop to discussions concerning the
desirability and/or feasibility of the state's commitment to ensuring 40
per cent gender representation on County Enterprise Boards.

At a less overt level, the state's commitment to industry, and
specifically to manufacturing as the 'main source of new employment'
(Third Programme for Economic and Social Development, 1969:91),
implicitly favoured men, since this sector has been, and indeed still is,
predominantly an employer of male labour. The majority of all women's
employment was, and increasingly is, in the services sector. Service
activities typically involve a level of personal contact and deference
which fits easily with female socialisation. This sector is also however
typically characterised by lower levels of pay, poorer working
conditions, lower levels of unionisation, etc. – factors which are
regarded as related to its gendered nature. In 1971, 66 per cent of
women were in paid employment in this sector, and by 1996 this had
increased to just over 80 per cent (see Table 2.6).

TABLE 2.6

WOMEN AT WORK BY BROAD SECTOR 1971-1996 (ROUNDING %
AND N IN 000S)

Sector	1971	1981	1991	1996
Agriculture	9% (25.5)	4% (12.8)	3% (12.4)	3% (14.7)
Industry	25% (68.4)	21% (68.7)	18% (70.7)	17% (80.7)
Services	66% (184.4)	75% (247.7)	78% (303.2)	80% (392.6)
Total	100% (278.3)	100% (329.2)	99% (386.3)	100% (488.0)

CSO, (1997)

In 1996, 62.1 per cent of all of those at work were in the service
sector, as compared with 27.3 per cent in industry and 10.6 per cent in
agriculture (CSO, 1997:24). Yet the state has been very slow to endorse
the services sector as the chief source of future employment although it
was so identified in national economic and social development
publications as early as 1979, and was explicitly endorsed in the White
Paper on Industrial Policy in 1984. There has been increasing evidence
to suggest that low national unemployment rates are associated with
high participation in service employment (Kennedy, 1992). However, it
was only in the 1990s that a task force was set up to explore the
employment potential of the service sector. It is hard to ignore the

possibility that, in a state where the higher echelons remained disproportionately male, an overt commitment to attempting to solve the unemployment problem through the creation of female services jobs would be unattractive other than under the most extreme economic and/or political pressure. It is not suggested that this process is a conscious one but rather that it reflects a kind of gendered myopia.

At a very different level, attempts to tackle overmanning in semi-state organisations came about at least partly because of the apparent opportunities being offered to those countries who could meet the Maastricht criteria outlined by the EU. The fact that overmanning existed in a number of semi-state organisations such as the Electricity Supply Board, Irish Steel, Telecom Éireann, and that it involved shedding predominantly male labour has been effectively ignored by social analysts. It can be seen as part of a process whereby state policies from the late 1980s, under pressure from Europe, and confronted by a dismal economic performance, challenged that overmanning in the interest of creating economic growth. The part played by such overmanning in creating this dismal economic performance has been ignored.

Not surprisingly, in view of the under-representation of women at the higher echelons of the civil service, gender related issues continue to be marginalised. Within semi-state training agencies such as FÁS, an attempt has been made to encourage the participation of women in non-traditional occupations. Interestingly, however, although the objectives of the FÁS First Positive Action Programme in 1990 included actively promoting the participation of women in managerial occupations (1993:2), most effort appears to have been concentrated in the apprenticeship area, an area of declining employment. Furthermore other agencies such as Coillte, Teagasc, and An Bord Iascaigh Mhara have made little attempt to break down traditional stereotypical occupational patterns (Report of the Second Commission on the Status of Women, 1993).

The creation of agencies such as the Employment Equality Agency, the National Women's Council (formally the Council for the Status of Women), the initiation of programmes by the EU-funded New Opportunities for Women (NOW) and by the Department of Social Welfare, all in their different ways have contributed to changing the social milieu within which Irish women live. However, in the context of Connell's view of the state as both 'constructing and contesting patriarchy' (1995:130) it is important to note that the level of funding for such structures strongly suggests an implicit hope that they will provide no more than a token challenge. Indeed the allocation of 16 per cent of the Community Initiative Programme funds to the New Opportunities for Women Programme has been used to justify ignoring the issue of mainstreaming in relation to the rest of the Structural Funds (Community Workers Co-operative and the Northern Ireland Council for Voluntary Action, 1995).

Given the gendered nature of the state's employment policy, it is ironical that the inadvertent effects of the expansion of its own administrative and caring/controlling role (as outlined in the section on women and the economy) has affected the position of women in Irish society and particularly their participation in paid employment.

Women and the institutional church

Most commentators on the position of women in contemporary Irish society (e.g. Beale, 1986; Inglis, 1987; Mahon, 1987; Smyth, 1992a; Jackson, 1992; Second Commission on the Status of Women, 1993) have attributed the unique experiences of Irish women to the numerical and structural position of the Roman Catholic Church in Irish society. Internationally, relatively little attention has been paid to the importance of the institutional church in creating and/or maintaining the position of women although Daly (1986), Reuter (1983) and De Beauvoir (1972/ 1949) have highlighted the cultural marginalisation of women in and through religious ritual.

As previously mentioned, the European Values Study (Hornsby-Smyth and Whelan, 1994) revealed that the overwhelming majority (96 per cent) of Irish respondents identified themselves as belonging to a religious denomination, and of those who did, 97 per cent identified themselves as Roman Catholics (a proportion which has remained remarkably consistent since 1921). These trends persisted in the MRBI (1998) study, with 92 per cent of all respondents identifying themselves as Roman Catholics. In examining the importance of the institutional Roman Catholic Church it seems useful to focus on two levels: firstly, its impact at an individual level on behaviour and attitudes, and in terms of the continued relevance of individual control mechanisms such as confession; and secondly, in terms of its impact on the parameters within which various issues are discussed, e.g. through its direct and indirect influence on the 'ethos' of schools and hospitals, and on specific pieces of legislation.

Various studies have shown that the majority of Irish Roman

Catholics are at least weekly church attenders (81 per cent of those in Hornsby-Smyth and Whelan 1994 and 82 per cent of those in Mac Gréil 1991) – a pattern which contrasts with a European average of 30 per cent. Perhaps even more revealingly, only 12 per cent of the Irish respondents limited their church attendances to Christmas and Easter, as compared with roughly three fifths of their European counterparts. There is recent evidence (MRBI, 1998) to suggest that this pattern is changing, with 58 per cent of those in that study attending mass weekly or more often, and 24 per cent saying that they attended less often than every 2-3 months. Research also showed that Church attendance was highest among women (especially those who were full-time in the home); those over 40 years old; in rural areas and with less than third level education. They also found that the Irish were much more likely than their European counterparts to believe in heaven, sin, life after death and the existence of a soul. Again endorsement of these beliefs was highest among women, among middle aged and older respondents and among those in rural areas (Hornsby-Smith, 1992).

On the other hand, however, the majority of Irish Catholics (58 66 per cent), like their average European counterparts, did not have confidence in the church's ability to deal with either the problems of family life, the moral problems and needs of the individual, or the social problems of the country (Hornsby-Smith and Whelan, 1994). This lack of confidence increased slightly over the 1980s, and would arguably be even higher today because of the spate of widely publicised church scandals (involving clerical non-marital children, sexual abuse of children, etc).

There is also some evidence that the influence of the Roman Catholic Church over an individual's conscience, through confession, has weakened. The practice of at least monthly confession, which had characterised almost half the population studied in 1974, had declined to less than one in five (18 per cent) by 1989 (Mac Gréil, 1991). Indeed, only 1 per cent of those in the most recent MRBI (1998) study attended confession more often than once a month. Hornsby-Smith and Whelan (1994) suggested that before Vatican 2, the Irish Roman Catholic Church stressed loyalty, certainty, and unquestioning obedience by the laity within an extremely hierarchical Church. Vatican 2 offered an alternative view in the sense that it opened up possibilities in terms of private conscience and a more organic structure. However, *Humanae Vitae* – a widely discussed Roman Catholic encyclical in the 1960s – condemned 'artificial' contraception as immoral.

Nevertheless, what evidence is available suggests that the opportunity presented by the contraceptive pill was widely embraced – despite condemnation by the Roman Catholic Church. According to Seager and Olson (1986) 60 per cent of women in Ireland were using contraceptives in the 1980s while Nic Ghiolla Phádraig and Clancy (1995) found that among their Dublin sample in the late 1980s, 78 per cent had used contraception at some stage. These findings were very similar to the trends emerging in Noonan's (1993) study where 84 per cent of those aged 17-49 years had used contraceptives. These patterns may not be unrelated to the fall-off in confessions documented by Mac Gréil. Indeed, 70 per cent of the substantial majority of those in the MRBI (1998) study who said that they were familiar with the Roman Catholic Church's attitude towards contraception disagreed with it.

Inglis, in an intriguing analysis, suggested that historically there was an important relationship between the Roman Catholic Church and Irish mothers. He argued that from the nineteenth century onwards, the Roman Catholic Church developed an alliance with the mother and provided her with power and status to which she had no other access:

> It was not simply that the church gained control of women but that, due to their isolation within the domestic sphere, women, and especially mothers, were forced in their struggle for power to surrender to the control of the priest and ally themselves with the church (1987:201).

Their lives of service, self-sacrifice, collective orientation and self-abnegation fitted easily with the values endorsed by the church. However, as Inglis was at pains to highlight, this took place in a context where there was a decline in the economic importance of women's labour, especially among the more prosperous and increasingly numerous tenant farmer class. In this situation:

> The mother maintained her power within the home in the same way as the church did in the wider society. She did the dirty, menial tasks involved in the care of members of the household. She looked after the young, the sick, the elderly, the weak and the distraught. In Humphrey's term, she 'dominated by affection' (1987:220).

Inglis thus argued that the servicing role of the Irish mother provided her with a source of emotional and moral power. She created a position of prestige for herself, a position underpinned by the Roman Catholic Church, which however made it effectively impossible for her to curtail family size. This in turn necessitated late marriage, prolonged sexual repression for some of her children, and imposed permanent celibacy and emigration on others. Such a pattern, Inglis argued, increased the family's standard of living among substantial tenant farmers by avoiding subdivision. In this context, men's negative attitudes to marriage were supported by the bachelors' drinking group. They married mainly to 'keep the name on the land'. They generally lacked any experience of women, other than their mother, and within marriage maintained an emotionally distant relationships with their wives.

Inglis's analysis helps us to understand why an institution which excluded women from the higher echelons by virtue of their sex, should have enjoyed the wholehearted support of women. It implicitly raises questions about the tensions within this alliance today in a context where women are becoming more aware of the extent to which they are not represented in the church hierarchy. Almost half of those surveyed in a nationally representative study saw women as being very unfairly represented in the church (Drudy, 1993). On the other hand, however, within a society which is increasingly materialistic and individualistic, the moral integrity of the position of women as unpaid workers within the home cannot be legitimated within current economic thinking. The church does provide a potential discourse within which women's lives of service and love have meaning. The stages of their family-based lives are marked out by religious ritual involving Christmas, Easter, Church Holidays, First Holy Communion, Confirmation and indeed marriage (Nic Ghiolla Phádraig, 1991). However, the attitude of the Roman Catholic Church to 'artificial' contraception is at odds with the individualistic and/or economically rational decisions of women to limit family size – and the dramatic decline in marital fertility suggests that women have indeed been making such decisions (Clancy, 1991; Nic Ghiolla Phádraig and Clancy, 1995; Second Commission on the Status of Women, 1993).

Although the power of the Roman Catholic Church over aspects of the individual's conscience is arguably declining, it is still evident in areas such as education, health, and welfare services (Mahon, 1987; Curry, 1993). Breen *et al* (1990) noted that the original 1922 Constitution which was negotiated with the British government contained no explicitly religious overtones. The 1937 Constitution, framed by de Valera, formally affirmed the 'special' position of the Catholic Church in Article 44. It also reflected and reinforced Roman Catholic social teaching in endorsing the family as the primary unit of society; stressing the importance of private ownership of property and defining womanhood in terms of motherhood (Hornsby-Smith and Whelan,

1994). The significance of many of these articles only became clear many years later.

As the power of the Catholic Church became obvious, various attempts were made to separate church and state. The church itself did not oppose the deletion in the 1970s of the Constitutional article referring to the special position of the Catholic Church. In 1973 the hierarchy issued a joint statement in response to Senator, later President, Mary Robinson's bill on contraception, indicating that the state was not obliged to defend the position of the Catholic Church by legislation (Whyte, 1980). Nevertheless, as the recent debates about church/state relationships in education have shown (Coolahan, 1994) the church sees the maintenance of its control over education as an important part of its mission and one which it wishes to legally copperfasten rather than entrust to the 'people of God'. However, dissident voices have appeared within the institutional church. For example, the Conference of Religious in Ireland (CORI, 1997) have questioned the extent to which the school management role is compatible with providing a radical critique of the educational system (which they see as the proper role for religious).

Because of the predominantly Catholic composition of the population, the position of the other churches has attracted little attention. Quite clearly they have benefited from a state system which has encouraged denominational education. However, their structures have, at least potentially, been more open to women. Women have been ordained as priests in the Church of Ireland, the Presbyterian Church of Ireland, the Methodist Church in Ireland, and the Lutheran Church in Ireland (First Report of the Monitoring Committee, 1994). However, to a degree which is only now becoming clear, these churches have felt constrained in contributing to a public discourse. Indeed, it was only with the second divorce referendum that the position of churches other than the Catholic Church was publicly articulated (Girvin, 1996).

Church and state – focusing particularly on education

It has been suggested that the Catholic Church achieved its pre-eminent institutional position in Irish society because of historical factors, including its willingness to provide facilities and staff in the educational, health, and welfare areas at reduced cost to the state, in return for the acceptance by the state of the legitimacy of its influence and 'ethos'. (Inglis, 1987; Hornsby-Smith and Whelan, 1994). This 'arrangement' was effectively in the realm of 'taken-for-granted' legitimacy until very recently, although episodes such as that involving the Mother-and-Child-Scheme in the early 1950s were harbingers of later developments in church/state relationships (Curry, 1993). Most of the work which has referred to this area (e.g. Beale, 1986; Mahon, 1987; Curry, 1993) has focused particularly on the church's control over education.

Within a predominantly Catholic society, the appropriateness of Church control over education was seen as unproblematic until the mid 1970s. Challenges to it since then have been sporadic and have mainly revolved around issues related to the role of the church at a management level (particularly in relation to the composition of management boards and the recruitment and promotion of teachers); the rights of parents to choose whether or not their children should receive religious instruction in primary schools, and the difficulties of respecting their rights within a context where a religious ethos permeates the school; access to buildings for community schools (at second level) and access to under-utilised buildings for multi-denominational schools (at primary level).

In the educational area, the central position of the churches is indicated by the fact that it is impossible for a non-denominational primary school to be supported by the state. Only 10 multi-denominational primary schools exist out of a total of 3,235 schools (Curry, 1993). At primary level, more than 96 per cent of children attend state supported national schools, and 93 per cent of these are under the patronage of the Catholic Church (Clancy, 1995). Since only baptised people can attend teacher training colleges (which are denominational) and since there is an emphasis, since 1973, on an 'integrated' curriculum in primary schools, religion is inevitably part of the 'ethos' of primary schools, although most of the cost of the building and all of the teachers' salaries are paid for by the state. The schools close on church holy days to enable students to attend mass. Parish clergy have access to the schools and, as Nic Ghiolla Phádraig (1995:603) has noted, they 'use the situation to evangelise'. This indeed may conform to the wishes of the parents. We do not know, however, because parents do not yet for the most part have a choice in the matter. Cook's (1997) study of Marley Grange in the 1970s illustrates the process through which this position was maintained at least in that locality.

Since the 1970s the patron, who is typically either a bishop or archbishop, has played a central role in the appointment of the school management board, nominating the chairperson, and having an important voice in the appointment and promotion of teachers. Under

the 1997 Education Bill as introduced by Niamh Bhreathnach the extent
of this power was somewhat curtailed. Thus on the boards of
management of large primary schools there were to be two parent
representatives, two teacher representatives and only two nominees of
the patron (including the parish priest) – the remaining two members to
be selected unanimously by the board from the community. However,
with the fall of government in 1977, the Bill was redrafted, with the
responsibility for appointing the board returning to the patron.
Furthermore, in the event of the composition of the board not being
agreed (i.e. between the patron, the national association of parents, the
school management organisations, trade unions and the minister), the
Bill suggests that governors are to be appointed by the patron. Quite
clearly, the position of the patron is considerably stronger in this version
of the Education Bill (1997).

Furthermore, the Employment Equality Bill (1997) specifically
recognised the rights of the churches to protect the ethos of the schools
they owned and/or managed by giving priority in recruitment to
members of their own denominations. Despite considerable agitation,
especially by the primary teachers union, these sections of the Bill were
not redrafted, and were found to be constitutional when the whole Bill
was referred by the President to the Supreme Court to assess its
constitutionality. These elements thus remain unchanged in the redrafted
Employment Equality Bill. Effectively the control of the Churches over
the primary educational system has been legitimated.

The effective institutionalisation of religious discrimination as regards
appointments and promotions has implications for secondary schools
which are owned and/or managed by the institutional churches. Clancy
(1995) noted that at second level, 62 per cent of pupils attended
secondary schools, with 89 per cent of these being owned and controlled
by Catholic religious communities. The remainder 'are divided between
those which belong to other religious denominations, and those which
are either privately or corporately owned by lay Catholics' (Clancy,
1995:474). Through a combination of expansion in educational
provision and a decline in religious vocations there has been a virtual
disappearance of religious as teachers (Nic Ghiolla Phádraig 1995;
Hornsby-Smith and Whelan, 1994). However, it is clear that the
churches will continue to exert considerable influence through the hiring
and firing of teachers. In the mid 1980s church power was used in the
controversial case of Eileen Flynn – a secondary school teacher who
became pregnant by a married man and who was fired because her

lifestyle was seen as incompatible with the ethos of the Roman Catholic school where she was employed. Such actions were effectively legitimated under the recent Employment Equality Bill – to the considerable chagrin of the teachers' unions.

The Roman Catholic Church has had some influence on certain areas of legislation over the past forty years (Inglis, 1987; Whyte, 1985). This influence has been most obvious in legislation related to sexuality and family issues prior to the 1970s. However, the Roman Catholic hierarchy became involved individually and collectively in the first abortion and divorce referenda (in 1983 and 1986 respectively). Increasingly, in morally sensitive areas such as the second abortion referendum (1992) and the second divorce referendum (1996) its public face was a lay one (Inglis, 1987; O'Reilly, 1992). The Irish Medical Organisation's vote against abortion (1992) and the active involvement of 'Pro-Life' campaigners in Parents Against Stay Safe Programmes in primary schools, in the Housewives Union, and in the Association for Mothers Working at Home, are suggestive as regards future alliances between middle class legal and medical professionals (mainly male), right-wing women (Dworkin, 1983) and the more conservative elements of the Church hierarchy.

It has been suggested that women's attitudes to the Roman Catholic Church, and their support of it, are likely to become more fraught in the face of rising levels of individualisation. Nic Ghiolla Phádraig (1995:617) suggested that the church's direct and indirect sphere of influence was likely to become increasingly attenuated, 'limited in many respects to a declining constituency of orthodox Catholics'. It is equally plausible, however, to suggest that the institutional church will remain important, especially insofar as it continues to retain its control over education; continues to provide moral validation for the unpaid love and labour of the majority of Irish married women, and continues to reinforce its structural and ideological power base by forming key alliances with middle class groups.

The influence of the institutional church has also been felt in other areas. There has been some evidence to suggest that 'the provision of female sterilisation services through the health system has been blocked in a number of public hospitals' (Barry, 1992:116). Nic Ghiolla Phádraig (1995) also noted that church influence was still very much a reality on Medical Ethics Boards (e.g. in the National Maternity Hospital) and was reflected in the prohibition of sterilisation in such hospitals. (Indeed although the Department of Health (1995) recognised the state's responsibility to facilitate a woman's desire for sterilisation, the picketing by medical practitioners of a clinic providing this service in the North Western Health Board in 1996 by these same practitioners indicates the difficulties that still arise.)

The continued acceptance by the state of the influence of the church at a societal level is closely related to the extent to which alternative sources of moral authority can be identified to underpin the legitimacy of the state; by the extent to which situational changes (such as the decline in vocations) affect the church/state relationship in areas such as education, and by the visibility of church control to Northern Protestants within the context of discussions about the political future of Northern Ireland.

Social and cultural construction of heterosexuality

The Oxford English dictionary defines heterosexual as 'relating to or characterised by the normal relation of the sexes'. It has been increasingly recognised that such relationships are socially and culturally constructed. Furthermore Richardson (1996:9) observed that:

> If we are to develop social theory which can adequately theorise and challenge the way in which our everyday lives are structured by heterosexual practices, within a variety of institutional domains such as families, religion the economy and so forth, we require more than a querying of the sexual. Much more significantly, we need to rethink the social.

She went on to recognise her own sense of unease at this distinction, asking: 'how can the sexual be separate from the social?' (1996:9). However, it has been increasingly recognised (Vance, 1989:14) that:

> Gender and sexuality have been the last domains to have their natural biological status questioned.

Connell (1995a) noted that much of the early debate on this topic was initiated by women and gay men. Rich (1980:647) put forward the notion of 'compulsory heterosexuality' and suggested that a heterosexual preference was inculcated in women by a variety of mechanisms (including romantic love) as a way of 'assuring male rights of physical, economic and emotional access'. Egan (1997) went further and suggested that assumptions that the world is and should be heterosexual reflected and reinforced homophobia – and ultimately ensured that all women could be controlled by the fear that they might be seen as lesbian.

Underpinning the construction of heterosexuality lies an implicit devaluing of other sexual choices – which by definition need to be 'explained'. Increasingly, however, it is accepted that it is legitimate and appropriate to examine heterosexuality, as it is currently constructed, as a social and cultural institution (Richardson, 1996). Thus for example Connell (1995a) has observed: 'I am a heterosexual man, married, middle aged, with a tenured academic job in an affluent country …. I owe an account of what I am doing here.' It is obvious that for Connell heterosexuality as an institution transcends a discussion of sexual practices, and is concerned with social and cultural privileging. He dismisses the notion that men are equally oppressed – seeing it as 'demonstrably false'. He does however suggest that heterosexual men have something to gain from a change in this institution.

Two aspects of the social and cultural construction of heterosexuality are explored here: firstly, the underlying idea that the 'normal' relationship between men and women involves dominance and submission, reinforcing the expectation that women must 'service men emotionally and sexually' (Richardson, 1997); and secondly, the idea that the ability and the willingness to use force is a 'normal' element in the definition of masculinity and one which underpins the social and cultural construction of hegemonic heterosexuality.

MacKinnon (1992) has been among those who have argued that in western society, heterosexuality incorporates an erotisisation of dominance and subordination. 'Being a man' becomes tied up with female submission, however 'submission' is defined. Obviously insofar as what Bell and Newby (1991) called 'the deferential dynamic' exists, the issue of dominance or submission does not overtly arise. It is reflected in the prioritising of men's needs and schedules and more generally in the perceived legitimacy of women's 'servicing relationship' with men.

> Within heterosexual relationships women, emotionally and materially as well as sexually, service men. Women support men more than men support women. Women are more emotionally responsive to men than vice versa, since men are both unprepared, because of their masculine upbringing, and unwilling because of their dominant position, to reciprocate fully (Walby, 1990:120).

It is arguable that within Irish society this aspect of the current social and cultural construction of heterosexuality is still taken for granted. It is seen as 'natural' that women should look after men, at least emotionally. It will be shown (Chapter 5) that in Ireland, to an even greater extent than in most other EU countries, it is women who undertake the bulk of household labour, including the care of children – despite the fact that they are increasingly participating in paid employment, largely on a full-time basis. It will also be shown (Chapter 4) that although men typically own land and control economic resources in the household when they are relatively plentiful, their day-to-day power within the family may be limited although they do continue to have disproportionate access to money to spend on themselves. Holland *et al* (1992:650) suggested that:

> The control that men exert over women in the private sphere cannot be separated from the legitimating of male dominance, the greater value of men and the dominance of patriarchal political and economic institutions in the public sphere.

It seems plausible to suggest that there is considerable male ambivalence about women's access to positions of power or prestige within the public arena – particularly in areas which are seen as relevant to definitions of masculinity. For example the treatment by the media and other organisations in 1996-97 of Ireland's two most successful female athletes was extraordinarily vicious, and had no precedent in a similar treatment of male athletes. However, for the most part, the former President Mary Robinson avoided such odium, while the selection by the main political parties of three female candidates to contest the 1997 Presidency of Ireland does suggest that, under certain conditions, male ambivalence about women's access to positions within the public arena may be offset by other considerations.

Walby (1990) has argued that although MacKinnon's arguments are important in understanding women's subordination, some forms of male power are not expressed through sexuality. Holland *et al* (1992) challenged the depiction of men's erotic behaviour as necessarily violent, and women's as never so. One might suggest that there is a certain cultural ambivalence in Ireland about force as an element in the definition of masculinity. It is impossible to provide evidence for this although many TV viewers will see it as being reflected in the depiction of Miley in the rural soap opera, Glenroe. It seems possible to suggest that these attitudes have traditionally been reflected in the positive valuation of such passive 'quiet' men combined with tacit admiration of 'hard' men.

The idea that the ability and willingness to use force is a 'normal' element in the definition of masculinity and hence an element in the social and cultural construction of heterosexuality offers a potentially fertile source of legitimisation for male violence whether in physical violence towards a spouse or indeed towards any woman, and also in pornography, rape, and sexual abuse. Evanson (1982) has suggested that the causes of marital violence were 'the deeper assumptions of husbands that they have a right to dominate and the powerlessness of wives which make them legitimate outlets for aggression which cannot be vented on others'. Typically, however, such issues and those relating to men's greater cultural value, and the legitimacy of their dominance, are ignored.

In Western society it is recognised that official statistics on crime vastly under-estimate the extent of domestic violence. Dobash and Dobash (1992) have suggested that the crime of violence against women in the home occurs in between one in four and one in ten families. Walby (1990), on the basis of a wide-ranging review of work in the US, suggested that one in five women who had ever been married had been beaten by their husbands at some stage, rising to over one in four when rape as well as beating was included. Broadly similar trends have emerged in a Canadian national sample study, while smaller more local British studies (e.g. Andrews and Brown, 1988) showed that approximately one in four of the women in their working class sample had experienced marital violence.

Using an Irish national random sample, Kelleher and Associates and O'Connor (1995) found that just under one in five (18 per cent) of the women who responded had experienced violence within their intimate relationships. Just under three fifths of those in this study knew a woman who had been subjected to violence by a partner. Their in-depth study of women in doctors' waiting rooms in North East Dublin found that just over three fifths (66 per cent) of those interviewed knew a woman who had been subjected to domestic violence; over one third (36 per cent) said that they had experienced it themselves. Thus it seems possible to conclude that between one fifth and one third of Irish women have been subjected to violence by a partner – a trend which is broadly similar to that emerging in British and US studies. It clearly gives the lie to the idea that such violence is a rare or exceptional phenomenon.

Significantly, perhaps, in terms of the perceived role of the state in implicitly colluding with these patterns, only one in five of the women in that study had reported the violence to the Gardaí. According to the women, the Gardaí rarely arrested the man. The social services (the 'compassionate' face of the state) were seen as lacking any strategy for responding to this issue and only 3 per cent of the women reported it to them. Indeed, both this study and McWilliams and McKernan's (1993) noted that the training of social workers failed to recognise marital violence as an issue.

The perception of violence as a private problem is also evident in the uneven and unsatisfactory provision of, and funding received by, the eleven refuges in Ireland which serve a population of 3.6 million. The level of such provision itself contrasts vividly, for example, with Norway which has 400 refuges for a population of 4 million (see Maguire, 1988). On the other hand, Irish legislation has been introduced to limit men's abuse of power, both by defining marital rape as a crime and allowing Health Boards to apply for a barring order on behalf of 'an aggrieved person'. In these ways, the state is taking upon itself the responsibility to curtail the extent of men's power within the family.

In Ireland there has been very little discussion of the appropriate extent and nature of male control although there is considerable cultural unease about the abuse of various kinds of male power. Five incidents in 1992-93 received very widespread media coverage: the 'X' case taken by the Attorney General to legally restrain a fourteen-year-old rape victim from leaving the country with her parents' consent to procure an abortion (for a detailed description of the case and its consequences see Smyth, 1992a); the case of Lavinia Kerwick who, because of her willingness to identify herself as a rape victim, raised the issue of the personal effect of rape and the implications of lenient sentencing by a legal system which she perceived as effectively colluding with her violation (Shanahan, 1992); the Patricia O'Toole murder by an army recruit, which implicitly raised the issue of the extent to which the state was actively colluding with physical violence since the man who was found guilty of her murder wore his army uniform during the trial (which he was legally entitled to do); the personal revelations of a 27-year-old incest victim in Kilkenny, and subsequent official enquiry, which exposed the reality of 16 years of sexual and physical abuse by a father, and the attitude of the state to domestic violence against women and children (South Eastern Health Board, 1993). Finally, the Gay Byrne interview with Annie Murphy, the mistress of the former Bishop of Galway by whom she had a child, which inadvertently stimulated a public debate about the double standards latent in our attitudes to single mothers and fathers, in terms of their responsibility for contraception and the moral value of their contributions to their child's well-being.

The experiences of these individual women, and the public discussions they inadvertently generated, have played an important role in raising the question of the appropriate nature and extent of male control. The sequence of 'victims and saviours' (O'Connor, 1995c) has continued, including the murders of Imelda Riney and her son; Marilyn Rynn, the journalist Veronica Guerin, and many others. The intimidation and death of Brigid McCole and the infection of approximately 1,000 other women with Hepatitis C contracted from infected blood administered by semi-state agencies has further challenged naïve notions of trust which are a key element underpinning the social and cultural construction of heterosexuality in our society.

Even documenting them can be assessed as 'having a go at men', blaming them entirely, seeing them as bad, etc. This is not what is intended here. It is recognised that the structural and cultural patterns which surround heterosexuality raise issues for men who do not wish to perpetuate those patterns. Indeed it is suggested that an alternative discourse as regards masculinity exists but is not yet valued. Discussion of such a discourse remains very muted indeed.

The women's movement

Dahlerup (1986:2) has suggested that a social movement

> is a conscious, collective activity to promote social change, representing a protest against the established power structure and against the dominant norms and values.

As implied by Dahlerup, the women's movement is an attempt to promote change within what are seen as patriarchal power structures and cultural systems which reflect and reinforce a differential valuation of men and women. For Dahlerup this is a conscious collective activity. However, as was suggested in Chapter 1, until a social movement has reached a certain stage, such consciousness may not emerge. Faith's (1994:37) focus on 'resistance to invisibility and silencing' is useful in describing this stage. Implicit in it is the idea that the process of challenging 'gender disparities as a universal but unnatural power reality' involves an increasing politicisation – or at least raises issues which have been ignored or devalued by patriarchal structures. Prior to achieving this a protest element may be muted, as an attempt is made to bring about social change with the minimum social, psychological and economic cost to those involved through the use of 'non-compliance, foot dragging, deception' (Scott, 1985:xxvi). This has often seemed to be the case in Ireland, where many women, effectively resisting particular power structures, can often be heard to say 'I'm not a feminist but ....'

Because of their inchoate nature social movements are extremely difficult to study (Mahon, 1987 and 1995; Connolly, 1996 and 1997; Conroy Jackson, 1986; Smyth, 1988; Mulvey, 1992 and Barry, 1992). Nevertheless it seems important to attempt to do this since, as Stacey (1986) has noted, purely structural explanations of the position of women in society are unsatisfactory – not least because they portray women as 'victims, robots or fools' – depictions which do not correspond to the subjective reality of most women at most points in their lives. In an attempt to deal with this inchoate nature Connolly (1997) focused on key organisations within the Irish women's movement. She traced the processes through which such organisations developed and the political structures which facilitated such development from the foundation of the state up to the 1990s. This approach does raise questions about the kinds of organisations which should be included. Furthermore it implicitly ignores the fact that 'the movement is more than its organisations: it represents endeavours to reach beyond its own boundaries' (Dahlerup, 1986:218). For example, the very success of the women's movement (and indeed of any social movement) lies in its ability to transform the wider institutional and cultural context. Connolly did suggest that there was a dynamic interplay between the established power structures and those resisting them, so that it was politically expedient or socially desirable for certain kinds of initiatives to be taken at particular moments in time (e.g. the introduction of the Unmarried Mother's Allowance in the 1970s or Maternity Leave in the early 1980s). Equally, under the direct or indirect influence of the movement, individuals or groups may set up organisations which are of particular relevance to women, or they may take legal action at national or European level (see Connolly, 1997; Smyth, 1992a). Thus the relationship between the women's movement and established power structures is a dynamic one, the emergence of new organisations, structures and agendas indicating its continuing vitality.

The start of the second wave of feminism has been popularly located in the 1960s and 1970s. It has been noted that in the late 1960s despite women's under-representation in the political, legal and economic structures, Irish women showed a formidable ability to use organisational structures. The request in 1968 to set up the First Commission on the Status of Women came from an ad hoc committee of ten women's organisations, including the Irish Housewives Association, the National Federation of Business and Professional

Women's Clubs, and the Soroptimists (Smyth 1988 and 1993; Mahon, 1995; Connolly, 1996 and 1997). These organisations very adroitly exploited the possibilities created by a UN Directive in 1967 asking member governments to examine the status of women in their countries. The First Commission on the Status of Women was set up in Ireland in 1970 – not a great deal later than in the US (the President's Commission on the Status of Women being set up there in 1961: Mahon, 1995).

The 1970s have been seen as a period of considerable activity involving confrontation, direct action and organisational development (Connolly, 1996 and 1997; Mahon, 1995; Smyth, 1988). Mahon (1995) suggested that the main focus in the early 1970s was on equal rights for women at work and the legalisation of contraception. This period is best remembered for the emergence of the Irish Women's Liberation Movement in 1970 (Levine, 1982; Smyth, 1983; Connolly, 1997). Their 1971 six point Manifesto (*Chains or Change*) looked for equal pay, equal access to education, equality before the law, the availability of contraception, justice for deserted wives, unmarried mothers and widows, and one house, one family (Mahon, 1995). Their strategies were spectacular and in 1971 they included the public launch of the Irish Women's Liberation Movement on the most popular television programme of the time (The Late Late Show); the organisation of a mass public meeting in Dublin, and the staging of what became known as the 'contraceptive train' – involving travel to Belfast and the purchase and public importation of contraceptives. These activities generated widespread public comment and galvanised substantial numbers of women to publicly voice their support (Smyth, 1993). As Connolly (1997) noted, the effectiveness of such strategies was not unrelated to the fact that many of the core members of the Irish Women's Liberation Movement were either journalists or had close ties with the media. Such strategies played an important part in transforming public consciousness, and the process was facilitated by the non-hierarchical consciousness-raising style of mobilisation used. This very structure however made it very difficult for the movement to organise nationally and it fragmented within two years.

It is widely accepted that there has been no subsequent mass-based women's liberation movement in Ireland (Connolly, 1997). However, according to Smyth (1988) and Mahon (1995) radical feminism surfaced with renewed vigour in 1974 with the emergence of Irish Women United, which included not only free legal contraception among its objectives, but also asserted the rights of women to a self-determined sexuality, as well as to equality in education and work. It is impossible to assess the impact of Irish Women United, but it is arguable that it set in train processes which ultimately modified the institutional and cultural reality.

In the 1970s a wide range of organisations emerged from within the women's movement to provide support and services for women which were not provided by the wider institutional structures. They included organisations such as the Fertility Guidance Clinic (1969); Cherish, to support pregnant single women (1970); the Women's Progressive Association (1971) which later became the Women's Political Association; Rape Crisis Centres; AIM, founded in 1972 and committed to family law reform; the Irish Women's Aid Committee, which established the first hostel for battered wives in Ireland (Mahon, 1995). Connolly (1997) has argued that the 1980s were characterised by increased formalisation and mainstreaming of the service organisations which had been established in the 1970s; and the development of the Council for the Status of Women, whose roots lay in the initial ad hoc Committee and which has now become the National Women's Council.

The 1980s were an economically difficult period, characterised by high levels of emigration and the effective mobilisation of a counter movement. These were years of demoralisation for those involved in the more radical sector of the women's movement in Ireland. Radical action centred mainly on the two abortion referenda (1983 and 1992) and two divorce referenda (1986 and 1996) and on legal initiatives taken by individuals and groups mainly around the legality of access to information and the provision of counselling in the wake of crisis pregnancies. A woman centred discourse was marginalised during this decade. Barry (1992:114) noted that a new phenomenon emerged, viz. the presence of women on the 'pro-choice' and the 'pro-life' sides.

> So while it was women and the women's movement who had organised and demanded change in the 1970s, seeking greater control over their bodies and their lives, it was also women who formed the basis of PLACs [Pro-Life Amendment Campaign] across the country.

In the 1990s there have been what Connolly called 'general movement gains' – including the election of Mary Robinson as the first woman President of Ireland in 1990; the election for the first time of 20 women to the Dáil in 1992; the establishment of the Second Commission on the Status of Women and the publication of its report in 1993; the establishment of a Department of Equality and Law Reform in

1993 charged with the 'elimination of inequality'. However, it is unclear to what extent such gains can be maintained. In 1997 the Department of Equality and Law Reform became absorbed into the Department of Justice. Virtually all the women who had been prominent in the Dáil lost their seats. On the other hand, the main political parties all nominated women to contest the Presidency – with victory going to Mary McAleese, the Fianna Fáil candidate who had won the nomination in the face of strong opposition from the previous leader of that party, i.e. Albert Reynolds.

By the early 1990s there were approximately 40 Women's Studies courses in existence (Drew, 1993; Ní Charthaigh and Hanafin, 1993), with all the universities in Ireland having Women's Studies at undergraduate and/or postgraduate level. Typically, however, women's studies remains under-resourced, with inadequate staffing levels (Connolly, 1996; Byrne *at al*, 1996). There is a tension, of course, in the presence of Women's Studies within what are essentially male hierarchical structures (Byrne 1995:26-27) and there are enormous risks of co-option. At its best, however, the existence and vitality of Women's Studies is a radical challenge to the structure and ethos of these institutions. In the 1980s and early 1990s feminist publishing flourished in the shape of the emergence of a feminist publisher (Attic Press); the launching of an Irish Journal of Feminist Studies and the production of monographs by the Women's Studies staff and students in most of the universities. These publications both increased the range of material available and contributed to the vitality of the intellectual scholarship in the area of Women's Studies. Such developments marked the penetration of the movement into areas where it had previously been notably absent.

The 1990s also saw the rapid growth of locally based (mainly working class) women's groups concerned with women's poverty. Connolly (1997) has suggested that these groups are indicative of the vitality and changing form of the women's movement – a position which has been challenged by Ward and O'Donovan (1996). Like the radical groups in the 1970s, these are often non-hierarchical structures. They are concerned with empowering women within their families and communities. Inevitably, perhaps, because of the paucity of their resources, and their marginalisation, the opportunity for such groups to transform society is very limited. A notable exception to this is the Married Women for Equality group in Cork, a largely working class grass roots group, which successfully took on the state and forced it to honour its obligation to the estimated 75,000 women entitled to Social Welfare equality payments (arising from discrimination by the state in its attempt to implement the 1976 EC Social Welfare Equality Directive).

It is interesting to note that the issues which came into focus in the Irish women's movement were very similar to those emerging across Europe (Women of Europe, 1987) and in the United States:

> The spread of feminism in these circumstances showed the force of the pressure for change, and the ability in the right climate for ideas to be carried across the boundaries of socio-economic conditions and across frontiers (Hoskyns, 1996:34).

To a degree which we perhaps have only begun to appreciate, the women's movement in Ireland reflected and reinforced 'ordinary' Irish women's positive evaluation of themselves. However, since their evaluation of themselves was predominantly based in the private arena, there were tensions around those issues which were seen as key in a wider European/American context, viz. paid employment and the right to abortion, since they could be construed as an attack on the choices made by those married women who were full time in the home.

The strength of Irish women's evaluation of themselves was very clearly revealed when a national sample study directed at women (MRBI, 1992) showed that between 76 per cent and 92 per cent of the respondents felt that the Government should listen to men and women equally on jobs, employment, taxation, savings, divorce, issues related to children, teenage drinking and Green issues; with between one third and a half feeling that the Government should listen to women only on issues related to contraception and abortion. Such attitudes indicate the importance, in women's own estimation, of their contribution to the 'public' arena. They are compatible with the fact that, despite the highly constrained nature of the lives of women from the late 1920s up to the mid 1960s, Irish women enjoyed disproportionate access to education when compared to women in other countries. Of thirteen OECD countries, only in Ireland were women aged 55-64 years more highly educated than men of the same age. Furthermore, although women aged 25-34 years were more highly educated than men of the same age in six of the thirteen countries, the difference was greatest in the case of Irish women (Rubery et al, 1996).

Ironically, however, feminism and the women's movement are often portrayed as being viewed with ambivalence by many women. In part, this arguably reflects a fear on the part of women, as well as men, of shattering the possibility of co-operation between the sexes (of 'splitting the sexes', 'making things worse than they already are'). In part, it also arguably reflects a resistance to an individuated concept of the person, and especially an individuated concept of woman. The evidence also suggests that what is often presented as popular antagonism to feminism and the women's movement is in fact very much a minority phenomenon. A national poll (MRBI, 1992) found that nine out of every ten Irish women had heard of feminism. Four out of every five of these women said that they knew what it meant, with 87 per cent seeing it as 'developing women's confidence in themselves'; 84 per cent subscribing to the view that its aim was to ensure that the things in life which women value receive full consideration in how the society and the economy develops; and 76 per cent seeing it as 'developing a society in such a way that women play a greater part' – all of which, the report notes, are very far removed from 'old images of feminism' (MRBI, 1992). These patterns were very similar to those which emerged in a study of *Woman's Way* readers in 1991 (Council for the Status of Women, 1991). That study also showed that nine out of ten of the readers felt that their lives had improved as a result of the women's movement.

One can suggest that changes in the position of women in Irish society might have come about anyway. It is certainly true that changes were facilitated by transformations in the wider economic, political and cultural systems; by our relationship with the EC/EU; by a shift in relationships between church and state; and by women's rising levels of education and changes in their consciousness and perceived life options. Nevertheless, the contribution of Irish women to changing the position of women in their society has been diverse, incorporating institutional reform and service provision, radical action, the utilisation of individual cases to highlight issues and, increasingly, the mounting of an intellectual challenge to dominant ideologies. Perhaps the most striking change has been in the behaviour and attitudes of 'ordinary' women, about whom we know all too little, but whose behaviour, as will be described in subsequent chapters, clearly suggests that they are actively shaping the future for themselves and their children.

Summary

This chapter has put forward a broad framework for understanding the position of women in Irish society. It has built on the work of those who have stressed the importance of the economic system, and those who have located it in the context of a wider understanding of the nature of a specific society. Within the parameters of Irish society, it is impossible to ignore the role of the state and the institutional church, and hence these have been included. Finally, drawing on Connell's (1995a) work and on an increasing unease about the depiction of women as victims, it has included a discussion of the part played by women themselves in changing the structure of Irish society.

Implicit in this book is the assumption that depending on a woman's age, ascribed class position, life stage, participation in paid employment etc., the impact of these structures may vary. As has become very evident in the 1980s and 1990s, women may ally themselves with the state, the institutional church, or with neither. Furthermore, as is increasingly recognised, regardless of the similarity or difference in their actual experiences, women's feelings about their situation may vary. Hence, it is necessary to look at the position and experiences of particular groups and categories of women within the context of the framework outlined in this chapter. First, however, we examine more closely the ideological parameters within which Irish women construct their lives.

3

Concepts of Womanhood

Introduction

To many young Irish women it is inconceivable that women in Ireland twenty-five years ago did not feel oppressed, discriminated against and trivialised. They cannot envisage the existence of the marriage bar; are amazed at the highly ambiguous status of contraception, the absence of divorce, the existence of separate pay scales for men and women, and women's under-representation in positions of economic, legal and political power. Until very recently all these (and indeed many other phenomena) were presented as virtually inevitable, underpinned by ideologies which explained and justified them. They can be located in a wider context in which the positions, roles, identities and attributes of men and women were socially and culturally constructed in a particular way. Gardiner (1996:40) has noted that it was 'men's values' which defined this context, women's values being part of 'what is virtually a subculture'.

Inevitably perhaps, in view of the social and cultural construction of heterosexuality, the concepts of womanhood generated by the dominant institutional structures have included elements of service and subordination. Gardiner noted that such concepts of womanhood have made women 'the natural ally of a capitalist patriarchal state'; that 'acceptance of the status quo separates the functional worlds of men and women, depoliticises women and postpones political competition between women' (1996:40). Implicit in them is the idea that essential biological differences exist between men and women. This chapter is not concerned with adjudicating on this issue. It is however concerned with speculatively exploring these ideas since they are part of the cultural tradition out of which Irish women weave the fabric of their own identity and the meaning of their lives. These concepts of womanhood are not, for the most part, peculiarly Irish. Neither do they relate solely to marriage and family life. Indeed it can be argued that they underpin the huddling of women into the lower levels of a small range of (mostly poorly paid) employment right across Western society (Kaplan, 1992; Ungerson, 1987).

It must be stressed that although in this chapter attention is focused on these dominant definitions, it is recognised that individual women have been able to exercise considerable agency and ingenuity in constructing their own definitions of self. Furthermore, individual women and groups of women, by differentially prioritising the various elements, have begun to transform them.

Although the main focus in this chapter is on concepts of womanhood, these are seen as being located in a wider discourse about women and their lives and an increasing acceptance that taken-for-granted ideas need to be located structurally. This discourse includes ideas about who can speak authoritatively on the lives of women and their experiences (e.g. the medical profession, clerics); ideas about how women should feel and act in particular situations (e.g. childbirth, full time housewifery). The idea of discourse is particularly useful in this context since it implies that it is possible to identify dominant and submerged discourses – the former being reflected and reinforced by the institutional church, the state etc., and the latter by those structures and processes which are part of a women's movement. Furthermore it enables us to see this ideological challenge as part of a much wider legitimacy crisis across Western European society.

Drawing in a speculative way on the scattered and limited evidence which is available, it is suggested that the concepts of womanhood generated by the dominant discourses revolve around themes related to caring, reproduction, familism, love, sexual attraction and 'women's place' within the paid employment arena. Under the influence of the women's movement, it has become possible to suggest that these are neither 'natural' nor appropriate for all women and that new – albeit inchoate – definitions of womanhood are emerging. These are revolving around ideas of personhood, whether this is construed in terms of an identity which transcends the familial one; in terms of a degendered concept of self revolving around paid work, or simply in terms of an idea of womanhood which accepts 'difference'. It seems useful to briefly explore what is known about the wider ideological context within which these definitions of womanhood are located before examining these themes in more detail.

Wider ideological context

As previously noted (Chapter 1) the concept of ideology has been used to refer to 'common-sense knowledge, which legitimates the social structure'. Such ideologies have identity implications at an individual level. The increasing influence of what has been called post-modern theoretical perspectives has contributed to 'the deconstruction of historical myth and the interrogation of essentialist cultural identities' (Bell, 1991:85). Within this context concepts of womanhood can more easily be explored.

A steady interest in ideology emerged among sociologists in Ireland in the 1980s (Curtin *et al*, 1984, 1987). However, with a number of notable exceptions (including Drudy and Lynch, 1993; Peillon, 1982 etc.) few attempts were made to explore the relationship between ideology and social structure. In part, this has reflected the ideologically monolithic, authoritarian, conservative, male-dominated nature of Irish society (Breen *et al*, 1990). In the context of this consensual perspective Ireland was depicted as a place

> devoid of class conflict and dissension; it is represented as a repository of Catholic virtue, neighbourly solidarity, and good will. There is no reference to the socio-economic and sexual inequalities that exist within it in the real world as opposed to the ideal one (Drudy and Lynch, 1993:64).

In this context, there was no intellectual framework within which a challenge could be mounted. By definition, dissenting voices were marginal, unintelligible and illegitimate. The question of the relationship between ideology and social structure had no real importance: indeed it literally made no sense (Drudy and Lynch, 1993). Within such a society, even problematising the taken-for-granted ideological structure and exploring the extent to which it reflected what Drudy and Lynch (1993:113) called 'the conflict of interests between the various power groups, classes and strata ... which make radical change difficult', was a scientifically suspect exercise. The difficulty of examining the structural bases of ideologies which perpetuated women's position in society, or of generating a critique of these ideologies, was even more formidable.

Within a gendered social and cultural milieu, it is difficult to see how our sense of ourselves could be other than incomplete insofar as it effectively ignores those ideologies which underpin the lives of one half of the population. Conroy Jackson (1986) noted the scarcity of female intellectuals in Ireland and the fact that 'the women's movement failed to explore in depth many cultural, political and ideological issues during (the) early years.' This was not unrelated to the very low representation of women at the higher echelons of third level institutions (Smyth, 1988; Hayden, 1990; O'Connor, 1998). Indeed, the likelihood of individuals who might mount such a critique achieving the position to engage in it was remote, given both the highly controlled nature of the system and the availability of emigration. Quite simply many academics went abroad, following the well-worn path of creative writers, or buried themselves in teaching and administration.

Drudy and Lynch, focusing mainly on education, identified essentialism as a key element in Irish ideology. They pointed particularly to its implications regarding intelligence. Within a wider debate, this theme, translated into a biological essentialism which defines women in terms of their biological nature and/or their reproductive potential, is particularly important. Drudy and Lynch (1993:55) were at pains to highlight the extent to which essentialism is not peculiarly Irish, but argue that: 'What makes Ireland unique is that consensualism has forestalled any critique of essentialism.'

O'Dowd (1987) highlighted the role of church and state (and the 'accommodations' between them) in perpetuating ideologies which legitimated a familial, self-sacrificing, role for women. He noted that such ideologies obscured the reality of women's own experiences and the extent of women's 'subordination'. It is arguable that this constitutes one of the central difficulties for women in Irish culture. Only relatively recently has it been possible to suggest that this 'natural order' was 'a particular construction of sexual and familial roles' (Meaney, 1991:6). In this context, definitions of womanhood were mechanisms through which women were controlled and men defined. They valorised images of what Meaney calls 'all-powerful, dehumanised figures' (1991:4) including 'Mother Ireland', and the 'self-sacrificing Irish Mother' – images which reflect and reinforce men's fear and loathing of women, and their self-definition of themselves as men.

> [Women become] guarantors of their men's status, bearers of national honour and the scapegoats of national identity. They are not merely transformed into symbols of the nation, they become the territory over which power is exercised (Meaney, 1991:6/7).

The ideological choices offered to women within such a context are stark indeed. One could either be a self sacrificing Irish mother or an a-sexual employment-oriented being. Attempting to challenge this, Peillon argues, involves a radical reworking of Irish ideology:

A truly critical orientation to Irish ideology would apparently require dismissing the relevance of these opposites or else dismissing their dichotomous nature (1984:57).

Within a consensualist, essentialist perspective, there are no inequalities, other than those deriving from the 'natural order', between men and women. The identification of 'women's issues' in the public arena is perceived as provocative; and discussion of women's feelings about being wives and mothers is unnecessary, since their attitude to these is assumed to be 'natural'.

Meaney (1991) and Smyth (1991) have noted that, within this ideological context, insofar as women use their own 'voice', they put themselves outside the dominant discourses. Smyth has vividly depicted the alienation of woman's voice from the symbolic order:

> In the end I couldn't speak for Irish women. Can barely speak for myself. Can barely speak.

Paradoxically, as Smyth noted (1991:25), as long as she remained the 'Other' she had a place in the Irish cultural and social context:

> Irish Woman enables definition of Irish Man. I am the edge, defining the centre. Border country. Margin. Perimeter. Outside.

Although church and state are seen as the main institutional structures involved in the creation of the ideological parameters of our lives, the economic structure has also played a role. The economic discourse generated by the socio-economic forces (i.e. unions, employers and farmer organisations) implicitly devalued the unpaid work of women in the home and incorporated ideas about the secondary and/or subordinate position of women in the world of paid employment. It is popularly suggested that the economic discourse is becoming increasingly dominant as Irish society becomes more materialistic. This seems somewhat simplistic – although concepts of womanhood involving caring and familism are gradually incorporating materialistic elements.

Bell (1991:88) has argued that sociology has 'permitted the appropriation by the literary imagination of identity talk'. Such 'talk' has been particularly concerned with issues related to national, religious, cultural and political identities – with Langley (1990), Meaney (1991) and Smyth (1991) highlighting the use of women as nationalist images, e.g. Cathleen Ni Houlihan, Dark Rosaleen, Mother Ireland (Langley, 1990). In looking at concepts of womanhood in this chapter, issues explicitly related to women's Irish, national identity are left to one side since to tackle them would simply over-extend its focus.

Concepts of womanhood: main themes

Oakley (1972) early differentiated between sex and gender – defining the former in terms of the anatomical differences between men and women, and the latter in terms of the socially and culturally constructed differences between men and women. Over the past twenty-five years there has been a good deal of interest in the social and cultural construction of womanhood, and in particular, the extent to which patriarchal ideology has attributed to women those characteristics, such as submissiveness, passivity and self-sacrifice, which are particularly conducive to patriarchal control. Internationally, liberal feminists who exhorted women to follow male role models have been criticised. Some radical feminists have argued that there is a need either to move towards more androgynous definitions of womanhood and manhood or to 'revalorise' female characteristics, within a context which recognises that:

> Womanhood is a man-made construct, having essentially nothing to do with femaleness (Daly, 1978:68).

In the argument about whether women 'should' be self-sacrificing or emotionally detached, dependent or autonomous, what can be seen as the central issue gets lost sight of, viz. the idea that stereotypical views about the 'nature' of men and women are unhelpful. Such views simply impose a culturally laden veneer of prescriptive emotional 'states' on men and women based on biological status. They implicitly suggest that these 'states' are in fact biologically based, although it is now well recognised that it is impossible to know to what extent traits, states or dispositions are due to nature and/or nurture.

Caring

It is widely assumed that 'caring' is a strong underlying element in the concept of womanhood. There is very little quantifiable empirical evidence to support this view but it seems possible to suggest that the definition of womanhood in Irish society is closely interwoven with 'tending', i.e. caring for children, seeing to housework and looking after vulnerable or dependent members of the family or community. The term is interwoven with ideas about self-sacrifice (particularly to a husband and/or children), submissiveness and self-effacement. It suggests that the appropriate contribution of all women – regardless of their age, life stage, domestic situation, talents or wishes – lies within the family, and that manhood is appropriately expressed outside this arena. Thus implicit in Peillon's work (1982, 1984) is the idea that:

the traditional status of women is justified (and after all, ideology is about justification) by recourse to the Catholic doctrine which insists on the spiritual and affective role of women and which places women at the centre of family morality (1982:138).

Parker (1981) and Graham (1983) have differentiated between 'caring for' other people in the sense of tending them, and 'caring about them' in the sense of 'feeling for them'. Dalley (1988) noted that at an ideological level these two elements were indissolubly linked in the case of women, but not in the case of men. She suggested that although it is possible for men to care about someone without being expected to care for them, this is not so for women. This definition of womanhood in terms of caring is not restricted to Ireland although it is particularly important here because of the fact that the majority of Irish married women are still full time in the home. However, Barrett and McIntosh (1991) and Dalley (1988) argued that throughout Western society familial ideology assigns caring activities to women both inside and outside the home – and affirms that women 'have a natural inclination towards and aptitude for performing the monitoring, servicing tasks within the family setting' (Dalley, 1988:24). Implicit in the equation of caring with tending is the idea that cleaning the lavatory is

> given the same affective value as the feelings she [the mother] has about the family members for whom she is performing these tasks (Dalley, 1988:8/9).

The image of a passive, self-sacrificing mother has strong roots in Irish Catholicism: linked indeed with an image of Mary as a woman who obeyed without question and who devoted her life to the service of her Son. These themes have been steadily echoed by the Irish Roman Catholic hierarchy over the years: the idealisation of motherhood, the importance of family life, the nature and importance of women's lives of service and self-sacrifice, fitting together easily within a critique of materialism, selfishness and interference with nature (Peillon, 1984). Nic Ghiolla Phádraig (1995) noted that the 'Marian cult' pointed to a silent, domestic role for women. Endorsement of this persisted in the guise of, for example, May Processions, Children of Mary etc. at least up to the end of the 1960s. At that time, and indeed since then:

> Not only did the churches strongly project a predominantly private and familial role for women, they provided exemplary models of patriarchy in their own organisational arrangements (O'Dowd, 1987:12).

Pope John Paul II has been particularly vociferous on this topic, calling on women to remember their true role in life:

> May Irish mothers, young women and girls not listen to those who tell them that working at a secular job, succeeding in a secular profession, is more important than the vocation of giving life and caring as a mother (Quoted in Beale, 1986:50).

The attitude of church and state to the centrality of such 'duties' in the lives of women is implicitly reflected in Article 41.2 of the Constitution, which pledges that mothers will not be obliged by economic necessity 'to engage in labour to the neglect of their duties in the home'. The fact that housework is unpaid and 'has' to be done by wives and mothers is reflected in and reinforced by the state in its social welfare system (see Chapter 2). To change this would potentially undermine the ideology as regards the appropriateness of 'unpaid care' being provided by woman in 'exchange' for financial support, in a relationship of dependency in which 'people are recruited (obliged) to do this work by kinship and family relationships' (Delphy and Leonard, 1992:100). It is reflected in the continuing difficulty that married women with children experience in being identified as available for work, and hence in getting Unemployment Assistance Payments (Second Commission on the Status of Women, 1993; Cousins, 1996). For those women who are supported by the state because of their past relationship with a man (e.g. lone parents), the payment, ironically, as Daly has noted (1989:67), is higher than that provided to those women who are currently with a man, because:

> not having a man to provide for them, the welfare of their families is in their hands and, if they had to work outside the home, they might neglect their duties.

The state has not shown itself willing to share responsibility with women for day-to-day child care on a routine basis. Among policy makers and civil servants, resistance to the provision of such care is justified on the grounds that if it were available 'everyone would use it'. There is an implicit contradiction here since, if the rearing of children is so 'natural', then an attempt by the state to share it in a non-stigmatising way (e.g. through the provision of free day-care, crèches, after school care, etc.) would not 'open the flood gates'.

It is arguable that in Irish society, the interweaving of womanhood with the giving of domestic service to a husband has weakened. Within the concept of marriage as a partnership, such servicing is seen as inappropriate, although in fact it may still happen because of 'pragmatic' factors, such as the wife being at home during the day. Anecdotal evidence would suggest that female caring is acquiring an additional element, viz. the provision of consumer goods and services (toys and 'treats') – funded through women's participation in paid employment. Nevertheless, tending in the area of housewifery and child rearing continues to be highly valued. It reflects ideas about the role of the mother, the division of labour within the home, and the wider nurturing and servicing role of women in the community. Such ideas implicitly reinforce women's economic, social and/or psychological dependence on men. They underpin other social phenomena such as the undervaluing of women's skills, the marginalisation of men as emotionally significant people in their children's lives, and the lack of awareness of the high incidence of psychological distress among women who are full-time housewives (Whelan *et al*, 1991). Caring is thus an important element in that concept of womanhood which is endorsed by the institutional church and state, and one which is indeed an important element in the definition of 'normal' heterosexual relationships.

Familism

Within an Irish cultural tradition the family is an important symbol of collective identity, unity and security – although interestingly many aspects of the lifestyle which we see as peculiarly 'Irish' (e.g. pub-culture, the non-sexually based sociability captured by the concept of 'craic') take place outside the family setting. It is revealing that Peillon (1982:84) does not identify 'family' as a key theme within Irish culture; indeed it may not be so from a male cultural perspective since the family does not require any great commitment of men's emotional or physical energy (Kiely, 1995). On the other hand, ideologically, women's 'destiny' lies in subsuming their identity in, and committing their time and energy to 'the family':

> The woman was subsumed under the family, in the name of protecting individual freedoms against state 'control' (Rowley, 1989:46).

Underpinning this familial ideology, Barrett and McIntosh argue, is a 'possessive individualism', involving notions about privacy, autonomy and self determination – concepts which are used to define the boundaries of the family unit. Within this unit however the issue of the rights of all the individuals involved – particularly those of women and children – to such privacy, autonomy and self-determination is obscured, the implication being that, by some process of osmosis, their identities, wishes, etc. will coincide with that of the head of the household. This has been very obvious in discussions regarding farm families:

farm women rarely feature in debates about the evolution of European Rural Society ... the family farm is treated as a consensual unit with the male farmer as 'head' of the farm (O'Hara, 1993:1).

The 1937 Constitution, essentially a conservative document, gave special importance to 'the family' but included both conservative and libertarian principles. The latter formed the basis for a recognition of the rights of the individual members over and above the competing rights of the unit, this being reflected in, for example, the Status of Children Act, 1987 which abolished the concept of illegitimacy. The relevance of these ideas for the concept of familism has not really begun to be discussed.

The family, usually implicitly defined as the heterosexual family unit, is seen by the institutional church and state as the 'natural' basic unit in society. In fact, however, there is a good deal of evidence – anthropological, historical and sociological – which challenges this view (Finch, 1996). It has been shown that although certain tasks need to be performed in a society, it is not necessary that these be performed by the structure that we define as the family. There is a good deal of evidence to show that the structures which have performed these activities have varied considerably over time and place. Indeed in its taxation and social welfare regulations the Irish state has recognised cohabiting couples, as it does under the 1991 Social Welfare Act, or a lone parent and his or her children as families. It is arguable that the very concept of 'family' is being redefined in Irish life. However, outside the limited context of pragmatic rules and regulations, such patterns still tend to be viewed by the state as social problems – a view which is even more strongly endorsed by the Roman Catholic Church.

The endorsement of familism effectively copperfastens the privileged position of the upper and middle classes in Irish society. Interestingly this has not been recognised at an ideological level despite the fact that it has been clearly established that:

> It [the family] is also, of course, the central mechanism for the transfer of property rights and the economic and political power associated with property. Family and kinship connections also provide a basis for recruitment to positions in economic and political organisations (Curtin, 1986:155).

However, the obvious question as to how equal access to property, employment, and political power can be provided to the children of families who lack such resources, has not been faced. Familism is most likely to be 'attractive' to the upper and middle classes in a situation where education is increasingly the route to paid employment; and where the greater the family's social and economic resources, the more likely their children are to' gain access to educational and employment opportunities. This however may well be obscured by an idealisation of working class family ties within a context where such ties may provide 'free' child care.

Within a society where rhetorical commitment is given to equality but where education is particularly important in ensuring the future economic and social well-being of children (Drudy and Lynch, 1993), and where access to it is related to family resources (Breen *et al*, 1990), the interests of women, especially upper and middle class women whose lives are absorbed with their children, are well served by maintaining these ideas, despite the fact that the family remains 'an effective mechanism for the creation and transmission of gender inequality' since it is also 'a vigorous agency of class placement' (Barrett and McIntosh, 1991). Obviously whereas in the past familism was used to legitimate women's investment of time and energy in their children, it can be redefined to legitimate their participation in paid employment.

Reproduction

Being female in Irish society is very closely tied up with the bearing of children. This idea emerged in the ideological positions endorsed in what has become known as the 'abortion debates' held prior to the 1983 and 1992 referenda. It was clearly spelt out by Ingram who noted that:

> Vesting the unborn with an absolute right to life can be thought consistent with the mother's equal right to life only if our image of woman confines her to a natural and social role of reproduction and nurture ... The trick is performed by supposing that her natural human identity and proper social role is reproduction (1992:154/155).

The same interdefinition of womanhood with motherhood is evident in the Irish Constitution where the word 'mother' is used, interchangeably, with the word 'woman' in Articles 41.2.1 and 41.2.2 (Rowley, 1989). Ingram (and indeed also Barry, 1992 and Smyth, 1992a, 1992b) argued that this reflected an important element in the Roman Catholic Church's view of women:

> It is still the case that womanhood and motherhood are represented as synonymous realities ... for the bishops, only mothers are real women. ... womanhood is symbolically and materially non-existent until non-sexually osmosed into 'motherhood' (Smyth, 1992b:143, 144).

Within the context of the dominant discourse, as reflected in the Constitution and in the statements of the Roman Catholic Church, a concept of womanhood which did not involve reproduction is effectively a non-issue. If we accept that womanhood is naturally, inevitably and totally expressed in reproduction, then the question of a possible conflict between her rights and that of the unborn simply revolves around the extent to which birth is likely to endanger her physical life: this indeed became defined as the 'substantive issue' in the second referendum on abortion in 1992.

The very facts of the 'X' case in the 1990s made it almost impossible to ignore this issue. A fourteen-year-old girl was raped and her parents wished her to have an abortion, thereby implicitly evoking the theme of familism which was perceived as being challenged by an intrusive state. The subsequent Supreme Court ruling in the light of the 'X' case that the 1983 Eighth Amendment to the Constitution had in fact introduced a right to abortion in the event of there being a real and substantial risk to the life, as distinct from the health, of the mother, inadvertently generated an awareness that, in certain circumstances, the rights of a woman could conflict with the rights of the foetus.

The judgement of the Supreme Court on the 'X' case did not rule conclusively on the right of pregnant women to travel abroad to obtain an abortion:

> The construction (destruction) of 'woman' which emerges overwhelmingly from these and other statements by both the male judiciary and the (even more male) Catholic Church leaders is of a subordinate being (hardly a 'citizen'), morally irresponsible and intellectually unreliable, whose 'agency', insofar as she is allowed agency at all, requires to be controlled by the (patriarchal) state for the 'greater good' (Smyth, 1992a: 16-17).

In their non-binding asides three of the five judges held that the right to travel was subordinate to the right to life. This implied that unless there was a real and substantial threat to her life, a pregnant woman was not entitled to travel abroad for an abortion. It implicitly raised the issue of screening women to ascertain if they were pregnant and what their intentions were prior to allowing them to travel. This (and indeed *The Irish Times* famous cartoon showing Ireland surrounded by a fence and suggesting internment for pregnant fourteen-year-olds) vividly raised the question of the right to travel – an up to then basic and uncontroversial right. This right was affirmed by the majority of the Irish population in a referendum in 1992 (see Smyth, 1992a; Mahon, 1995; Connolly, 1997).

The issue was further extended by the debate on women's right to information in the wake of the 'X' case. Speed (1992), Barry (1992) and Smyth (1992b) noted that the censorship of information which followed the 1983 referendum on abortion had not been anticipated. It involved, for example, a ban by RTÉ, the national broadcasting station, on any live discussion of abortion on radio or TV; the removal of women's self-help books (such as *Our Bodies, Our Selves*), and even the removal of British telephone directories from public libraries. It also involved the taking of legal action against the Dublin Well Women Centre, Open Line Counselling and the Union of Students because these bodies were seen as providing such information. Such activities implicitly raised questions about the status of women as intelligent, moral beings. They demonstrated the economic, legal and political strength of those who saw state agencies as (appropriately) very much involved in the control of women's bodies. In such a context, one can only estimate the extent of self-censorship which existed, a bizarre indication of this being the decision by the Irish distributors of *The Guardian* newspaper not to distribute it for sale on the day it carried an advertisement for the Marie Stopes clinic (Smyth, 1992b).

It has been widely noted that in Ireland, even within the women's movement in the Anti-Amendment Campaign in the 1980s, the issue of 'women's right to choose', and ultimately to exert control over their own bodies, was marginalised (Jackson, 1996; Connolly, 1997). On the other hand, internationally, the feminist discourse within which abortion is located is one involving women's control over their own bodies (Tong, 1992; Jaggar, 1988; Hood, 1984). Within this context, American black feminists have been vociferous in arguing against the compulsory sterilisation of black women on social welfare. Such trends challenge facile depictions of feminists as 'anti-life/pro-death', concerned only with the position of women within the workplace. They underline the idea that individual desires, wishes and identities will vary; that these may or may not include procreation, domesticity, and/or paid employment; but that within the context of a liberal democracy, individuals have the right to make such choices.

The neglect, in the abortion debate, of the social and personal consequences of conception revealed the perceived irrelevance within the dominant discourse of the actual effect on women's day-to-day lives of rearing a child, e.g. her ability to cope with another child, the implications for the other children in the family and/or for the marriage. Yet in the overwhelming majority of cases, the mother is and will continue to be the main long-term carer. The moral debate did not deal with the social consequences of birth at this level (Gilligan, 1982; Porter, 1996). Indeed, there was the implicit assumption that, by guaranteeing the continuance to term of its life in the womb, the future care of a child would be guaranteed.

Although ideologies of reproduction are most obvious in debates about contraception and abortion, such ideologies also underlie notions of appropriate family size. It has been noted that the ideal family size in Ireland remains high: four or more compared to a European average of two or less (Whelan and Fahey, 1994). Scheper Hughes (1979a:137) pointed out how large families were idealised by the Roman Catholic clergy – and indeed this view, although rarely expressed directly, is still implicit in much of the thinking of the Church and key structures in family and community life (e.g. the Gaelic Athletic Association). It is arguable that although reproduction remains an important element in the concept of womanhood, the increasing presence and acceptance of lone parenthood reflects a concept of womanhood in which it is much less closely embedded in marriage than it has been in the past.

Love

Ireland has moved very rapidly from a situation where marriage was very clearly an economic contract between the families of the partners and concerned with property, social position, authority and legitimate sexual procreation, to one in which love is seen as the basis of and ultimately the rationale for marriage, a situation which is typical of America, North-western Europe and Polynesia (Restivo, 1991). As Beale noted (1986:65), in the 1970s in Ireland:

> A new ideal of marriage emerged; an ideal which can be found in the manuals for marriage guidance counselling and pre-marriage courses ... a love bond between a man and a woman is now accepted as the normal basis of the marriage relationship.

Implicit in this ideal were notions of personal commitment and sexual fidelity; ideas about open and honest communication; about emotional accessibility; about power; about time spent together; issues relating to working at the relationship and dealing with interpersonal problems. Beale (1986) argued that by the mid 1980s, this ideology had percolated into the Catholic hierarchy's concept of marriage. At that time the bishops in their pastoral letter, *Love is for Life* (1985:16), stressed that marriage was a 'partnership between equal persons'. However, the continued depiction by the Roman Catholic Church of good women as virgins and/or mothers was not conducive to women and men transcending stereotypical images of each other. Furthermore, there is a tension in the Roman Catholic Church's attitude to marriage insofar as, while defining marriage in terms of a personal love relationship, it does not accept the legitimacy of divorce as an option when that personal relationship is dead. As Beale (1986:83) has succinctly remarked:

> The debate about divorce centres on the question whether the relationship or the contract is the most important aspect of marriage. To those who see the contract as more important, marriage is for ever. To those who favour the relationship, permanence cannot be guaranteed and divorce is a human right that should be available to all.

It is clear that although romantic love is ideologically endorsed as the basis for marriage, it is not a realistic basis for stable married life. This is not surprising in the context of a definition of romantic love as:

> a wildly emotional state [in which] tender and sexual feelings, elation and pain, anxiety and relief, altruism and jealousy co-exist in a confusion of feelings (Berscheid and Walster, 1978).

This definition views love as an intense preoccupation with the loved object, characterised by possessiveness, exclusiveness and a desire to retain proximity. An ideology which builds a long-term relationship (potentially 50 years with increased life expectancy) on an intense emotional involvement, whose initiation has been shown to be highly associated with particular situational factors, e.g. fear or anxiety, has within itself the seeds of its own destruction. Berscheid and Walster (1978) suggest that over time such feelings are replaced by a calmer 'companionate love', although there is obviously no logical reason why people should not continue to seek intense romantic relationships after they are married.

Langford (1996) argues that the ideology of romantic love taught women that their lives could be meaningful and significant through devoting themselves to finding and keeping a man:

> The desire to fuse romantically with men in a hopeless attempt to overcome their own powerlessness shows that .... love is the psychological pivot in the persecution of women.

From this perspective, romantic love can be seen as a form of false consciousness which prevents women from recognising the reality of their situation. However, Stacey (1986) has argued that the desire among women for a long-term egalitarian love relationship is something which feminists underestimate at their peril. Indeed, it will be argued (in Chapter 5) that Western European concepts of love are feminised conceptions (Cancian, 1986) which implicitly value women's ways of relating and hence are a way of dealing with power within marriage. In these terms romantic love is a legitimisation and a validation of their desire for an equal, intense, emotionally open relationship, in which, because of the emotional vulnerability of both, both potentially have control:

> Ideas about romantic love were plainly allied to women's subordination in the home and her relative separation from the outside world. But the development of such ideas was also an expression of women's power, a contradictory assertion of autonomy in the face of deprivation (Giddens, 1992:43).

The separation of romantic love from power involves the assumption that gender differentiated patterns of access to power which exist outside marriage can somehow be nullified within it. This idea is peculiarly attractive to women in a society where in the public arena they are less valued than men. Langford (1996) has suggested that although it is necessary to locate an understanding of the popularity of love within this wider context, the idea that it is possible for love to dissolve power is illusory. She recognises that it is an illusion to which many women are very attached since it offers them the possibility 'to achieve in fantasy what they cannot achieve in reality'. However, she suggests that the kind of 'submissive ego-boosting behaviour' which is expected of women in love relationships simply reflects and reinforces the view that men's needs and wishes are of greater importance than those of women. Thus, it is necessary to reconsider

> whether investing our energies in the promise of salvation through an exclusive encounter with another human being is the best way to realise our hopes for a better world (Langford, 1996:32).

Beck and Beck-Gernsheim (1995:173-176) have suggested that love can be seen as a latter day religion in Western society. Love promises perfect happiness; it is 'communism within capitalism'; 'a utopia which grows from the power and persistence of sexual drives and deep personal wishes', and is particularly attractive in a society of 'uprooted loners'. For the most part, however, sociologists have ignored the fact that who we love, how we love, even what is seen as love is socially and culturally constructed (Restivo,1991). It seems plausible to suggest, for example, that in Ireland 'breadwinning' is seen as a much more integral expression of a man's love for his wife, than of a wife's love for her husband.

Sexual attraction

Within a heterosexual society, it is assumed that sexual attraction will occur between men and women, or at least that it is 'natural' and 'best' if it occurs in such a context. The idea of sexual attraction implicitly refers not only to physical attributes, but within the current social and cultural construction of heterosexuality, it implies the acceptance of a male-centred relationship.

It has long been recognised that the discourse of sexual attraction is constructed differently for men and women. In Western society sexual conquest is arguably an important element in the affirmation of men's identity. On the other hand, a very different attitude exists towards such behaviour in the case of women.

> Feminine sexualities as socially constituted in Western cultures are generally disempowering in that they are constituted in subordination to dominant masculine sexualities (Holland *et al*, 1992: 651).

Lees (1993) has vividly documented the way in which the 15-17 year old girls in Britain in the mid 1980s dealt with situations of sexual attraction. If they were 'too available', they ran the risk of being offensively labelled as a 'slag', a 'slut', a 'scrubber', an 'easy lay'; however, if they were too inaccessible, they ran the risk of being seen as a 'tight bitch'. They had to tread an uneasy line between passive and active sexuality – one which could really only be safely negotiated within the confines of a love relationship with a steady boyfriend, i.e. control by one man rather than by a wider patriarchy. In this relationship, love legitimised sexual activity – it steered female sexuality into an appropriate arena. Effectively then, Lees argued:

> The term slag functions as a pressure on girls to submit to a relationship of dependence on a boy, leading eventually to marriage . . . [it] lies behind the importance all girls lay on finding a boyfriend and leads to girls often colluding in their own oppression (Lees, 1993:53).

In Lee's study, the vocabulary of sexist abuse towards girls was very extensive and reflected a negative attitude to active female sexuality. This was in marked contrast to terms of abuse for boys, which were less common and reflected what was seen as passive male sexuality, e.g. 'queer', 'poof':

Feminine identity rests to a great extent on their sexual reputation. The only terms for active female sexuality are derogatory. Otherwise, girls are categorised as passive objects (Lees, 1993:63).

Similar trends emerged in Kitzinger's (1995) study of 19 and 20 year old Scottish women. Kitzinger suggested that this was because, despite the 'so called sexual revolution and 20 years of modern feminism', it was culturally very difficult for these young women to attempt to be 'self-determining heterosexually active young women' (1995:193-194).

Implicit in the notion of sexual attraction then is emotional and social dependence on men. We do not know to what extent these patterns are typical of young Irish women in the 1990s. It is arguable that the so-called sexual revolution has in fact changed little for them. The locus of control over women's sexuality has arguably changed from father/husband to peer group. Their needs regarding sexual pleasure and positive self-image are still not viewed as important within the dominant discourse.

The form of control of women through sexuality has changed ... There has been a move away from the more rigid private form of control of women's sexuality towards one that is freer and more public (Walby, 1990:127).

Increasingly there is pressure on young women to 'prove' their heterosexuality. Lees noted that among the girls in her study, the term 'slag' was used not simply to control sexual behaviour, but to control

any form of social behaviour of girls that would define them as autonomous from the attachment to and domination by boys. It acts as a censure against being unattached (Lees, 1993:52).

This reflects and reinforces assumptions that the only important affectional ties for young women are with young men. Indeed insofar as they are not interested enough in men they risk being seen as 'lessies' – lesbianism being a stigmatised and 'unnatural' identity. This view is strongly endorsed by the institutional Roman Catholic Church. At the same time, being too available is as likely to be problematic in Ireland as in England or Scotland. Although the situation is changing to some extent, it seems plausible to suggest that in Ireland a woman's sexuality:

is directed to one patriarchal agent for a lifetime and a plethora of practices exist to prevent her sexual interest from wandering, even though one of the side effects of these is to reduce her sexual interest in anything including marriage (Walby, 1990:124).

Issues related to sexual attraction are particularly salient in relation to teenage girls' perceptions of themselves. However, they are also relevant to adult women. Although the availability of the contraceptive pill has allowed the emergence of what Giddens (1992:2) has called 'plastic sexuality', i.e. 'sexuality freed from the needs of reproduction', Irish women's marital relationships are unlikely to be simply 'pure relationships', i.e. relationships which are sustained only so long as they provide personal satisfaction. Their sexual lives, for the most part, are firmly located within a network of domestic and family responsibilities. There has been indirect evidence for this pattern in the low level of reported extra-marital sexual activity (Noonan, 1993). The implications for marriage of a female centred sexuality have barely begun to be discussed.

What evidence we have suggests that in Ireland the sexual aspect of marriage seems to be less important than the wider relational aspects. Thus, 68 per cent of respondents in the European Values Study (Whelan and Fahey, 1994) saw sex as very important in making a successful marriage, as compared with the 81 per cent to 93 per cent who endorsed the importance of understanding and tolerance, mutual respect, appreciation and faithfulness. In Western society, women have considerable opportunities to meet and form relationships with men. Such relationships may become sexual and, given the stress on sexual exclusivity within marriage, they are highly likely to undermine that relationship.

Fahey (1993:118) suggested that in Ireland the institutional Church was 'preoccupied with the sinfulness of sex, with its dangers outside of marriage, and with the need to subordinate it within marriage to procreative ends'. Vance (1984) and Rubin (1984) have noted that little importance has been attributed to sexual pleasure in either a Judaic Christian tradition or a feminist tradition. British and American work has shown that assumptions about the importance of heterosexual experiences as a source of women's sexual pleasure are much exaggerated (Kinsey *et al*, 1953; Masters and Johnson, 1966; Hite 1987, 1976; Faderman, 1981; O'Connor, 1995d; Ehrenreich *et al* 1986). Ferguson (1989) suggested that the conditions which would allow a genuine reciprocal sexuality to emerge do not yet exist: that there is a 'gap between the romantic egalitarian ideology' which is at the heart of marriage in our society, and 'the continued absence of conditions for such a reciprocal sexuality'.

Female sexuality has been limited by economic and social dependence, by the power of men to define sexuality, by the limitations of marriage, by the burden of reproduction, and by the academic fact of male violence against women (Weeks, 1986:39).

There is little evidence to contradict the notion that, despite an increasingly consumerist attitude to sexual relationships and the uncoupling of the connections between sex, marriage and parenthood, a heterosexual cohabiting relationship continues to be seen as the most desirable status. It seems that, as in other countries, many Irish women are committed to emotional intimacy, and are willing to invest considerable time and energy to 'working at' heterosexual relationships even if they provide little pleasure, or indeed intimacy (Hite, 1987, 1976; Simonds, 1992; O'Connor, 1995d). For theorists such as MacKinnon (1989) this represents the triumph of patriarchal dominance; for Delphy and Leonard (1992) it reflects an economically dependent relationship between husband and wife where 'sexual servicing' and 'emotional work' are part of the 'class relationship' between husband and wife. Such interpretations, however, are likely to be far removed from the day-to-day experiences of individual women.

On the other hand the rise of consumerist attitudes to sex is compatible with the increasing commodification of relationships which is characteristic of a materialistic secular society. Furthermore this is occurring in a context where sexual boredom may occur – and indeed has been frequently identified in long-standing marriages (O'Connor, 1995d). Thus the whole issue of sexual attraction poses considerable challenges to concepts of womanhood revolving around caring, reproduction and familism.

Women's 'place' in the arena of paid employment

Insofar as definitions of womanhood in Ireland include paid employment, they are most compatible with gendered paid employment, preferably at non-managerial levels, and preferably undertaken 'for the sake of the family'. However, it does appear that there is still a certain cultural ambivalence about seeing paid employment, even gendered paid employment, as a central element in the definition of womanhood – something which has particular implications for young women, the majority of whom, whether married or not, are in paid employment.

Cousins (1996) noted that up to the 1970s at least, the state, employers, trade unions and the church stressed the importance of the role of women within the home – a position which was 'not unrelated to the fact that there was always a comparatively high level of unemployment and under-employment amongst Irish men' (1996:13). Even after the marriage bar was removed in 1973, industrial policy, wage disparities, lack of child care and discrimination in the tax and social welfare system continued to effectively discourage the participation of married women. Indeed that position was, and still is, endorsed by the Roman Catholic Church. Typically in Ireland women in their forties and fifties will have been out of the labour force for a considerable period of time. Indeed, in a 1993 study, almost 70 per cent of the women over thirty years who were unemployed were 'seeking a job after a period of non-activity', as compared with a European average of 49 per cent, and in contrast to Denmark where only 9.5 per cent of the unemployed women over thirty years were in this situation (Rapid Reports 1993: Diag. 10.5). It seems plausible to suggest that even insofar as such women enter paid employment, they are unlikely to see it as a key element in their concept of womanhood.

In Ireland, as indeed in other European countries, the majority of women are crowded into a small range of paid occupations which can be viewed as 'simply' an extension of their domestic and familial activities – manifestations of their 'essential' female nature – rather than as activities requiring skill and/or training. Whether women are in the professional or wider paid employment area, their work usually involves 'service', i.e. caring (e.g. primary teaching, nursing, cleaning). In a sense such gendered identities in the paid employment area fit easily within existing definitions of womanhood. The type of skills such activities require are not highly valued by the economic system (Lynch, 1989a; Tancred 1995). The educational system does not credentialise the intelligence required in many of these types of activity, and hence the skills involved are implicitly devalued and marginalised (Drudy and Lynch, 1993). Thus partly because of their 'unskilled' nature, and partly because they are predominantly performed by women, these occupations are low paid.

The position and status of nurses illustrates this issue. Their role has been seen as representing the ultimate fusion of caring, femininity and paid employment. Yet this very fusion, which was used to idealise them as women and as employees, was also used to legitimise their low pay and poor promotional prospects and so to perpetuate their economic exploitation and the subordination of nursing as a profession (O'Connor, 1995b and 1996a). Their attempts to redefine their role and renegotiate terms and conditions have been set within the discourse of professionalism, a concept which is gender neutral, but which includes elements of service. Within this discourse, it is difficult to see how issues related to appropriate cover for maternity leave or to job sharing, without prejudice to promotional prospects, can be raised, since implicit in the apparently gender neutral discourse is a male norm. Nevertheless, the mobilisation of the nursing unions does represent an interesting attempt to redefine a concept of womanhood within the paid employment area.

In Ireland the uneasiness about centring paid employment within a definition of womanhood is heightened when women's work involves access to positions of authority. Even in professional areas where ideologies of caring underpin their activities, (e.g. primary teaching), men have come to dominate the higher echelons. They also tend to be the spokespeople in such areas. It is possible that men may, in time, and in the face of increasing levels of unemployment, come to numerically dominate all these 'caring' professions (Hearn, 1982:188). In this situation, one would expect a reconstruction of womanhood, and manhood, and a redefinition of the gendered nature of the tasks associated with such areas: a process already in evidence in the depiction of intensive care nursing as involving a high level of technological skill.

A minority of women of course are in paid employment of a kind which is in tension with the dominant definitions of womanhood. Indeed, the women's movement in the 1980s encouraged women to enter areas of predominantly male employment, e.g. engineering. There is some suggestion that young women have difficulties in identifying these careers as appropriate career paths. There is also some suggestion that they experience difficulties in finding employment in such areas since these occupations are not perceived as 'normal' for a woman (Cronin, 1992).

In some cases indeed it is clear that the gender stereotyping of particular jobs is maintained by the industry itself. For example, although the electronics industry is uniquely suited to the employment of women with key-boarding skills (Murray and Wickham 1983):

> technocratic ideology is attempting to overcome older stereotypes which associate the hardware of information technology with the responsibilities and skill levels of the average typist (Sterne, 1984:178).

Hence, despite the economic advantages of employing women who already had keyboard skills, the industry depicted much of the equipment as 'masculine' and attempted to sell it to unskilled males so that power structures related to gender roles could be maintained.

Personhood – the family feminist, the degendered worker, or simply the acceptance of difference?

Up to now the definitions of womanhood which have been described are those which have been endorsed by the dominant institutional structures in Irish society. Here, however, we are concerned with identifying new definitions, definitions whose existence to a greater or lesser degree reflects the influence of the women's movement.

In her early work Daly stressed the importance of women saying no to 'the morality of victimisation', and yes to 'the ethics of personhood' (1973:105); that personhood in her later work being described as a state of 'be-longing, be-friending and be-witching' (1984:317-318), within a context which implicitly gave priority to women's own needs and values. A concept of womanhood linked to individual autonomy 'is counterproductive in a culture that thrives on social obligation' – that relies heavily 'on strong notions of kin, community, connections and social bonds' (Porter, 1996:293). In a society such as Ireland which stresses a 'culture of affiliation' (Woolf, 1993), a concept of personhood which leaves open the possibility that the self may be defined in and through relationships with others seems most appropriate.

It is suggested that the concept of personhood can include the family feminist, the degendered worker or simply the acceptance of 'difference'. Implicit in the idea of the family feminist is a definition of womanhood in terms of empowerment and connection in a context where women's ideas of themselves include, but transcend, the familial. The concept of a degendered worker implies that men and women are 'the same' in an employment, or indeed an educational or recreational context. To a surprising degree, this discourse, which obscures the 'aristocracy of sex', has become part of young women's taken-for-granted reality, although it sits uneasily with the gendered reality of Irish women's lives. The acceptance of 'difference' implies that women can and will vary in their needs and desires and that this diversity is an enriching manifestation of the reality of womanhood. It accepts that women's agency is legitimate, even when it is not controlled by individual men, whether husbands or employers, or by patriarchal forces within the area of paid employment or the state. This apparently innocuous definition is basically subversive. It is peculiarly attractive in the post-modern world where dominant discourses are fracturing.

Looking at these in more detail it is suggested that the grass roots, working class activities of the Women's Movement have played an important part in providing a positive and gendered definition of personhood which incorporates but transcends the family setting. Its contribution lies in validating women and their work as individuals in their homes and communities. Such a concept of personhood involves an element of connection. This idea has been captured in the concept of the family feminist. Home management, community and personal development programmes reflect and reinforce this new emergent concept of womanhood. Typically, the language used is that of 'empowerment', 'support', 'personal development' (Mulvey, 1991; Kelleher and Whelan, 1992). The focus is on recognising women's status as persons engaged in the highly responsible, exhausting and frequently isolated task of caring for children; on their entitlement to have that work validated and to have it shared in a non-stigmatising way, and on their entitlement to participate in other kinds of personally satisfying activities. As one of Mulvey's respondents said:

> I felt I only half existed, and I didn't count any more [before starting the course]. Now I want to be heard. I want my opinion to count. I don't feel like a child when talking to people like doctors, police, teachers. Now I have discovered I am an equal (Mulvey, 1991:21).

Implicit in such a response is a questioning of the ability of husbands and fathers to represent the interests of women to the state. Such views are radical within an Irish context. Less dramatic endorsements of personhood are evident in the perceived legitimacy of articulating feelings of exhaustion and isolation (Mulvey, 1991) and in legitimating married women's access to personal spending money or to time for themselves. The concept of the family feminist thus brings into sharp relief the value of family activity and connection, and the importance of transcending them.

The second definition of personhood is one which appears to obscure or degender the identity but which in fact implicitly adopts a token male identity. It assumes that society and culture are not gendered and suggests that the position of women in society can be addressed in terms of equity (Peillon 1982, 1984). The presence of women in public arenas is legitimated by the state on the basis of social solidarity and the need for a more broadly based democracy in terms of citizenship. For young women in the schools and work place, the 'official' definition of personhood seems to be a degendered one. In fact it is one which implicitly values male traits, behaviour and attributes. This is reflected in the widespread 'borrowing' by young women of dress styles, language and lifestyles which were stereotypically characteristic of males.

The third definition of personhood involves the acceptance of 'difference' – the idea that women will vary in their needs and desires, and that this diversity is an enriching rather than an inappropriate manifestation of the reality of womanhood. Implicit in it is the idea that women, whether they are in or outside paid employment; whether they have children or not; whether they are heterosexual or lesbian; and regardless of their race or class, have a reality which needs to be understood rather than be fitted into a Procrustean definition of womanhood. This does not reduce each one of us to instances of an abstraction called 'woman' (Lugones and Spelman, 1993:390). Equally, it avoids the essentialism implicit in a biological definition of womanhood. It recognises that women are oppressed, exploited and marginalised in different ways depending on their social and cultural and context. Its acceptance of that diversity, and the positive valuation attached to womanhood, implicitly undermines the basic premises of what Connell (1995a) has called conventional and hegemonic masculinity.

Thus, within a perspective which values diversity, neither women's heterosexuality nor their acceptance of subordination are seen as necessarily key elements in the concept of woman. This apparently innocuous relativist definition is basically subversive. It accepts the idea that what Smyth (1992a) calls 'women's agency' is legitimate, even when it is not controlled by patriarchy, whether in the shape of an individual man or the state. It raises questions about men's ability to define women, structurally or culturally; even more fundamentally it raises questions about how masculinity is to be defined, if it no longer necessarily involves the control, protection or subordination of women.

Meanwhile many women continue to see themselves in terms of their connectedness to patriarchal institutions so that new definitions of womanhood will come about only with the ideological transformation of these structures. The undermining of various kinds of male ideological control (sexual, physical, moral, familial) which has been evident in the 1990s (O'Connor, 1995c) is obviously one element in this transformation. However, given the under-representation of women in the ideological structures (church, state, academia) it is not clear to what extent this process will continue.

Coulter (1993) has noted that the educational arena is attempting to create institutions which would be more responsive to the needs of women, but these structures typically lack resources. As noted in Chapter 2, Women's Studies potentially provides an ideological challenge to the patriarchal structures from within (Fitzgerald, 1996; Byrne *et al*,

1996). It is possible that in a post-modern world, with the breakdown of what has been called the single narrative, male control will continue to be subtly eroded. In this situation, alternative discourses may be created and maintained in friendships (Oliker, 1989; Gullestad, 1984; O'Connor, 1992c) but we know comparatively little about them yet.

The key difficulty in formulating definitions of womanhood lies not so much at the level of content but of value, and with the implications of this for women's relationship with individual men and the wider institutional structure. This is not peculiar to Ireland, although the situation is arguably exacerbated here by the consensual character of our culture; the absence of a tradition of individuation; the continued strength of essentialism and its reflection in ideas about the centrality of reproduction and familism. The problem is of course particularly acute for young women without children, whose main option would appear to lie in the degendered employment arena.

Ideological closure: the ultimate illusion

The picture which has been presented here would seem to imply ideological closure. In fact, however, the ideological context is a good deal more open than this from the point of view of the individual woman. This arises firstly from the fact that structures do not act as homogeneous units; certain elements in the state apparatus endorse particular definitions while others effectively undermine them. Secondly, individual women can of course prioritise particular elements (e.g. love over reproduction). Thirdly, individual women and/or groups of women can exploit the symbolic significance of actions by 'high profile' women so as to effectively legitimise a redefinition of womanhood.

Drudy and Lynch (1993) among others have noted that institutional structures today are not monolithic entities. This is nicely illustrated by the fact that although the Department of Social Welfare reflects and reinforces women's caring roles within its mainstream income-maintenance programmes, a subsidiary activity of the Department reinforces women's personhood while providing grants to women's groups (Mulvey 1991) albeit attempting to effectively tighten the social control over them through home management courses. Indeed the same sort of tension has been observed by Ballaster *et al* (1991) in their analysis of romance in women's magazines – such romance being at one level ideologically oppressive, but at another level providing an opportunity for women to have their own dependency needs met and nurturant fantasies fulfilled, imaginatively at least.

Kelleher and Whelan (1992), Flynn and O'Connell (1990) and Hayes (1990) noted the part played by religious sisters in working with locally based women's groups: a position not without its tensions. Religious sisters are representatives of a male church, confidence in whose institutions has declined in the 1980s (Barker *et al*, 1992: 11) and which, particularly in working class areas, is seen as an extension of the male state (Kelleher and Whelan, 1992:67). Their work, laudable in itself, has a downside, but their status has ensured access to resources which have indirectly undermined the established concepts of womanhood. Similarly, lay community groups entirely dependent on the voluntary and unpaid involvement of women, although reinforcing personhood, can also be seen as perpetuating ideas about the availability of women's unpaid labour.

It seems possible to suggest that women have shown considerable agility in prioritising ideological elements. There is no hard evidence to support this, but it is at least arguable that in reducing their family size by half over a twenty-five to thirty year period, women have drawn on a concept extolling love rather than reproduction, although obviously their ability to do this has been facilitated by the development of the contraceptive pill. Similarly, the dramatic rise in married women's participation in paid employment may arguably reflect the endorsement of a particular definition of caring or indeed familism.

Individual women have emerged who, by their lives and performance, have challenged the essentialism of the ideological structure. A striking example is former President of Ireland, Mary Robinson. As a mother, a feminist and a wife, she has quite clearly shown a commitment to her children, husband and paid employment in a way which is in direct tension with the dominant discourse. Other women, by their own presence and performance in, for example, political arenas or sporting activities, have challenged the 'naturalness and inevitability' of restricting women to the 'private' arena. By any standard, these are exceptional women, whose presence does not negate the considerable structural and ideological barriers with which women have to contend. They do however have an important de-legitimating effect on essentialist ideological structures.

Summary

Definitions of Irish womanhood traditionally have revolved around two opposing images viz. the self-sacrificing Irish mother and the a-sexual, non-maternal, employment oriented being. Attempts to challenge this require, as Peillon (1984) has noted, a radical reworking of Irish ideology. It is suggested that that reworking is very much in progress. At the most fundamental level, it involves a reworking of concepts of essentialism, particularly ideas about women's 'essential nature', about their 'place', and perhaps even more importantly, about their value, and the appropriateness of their subordination to various kinds of male control (moral, physical, sexual). Ironically, although Irish society has traditionally been preoccupied with issues related to identity and ideology, there has been very little discussion of concepts of womanhood. Indeed given the social and cultural construction of heterosexuality there is little interest in doing so since such phenomena are assumed to be 'natural'.

It has been suggested in this chapter that caring, reproduction and familism are key elements in the concept of womanhood endorsed by church and state and that these sit uneasily with emerging definitions involving personhood, with all its implications as regards individual autonomy, individual choices, rights and responsibilities. Love and sexual attraction are also seen as important elements in the definition of womanhood, particularly since these effectively obscure the issue of male control. As such they are particularly alluring to women in a society where women are less valued than men. In a sense, however, both elements are implicitly subversive since they challenge definitions of sexuality which revolve exclusively around procreation.

Perhaps the most important element in the emerging concept of personhood lies in the acceptance of 'difference' – the idea that women vary in their needs and desires, and that this diversity is an enriching rather than inappropriate manifestation of the reality of womanhood. The acceptance of that diversity, and the valuation attached to womanhood, implicitly undermines the basic premises of what Connell (1995a) has called conventional and hegemonic masculinity. Thus, within a perspective valuing diversity, neither women's heterosexuality nor their acceptance of subordination are necessarily seen as key elements in the concept of woman. Thus, this apparently innocuous relativist definition is basically subversive.

Women, by prioritising different elements, make sense of their own lives. For single parents reproduction may well provide meaning, while for middle class married women, familism may be the key element. Indeed it could be argued that individual women's creativity and agency in Irish society is frequently more effective in creating meaning within their own lives, than in actually changing the dominant discourses within which they live. This is perhaps inevitable since, up to now, women have not shaped the dominant discourses in Irish society.

4

Family and Work – Unproblematic Realities?

Introduction

WE tend to assume that the family and paid work are unproblematic realities. However, such is not the case, as is shown in this chapter. Firstly, we examine the changing nature of marriage and family life. We think of the family as a static phenomenon, but it is clear from various indicators that family life has been changing dramatically in the recent past, both in Ireland and in a wider European context. Secondly, we describe the home as a physical reality, because although we think of families as emotional entities, their lifestyles vary depending on the material artifacts available to them. Thirdly, we explore the reality of the family as a small group, focusing particularly on power within the family. Fourthly, we present evidence on the issue of lone parenting. It is clear that although we think of the family as a heterosexual unit, lone parenthood is an increasingly common family form. Fifthly, we raise the issue of the extent to which paid work and family are permeable realities.

In this context, issues related to both the re-integration of married women into paid employment and to the boundaries between unpaid family/community work and paid work can be raised. This has a very real relevance to married women in Ireland insofar as the majority are not in paid employment, but are actively involved in creating communities. Finally, we examine the evidence that is available as regards how 'happy' women are with their lives.

The changing nature of marriage and family life

In this section we look very briefly at some of the basic indicators of the lives of Irish married women. Women, as members of married or cohabiting couples, are involved in just under 710,000 units in Ireland

(CSO, 1997). In what is often regarded as the 'normal' Irish situation, viz. housewives whose husbands are in paid employment, the figure is approximately 277,000 women. They made up only 39 per cent of all married or cohabiting couples in Ireland in 1996 as compared with just over 53 per cent in 1986 (see Table 4.1). On the other hand the proportion of couples where both were in paid employment doubled over that period (from just over 16 per cent in 1986 to 32 per cent in 1996). The proportion where neither was in paid employment has remained strikingly high (constituting just over 27 per cent of all married or cohabiting couples in 1986 and 24.5 per cent in 1996). There is still little evidence of role reversal: the proportion of couples where the woman only was in paid employment remaining very much a minority (just over 3 per cent in 1986 and 4 per cent in 1996: see Table 4.1).

TABLE 4.1

COUPLES CLASSIFIED BY WORK SITUATION 1986-96 (ROUNDING %S AND 000S-)

Work Situation	1986 %(N)	1991 %(N)	1996 %(N)
Both at work	16% (108)	22% (148)	32% (227)
Only the man at work	53% (355)	47% (320)	39% (277)
Only the woman at work	3% (22)	4% (26)	4% (31.5)
Neither at work	27% (128)	27% (180)	24.5% (174)
TOTAL	99% (667)	100% (674)	99.5% (710)

CSO 1997: Table 7

Traditionally Ireland was noted for late marriages and high proportions of people who never married. Even up to the 1960s, resistance to marriage was reflected in the high average age at marriage and the high rates of permanent non-marriage (Fahey, 1993; Breen *et al*, 1990). This phenomenon has been attributed to the economic climate, where marriage was not necessary for economic security and may even have been a threat to the living standards of individuals; and to Catholic moral teaching which saw little value in sexual or personal intimacy. That pattern steadily changed (Fahey, 1995). Marriage in Ireland reached a high point of popularity in the early 1970s, with a marriage rate of 7.4 per 1,000 of the population in 1973, as compared with a rate of 5.4 in 1961. The popularity of marriage has fallen more or less steadily since then.

The Irish pattern, however, although it is slightly more extreme than in other European countries, is not atypical. Between 1990 and 1992, the marriage rate in the European Community dropped from 6.4 to 5.6 per thousand. However, the lowest rate was in Ireland, with 4.5 in 1992 (Rapid Report, 1993:4), falling again slightly to 4.4 in 1995, and rising slightly to 4.6 in 1994 (Vital Statistics, 1995). The EU rate has continued to fall, with only Sweden now having a lower rate than Ireland (Eurostat, 1995).

> The institution of marriage is weakening in the European Community. More and more women are living alone and bringing up children alone . . . In the European Community and in most countries the gross marriage rate (number of marriages per 1,000 inhabitants) is falling (Rapid Reports, 1993:4).

These trends have been associated with a rise in the age at which people are marrying in Ireland and in the rest of the EU. The average age of brides in Ireland rose from 24 years in 1977 to 25.6 in 1986 (Clancy, 1991:12) and to 26.3 in 1992 (Eurostat, 1995). This trend has persisted. Indeed the mean age of women at first marriage rose in every member state between 1980 and 1990. However, in 1992, age at first marriage for brides was considerably higher in Ireland than the European average (i.e. 26.3 years, as compared with 25.5): with only Denmark, Sweden and Finland having a higher average age at marriage. In Ireland as Kennedy has noted (1993:4):

> Younger cohorts of women are at least postponing marriage. For how long, or to what extent permanently, remains to be seen.

In Ireland, as indeed in the rest of the European Union, women are having their first child later. Over the 1980-1992 period, the average age of women at the birth of their first child in what was then the EC rose from 24.6 to 26.3 years: although Portugal and Greece had significantly earlier first births, at 24.7 years (Rapid Report, 1993:4). In 1993 the average age of women at first birth in the fifteen member states of the EU was 28.6 years (Rubery *et al*, 1996).

During the period 1980-92, there was also a fall in fertility in the European Community from 1.8 to 1.5. In Ireland, although average fertility, at 2.11, was the highest in the European Community, it was very substantially lower than it had been in 1980 (3.25) or in 1970 (3.9). This fall has continued, reaching 1.93 in 1993, with Ireland, in common with other EU countries, not replacing itself in demographic terms for the first time in its history (Nic Ghiolla Phádraig and Clancy, 1995). There was a 37 per cent decline in family size between 1961 and 1981, and a further decline of 33 per cent between 1980 and 1993 (First Monitoring Committee, 1994). Indeed as Kennedy (1993:4) has noted: 'fertility per woman has been halved over the last 25-30 years'. Nevertheless, fertility in Ireland still remains high in European terms. Even in 1995, women in Ireland aged 35 years or less had the highest fertility rate in Europe – 2.39 children, as compared with an EU average of 1.7 (Rubery *et al*, 1996).

The home as a physical reality: material artifacts and their implications

For housewives the home is very much their place of work, as well as their place of rest. Its size and amenities have important implications for their lifestyles. Home ownership has traditionally been high in Ireland (67 per cent, according to Census, 1981). The 1994-95 Household Budget Survey (1997) showed that it had risen to 79 per cent. There has also been a substantial increase in the size of the average dwelling, particularly since 1971 (Fahey, 1992). The 1994-95 Household Budget Survey (1997) estimated the size of the average dwelling size at 5.5 rooms, for, on average, 3.3 persons. This has both positive and negative consequences. On the one hand, increased space is helpful in rearing children (e.g. in dissipating noise levels or reducing conflicts about space utilisation). On the other hand, however, this area has to be maintained and serviced. Fahey (1992:64, 67) noted that in families this work is usually not done on a commercial basis. Some services have become partly commercialised (e.g. 'take aways', paid child minding) while others (e.g. laundries) have declined. Overall, however:

> there appears to be nothing comparable to the armies of domestic servants which kept middle class households going a hundred years ago (Fahey, 1992:64).

The implications of this for the lifestyles of married women have not been recognised.

Certainly there have been very considerable improvements in basic domestic utilities which have, potentially at least, eliminated some household work. For example, by 1994-95, 99 per cent of households had piped cold water; 95 per cent had piped hot water and 97 per cent had an inside toilet (Household Budget Survey, 1997). The availability of vacuum cleaners (88 per cent) and washing machines (86 per cent) potentially reduces the level of domestic labour. The dramatic rise in ownership of microwave ovens (6 per cent in 1987; 47 per cent in 1994-

95: Household Budget Survey 1997) also suggests that women are attempting to cut down time spent on domestic labour (by using convenience foods and re-heating instead of cooking fresh). However, as Cowan (1985) has noted, the increase in domestic gadgets does not necessarily imply a reduction in the extent of domestic labour.

Indeed the equally dramatic increase in the ownership of video recorders (from roughly one in five households in 1987 to almost two thirds in 1994-95) suggests that the home is increasingly used as a place for forms of entertainment which were previously associated with areas outside the home. This tends to actually increase the extent of domestic labour. In any case, a rise in standards of hygiene has ensured that the actual amount of time spent on household work, internationally, has been little affected by the existence of technology (Coverman, 1989). It seems reasonable to expect that similar patterns exist in Ireland.

The quality of life for full-time housewives, especially for those living in rural areas (Byrne, 1993; Second Commission on the Status of Women, 1993), is likely to be strongly affected by the availability of a phone and/or the use of a car. In 1994-95, just over three quarters of households had a phone, as compared with half in 1987 (Household Budget Survey, 1997). Almost two-thirds had car(s) in 1994-95, a slight increase from 1987. The ownership of cars and phones was highest in rural areas, especially in farm households, with just under four-fifths of rural households having a phone and car(s). Clearly both these facilities are increasingly available in urban and rural areas, although sizeable minorities still do not have access to them.

The National Anti-Poverty Strategy (1997:30) suggested that:

> People are living in poverty, if their income and resources (material, cultural and social) are so inadequate as to preclude them from having a standard of living which is regarded as acceptable by Irish society generally.

In 1994 it was estimated that 34 per cent of the population were living on a disposable income which was below 60 per cent of the national average (National Anti-Poverty Strategy, 1997). Furthermore the proportion of the population below this poverty line had increased over the previous twenty years (from 25 per cent in 1973 to 34 per cent in 1994: Callan *et al*, 1996). Callan *et al* (1996) found that, in 1994, households headed by an unemployed person and households headed by someone working in the home were most likely to be in poverty. Whelan (1994a) found that, focusing on those aged under 65 years, the risk of poverty varied from one in a hundred households among the higher professional and managerial groups, to one in two among the unskilled manual groups. The groups which were at the greatest risk of poverty in 1994 were the unemployed; households headed by someone working in the home; lone parents; children and people with disabilities (National Anti-Poverty Strategy, 1997).

Callan *et al* (1994) also developed an eight item basic deprivation index covering items such as lack of adequate heating; spending a day without a substantial meal; having arrears on rent, mortgage, electricity or gas; going into debt in the previous six months to cover ordinary living expenses; not having a warm waterproof coat. They found that approximately one-third of the households in their study were deprived in one or more of these ways. They found that such households were not always those with the lowest level of income, suggesting that those currently on a low income might have savings which could tide them over. The researchers concluded that those who had both a low level of income and who suffered basic deprivation as assessed on this index could be regarded as consistently poor. In 1994, 540,000 people or 15 per cent of the population were poor in those terms (National Anti-Poverty Strategy, 1997:33).

It is clear that although the range of material artifacts available to Irish households has increased considerably over the past twenty-five years, access to these varies considerably. Furthermore, a sizeable minority (15 per cent) can be regarded as living in poverty, while an even larger proportion (34 per cent) are on a relatively low income.

The family as a small group: issues related to power

On the basis of a wide ranging critical review of research work carried out on Irish farm families, Shortall (1991) argued that the patriarchal parameters of Irish rural life have been taken for granted. For example, the fact that land is transmitted through the male line has not been integrated into a discussion of the distribution of power and authority within farm families. Mahon (1993) noted that the recommendation, by the Second Commission on the Status of Women, that all forms of income should be jointly owned, has not even been discussed. Research has generally assumed that the position of men and women within marriage is divorced from the wider institutional and cultural context. However, there are notable exceptions to this view:

> although the love bond between a man and a women is now the normal basis for marriage, being married involves much more than a relationship. Marriage is also a contract governed by the laws of both Church and State (Beale, 1986:74).

What limited evidence is available suggests that a high proportion of rural wives are not joint owners of the family home, 60 per cent of those in O'Hara's study (1994a, c) and 48 per cent of those in my own study (1995a) being in this position. In Ireland less than 10 per cent of women own farms and these typically are older women (Department of Equality and Law Reform, 1994). Three quarters of Irish farms are registered in the husband's name only. Quite clearly, at the level of ownership, women's economic power basis within the family is limited. Attempts to explore the extent to which resources and/or responsibilities within the family are systematically biased in favour of males are likely to be strongly resisted since they implicitly challenge the legitimacy and inevitability of male power and privilege. Indeed, the women themselves tend to collude with this (O'Hara, 1994a, b). This is understandable within a culture where women are not accustomed to think in terms of ownership and legal entitlements. It is almost impossible to imagine a parallel situation involving men.

For the most part, research work on power and authority within Irish homes has focused on who makes the decisions (Hannan and Katsiaouni, 1977; O'Connor and Daly, 1983). These studies have provided revealing insights into the balance of power between husbands and wives, insights which have, however, been obscured by the use of traditional/modern models. Thus, for example, Hannan and Katsiaouni (1977:50) using a Likert general power scale (including elements such as 'who has the final say in borrowing money to buy land?'; 'who is the general boss in financial matters?') found that almost three fifths of the families were characterised by husband dominance, and only 7 per cent by wife dominance. Similarly, O'Connor and Daly's study (1983) showed that decisions regarding a husband changing his job were predominantly made by the husband, whereas decisions regarding a wife returning to paid employment were made by both of them. Such findings have simply been recorded as part of an accepted reality. Their implications as regards the nature of Irish marriage have never been discussed.

It is not clear to what extent these patterns have changed. Using data on Dublin mothers with at least one child of school-going age, Kiely (1995) concluded that the wife had the greater influence on a variety of decisions involving the household and children (e.g. decisions about household furnishings, redecorating, the amount and type of food). In the majority of cases, moving house, changing the children's schools and having a night out were depicted as joint decisions. Nevertheless, Kiely suggested that the only significant decision-making role that husbands held was which TV programme to watch when the family were together. We do not know to what extent these patterns are typical. They point, however, to the collapse of the father's traditional position of authority within urban families:

> Headship is no longer vested in the father and authority tends to be based on competence. With the loss of headship and authority, decision making no longer rests with fathers (Kiely, 1995:155).

On the other hand, the existence of marital violence illustrates in sharp outline the locus of power within the domestic arena. Evidence in Chapter 2 suggests that between one in five and one in three women experience violence from a partner. However:

> until relatively recently, violence has remained a personal problem due in part to fears about intruding into the privacy of the home or interfering with the sanctity of marriage and also due to a reluctance to confront the myth of the idealised family where all is happiness, love and harmony (Ruddle and O'Connor, 1992:21).

A study of women in the Adapt Refuge by Ruddle and O'Connor (1992) found that financial dependence was characteristic of 95 per cent of these women. Perhaps not surprisingly then, three quarters of the women in Adapt returned to their partners following their first stay; and even after their most recent admission, more than one third went back to their partners. In the majority of cases, they returned to an unchanged violent marital situation. Furthermore there was a suggestion that violence by a partner could be seen as representing an attempt by him to retain control; and that violence was resorted to when all other attempts to maintain the 'appropriate' relationship with their partner had failed:

> Again, contrary to popular conception, the women who are victims of violence are not always those who subscribe to the traditional female role but in fact, are often more liberal than most in their attitudes (Ruddle and O'Connor, 1992).

In the Adapt study the level of physical violence was extreme, involving hospitalisation in some cases. A quarter of the women also reported that their children were severely beaten by their spouse. Similarly, in Casey's refuge study (1987), three fifths of the women interviewed reported being battered while they were pregnant; for approximately one third of these, the battering had brought about the loss of the baby. The Kelleher national sample study (1995) found that almost two thirds of those who experienced any kind of violence reported that they suffered from depression. Over 70 per cent of the women in that study who experienced physical violence reported that it resulted in physical injury, including broken bones, head injuries, loss of consciousness and miscarriages. Just under two thirds said that their children had witnessed the violence, and that the effects on the children had included a deterioration in their school performance, sleeping problems and being fearful and withdrawn. It is obvious that there are considerable psychological and social costs associated with men's violence within families, and that such violence occurs in a sizeable minority of families.

In the past ten years we have become aware of another unacceptable face of (predominantly male) violence within families, viz. child sexual abuse. It is not clear how common such abuse is in Ireland. On the one hand, the rate of confirmed child sexual abuse in the Eastern Health Board area in 1988 was 1.2 per 1,000. However, this is likely to be an under-estimation. Thus they noted that of the alleged child sexual abuse cases known to the Eastern Health Board, 52 per cent were confirmed sexual abuse, but only 5 per cent were confirmed non-abuse. The remainder included those where the case was closed; not enough evidence either way, etc. A retrospective study of adults using a sample of 1,001 adults (with a non response rate of 2 per cent) found that 15 per cent of the women had experienced sexual abuse, as had 9 per cent of the men. These figures would certainly suggest that child sexual abuse could be a relatively common form of abuse of power (IMS, 1993).

It is widely accepted that in the majority of cases such abuse involves people who are known to the child – for the most part men in the family. McKeown and Gilligan (1991) in the only published study in Ireland to date found that 90 per cent of the abusers were men; and that three quarters of the confirmed child sexual abuse victims were girls, with an average age of 9.2 years. The average age of abused boys was 7.9. Approximately one third of all the confirmed cases were less than six years old. The study also showed that 68 per cent of the confirmed sexual abuse cases in the Eastern Health Board area involved intra-familial males. Overwhelmingly the abuser was the father, sometimes a brother. For almost two thirds of the children the (confirmed) sexual abuse involved a variety of activities including actual or attempted vaginal penetration, as well as sex using fingers or objects and oral/anal sex. Ninety-one per cent of the confirmed cases came to light because of the child's disclosure, thereby implicitly suggesting that professionals were not reporting it. Indeed a variety of reports (including the Kilkenny

Incest Report: Wood, 1993) have adverted to the problem of non-reporting, and have recommended mandatory reporting by designated professionals. This has not occurred to date.

The trends that emerged in McKeown and Gilligan's study were broadly similar to those which have emerged in other European and American studies of child sexual abuse. They raise issues about male abuse of power within the family, and, more fundamentally, about men's ideas about masculinity and sexuality. They also implicitly raise issues about the role of the state in protecting the child. McKeown and Gilligan's study revealed that in roughly one third of the confirmed cases where the child and the abuser had been living in the same house, the child left (a pattern which is not seen as desirable); in a quarter of the cases where both were in the same house, child and abuser remained – a situation which appears even more unsatisfactory in view of the age of the children who were abused. Furthermore, despite the fact that child sexual abuse is a crime, civil proceedings to protect the child were taken in approximately only one in five of the confirmed sexual abuse cases. Criminal proceedings were taken in considerably less than 10 per cent of the confirmed cases.

Thus, the picture which emerges as regards power within Irish families is complex. On the one hand it appears, from the limited evidence we have, that although men typically own land and other property, their day-to-day exercise of power within the family may well be limited although it will be shown that they continue to benefit disproportionately from women's unpaid work within the family and to have disproportionate access to money to spend on themselves. On the other hand it seems that ideas about the acceptability of force continue to remain implicit in our ideas about manhood. These provide a fertile ground for legitimating abuse within the family – abuse which the state, to varying degrees, and for various reasons, finds difficult to confront.

The family – a problematic reality?

It is increasingly recognised that the family is far from being an unproblematic entity. Jackson (1993:180) suggested that, 'There is no simple single entity that can be defined as "the family" and compared across cultures'. Jackson (1993), Edholm (1992) and Finch (1996) noted that, for example, husbands and wives did not always live together; that the biological father was not always the social father; that ideas about the nature of blood ties varied cross-culturally; that biological motherhood was not always equated with social motherhood; and indeed that in some societies the mother was not seen as a blood relation of the child in the womb, but only as a container for it. These examples appear exotic. Yet even in our own society it is clear that despite the simplicity and attractiveness of familism at an ideological level, the family is by no means an unproblematic entity. Indeed it is increasingly recognised that it is more useful to speak of families, rather than the family. In Ireland, perhaps the biggest challenge to traditional notions of the family has come from the increasing presence of lone parents.

Lone parenthood: an alternative family form?

It has been noted that, across the European Community, 'more and more women are living alone and bringing up children alone' (Rapid Reports, 1993:4). This reflects the ability of women to survive on their own, and their willingness to redefine the family, excluding a residential hetero-sexual tie as the basic element in that unit. Furthermore as noted by Rubery *et al* (1996) the highest fertility rates are in countries such as Sweden where approximately one in two births in 1993 were outside marriage; such findings prompting the conclusion that fertility is no longer related to the existence of a two-parent married couple.

A similar sort of pattern is certainly visible in Ireland. For example, whereas in 1980 births outside marriage made up 5 per cent of all births, by 1996 they made up 25 per cent of all births (Vital Statistics, 1997). Up to the early 1960s, women who had children outside of marriage were perceived as 'Magdalenes', and were cut off from the community for most of their lives in institutions under Church control. Even in the early 1970s lone motherhood was so shameful that it was literally not spoken about (Levine, 1982). The introduction of the Unmarried Mothers Allowance (1973) reflected and reinforced public acceptance, if not enthusiasm, for single motherhood.

Even yet, however, lone parenthood is seen by the state as a social problem. It is implied that it overwhelmingly involves teenage girls. In fact, however, in 1996, less than a fifth of all births to lone mothers were to women under 20 years. Quite clearly it is impossible to dismiss this trend as an adolescent phenomenon although, overall, women giving birth outside marriage do tend to be younger than those giving birth inside marriage. Of course lone parenthood is in fact a heterogeneous category and includes single never married lone parents as well as those who are separated/divorced and widowed. Approximately one in five of all family units are headed by lone parents, again predominantly lone mothers (15.4 per cent: Census 1991, 1993).

What limited evidence we have is compatible with the idea that single never married lone parenthood constitutes an attempt, particularly among young poorly educated working-class women, to construct an adult status within a situation where there are very few options. Hannan and Ó Riain's (1993) study of secondary school leavers in the late 1980s highlighted the extent to which single never married lone parenthood was most likely to be characteristic of working-class women, whose mothers had low levels of education, whose fathers were unemployed, and who had themselves spent 60 per cent of their time in the labour force but unemployed. Thus single motherhood for them appeared to be a way of asserting an adult identity, within a very constrained situation.

Griffin (1985) argued that unemployed girls saw motherhood simply as an inevitable development, rather than as an alternative status to unemployment. Like Wallace's (1987) respondents they did not have a glamorised view of motherhood, but saw it as a virtually inevitable status. McCashin's work vividly suggests that both the single never married and the separated lone mothers in his Dublin study 'chose to be lone mothers – albeit not in circumstances of their own choosing' (1996:186). None of the single never married lone mothers in McCashin's study had conceived as a result of a casual relationship; the length of their relationships varying from four months to three years. They differed however in terms of their knowledge about contraception, their use of it, their desire to conceive, etc. Once they had conceived they did not consider for the most part any alternative other than keeping the baby. Their decision to be lone mothers reflected their deep concern for their children whom they saw as being central to their lives and decisions, and central to 'their experience and search for independence and control' (1996:186). Some of them found caring for their children a strain and some felt lonely, but overall they enjoyed the routine parenting tasks, and the independence and opportunity to make their own decisions that was characteristic of their lone parenting situation.

The lone mothers in McCashin's (1996) study saw shortage of money as their biggest problem, and in fact half were below the (60 per cent) poverty line. Social welfare was the only source of income for over two thirds of the respondents. Some of them could not afford basic necessities such as electricity, and many of them could not afford an occasional night out or new clothes. Most of them wanted to work, but were afraid that if they did they would be worse off, after covering the costs of child care and transport. However, although managing financially was a considerable worry, a number felt that at least now they were in control and could manage that money in their children's best interests. The trends emerging in McCashin's study as regards the poverty of lone mothers were not unusual. Callan (1994) noted that households headed by single, widowed or separated women under 35 years, with children under 18 years, were at particular risk of poverty; with almost three out of five of such households being below the poverty line.

In McCashin's (1996) study only 6 per cent of those who were separated or divorced received maintenance payments, and the others were not interested in pursuing such payments, not least because they feared a re-involvement in violent relationships, and an undermining of their control over their children's lives. Ward (1993) also found that the legislative arrangements as regards such maintenance were very unsatisfactory with only 13 per cent of maintenance orders made in the District Court being fully paid up (and that in a situation where 60 per cent were for amounts less than the lowest social welfare payment). Ward's data did not include either maintenance cases dealt with in the Circuit Court or those reached by agreement between the partners before going to court. Fahey and Lyons (1995) found that only 39 per cent of the legal aid cases in their study had a maintenance arrangement, whereas 65 per cent of the private cases had this. However, they also found that, even where a maintenance arrangement existed, an attachment to earnings existed in only a very small proportion of cases (7 per cent). Furthermore, the median payment per week was still quite low (for legal aid cases, £60 per week; and for private cases, £100 per week).

It has been widely recognised that states in Western society have been unwilling or unable to ensure that divorced fathers widely and consistently honour their maintenance obligations towards their children. The Second Commission on the Status of Women (1993) noted that in Manitoba, in Canada, the combination of an automatic monitoring system, and the automatic movement by the state to take proceedings within a month of a default, ensured that a very high proportion (85 per cent) of maintenance payments were honoured. Irish legislation does not include these arrangements.

McCashin (1996) noted that kin ties but particularly their relationship with their mothers were critical in affecting young women's experience of lone motherhood. Wallace's (1987) work also suggested that where lone mothers needed help it was normally provided by their mother. Flanagan and Richardson's (1993) five year study of never married single mothers in Holles Street, offered a further insight into their situation in so far as 50 per cent of the women in that study lived with their own parents after the birth, as compared with the 25 per cent who lived with the father of the child. Tensions arose in situations where lone parents lived with their parents, especially where the parents themselves had little money, or were in crowded accommodation. However, their expectations were that they were more likely to receive financial support, help and nurturance from their own mothers than from their sexual partners. Indeed only a quarter of the men involved in single women's pregnancies in McCashin's (1996) study were positive and supportive. These trends suggest a marginalisation of men within the family – a pattern which implies a radical challenge to our ideas about the family and to the cultural and social construction of heterosexuality.

Lone parenthood can partly be understood by situating it in a context where other life options are effectively closed to one group of women. However, it also reflects an assessment of the costs and benefits of male/female relationships.

McCashin noted the fact that young single women were coping and enjoying lone parenthood. This raises questions about why this pattern is seen as a social problem. Perhaps even more fundamentally it raises questions about the contribution of fathers to family life. Indeed the sheer existence of lone parenthood implicitly challenges the traditional 'unthinkableness' of a family life which is not based on a residential conjugal unit.

The nature of work

Overwhelmingly it is women who are engaged in 'non-work' activities. This situation is not peculiar to Ireland. For example it has been shown that across industrialised countries, although the overall proportion of work carried out by men and women is very similar, approximately two thirds of women's work time is spent in unpaid activities, and only one third in paid activities (among men the proportions are reversed):

> So men receive the lion's share of income and recognition for their economic contribution – while most of women's work remains unpaid, unrecognised and undervalued (United Nations, 1995:88).

For Irish women, the issue of what counts as work is particularly important, given the constitutional and cultural endorsement of the value of full-time work in the home and the fact that roughly three-fifths of Irish married women still work full-time in the home.

Feminist sociologists over the past twenty-five years have challenged the portrayal of housework and child care as non-work activities (Oakley, 1974; Benston, 1969; Dalla Costa and James, 1972). The sheer illogicality of excluding services produced for family consumption in the national accounts, while at the same time including, for example, the production of agricultural goods for home consumption has begun to be recognised (Lynch and McLaughlin, 1995). It has been estimated that 25-40 per cent of economic output is excluded from GNP and GDP – depending on the country and the method of measurement used. Various explanations have been put forward for these practices:

> Some commentators see them as the result of sexist bias against women's work, since unpaid housework is the main form of service production counted as non-economic, while the traditional explanation is that technical difficulties in placing a monetary value on non-market services account for the exclusion of such activity from measurement. The technical difficulties are no doubt real, although they seem no greater than those encountered and circumvented in other areas (Fahey, 1990:168).

Paying women the going rate for such activities is dismissed as economically impossible, while a Fine Gael proposal in the 1980s to pay a token figure was seen as derisory. The issue is resurfacing again in the shape of an argument concerning a social wage for all. This however constitutes a potential challenge to male economic control within the family. It is also potentially at odds with the market, since even if it were set at a subsistence level, it could be seen as discouraging employees from taking up low paid employment. From the point of view of the state it is both economically costly and unattractive. Strategies such as the three year part-time Job Opportunities Programme, stimulated by the Justice Commission of the Conference of Major Religious Superiors and operated in conjunction with FÁS, can be seen as an attempt to deal with this problem. Such strategies can also be seen as effectively copper-fostering the position of many women in 'feminised community' work, and hence (unless this work is revalued) in low paid, low status work.

The situation in farming can be seen as an extreme case in the context of a market model insofar as the bonds of loyalty and affection between husband and wife co-exist with a kind of employer/employee relationship. It illustrates the way in which the very definition of activity as 'work' reflects and reinforces a male model. Thus, although farm work is seen by the official agencies as constituting 'work', women's activities on farms do not automatically translate into an entitlement for economic remuneration. The National Report on Ireland (Department of Equality and Law Reform, 1994:54) noted that women provided more than a quarter of the total labour output on farms (their contribution being valued at £467.5 million by the Irish Farmers Association). At European level, in a study of non-salaried working women, it was shown that 60 per cent of farm wives received no payment for their work, although more than half found this work difficult and tiring and would give it up if they could (O'Hara, 1994a, 1994b). The majority of the women in O'Hara's sample were financially dependent on their husband, were perceived by the state as his dependant and were categorised accordingly in the taxation and social welfare systems. Unless they were legal partners (which the majority did not appear to be) they were only entitled to a widow's pension (based on their husband's contribution) and did not have cover for maternity, sickness, optical or dental benefits. Their situation, as O'Hara noted, is far from being unique in Europe. Thus the distinctions between paid and unpaid work are very significant indeed for the individuals involved.

Paid work and family: permeable realities?

Married women in Ireland face considerable difficulties as regards returning to the labour force despite the fact that in many cases they were 'pushed out' by the Marriage Bar – a policy that was supported by the institutional Church and state, by employers and by trade unions (Cousins, 1996). Even if they define themselves as unemployed and attempt to register as unemployed, because they have been out of work for a period of time they are unlikely to have sufficient insurance contributions to receive unemployment benefit, or even to register for credits. If the husband is in paid employment, the level of the household income (regardless of how it is distributed) will determine whether or not the woman will be entitled to the means tested unemployment assistance. If the husband is unemployed and is unwilling to 'swap eligibility', this option is closed to the woman. 'Splitting the claim', which is technically possible, is likely to reduce overall household income. Questions about availability for work in the context of responsibility for children are meant to be asked of both men and women. In practice, as Cousins noted, 'such questions are still likely to be asked mainly of women and to have a disproportionate impact on them' (1996:20). Hence married women are unlikely to be officially registered as unemployed (i.e. on the Live Register). Indeed, Conroy Jackson (1991) found that only 48 per cent of unemployed women were on the Live Register as compared with 85 per cent of unemployed men.

Employment and training schemes in Ireland are overwhelmingly targeted at those who are on the Live Register. They are thus very effective in excluding women. Insofar as such schemes are basically concerned with the re-integration of people into paid employment, this 'may constitute indirect discrimination contrary to the Employment Equality Act' (Cousins, 1996:4). In a country of high unemployment, focusing on women can be seen as controversial, particularly insofar as they are not part of the 'official' unemployment problem. However, because the growing areas of employment are in 'women's work', it is indeed difficult to justify this on a financial or political basis (Cousins, 1996:49). It reflects and reinforces the idea of male entitlement to paid employment and a perception of the state as the upholder of the rights of (male) citizens to paid employment/training. The situation is further compounded by the gender bias implicit in the widespread failure to facilitate women's access to training schemes by providing child care facilities. Similarly little attempt is made to facilitate women as regards the timing and location of courses; providing information on them in a way which is relevant to women returners and ensuring that staff in the Local Employment Services are trained to clearly identify and cater for the needs of women.

Thus through a myriad of apparently innocuous gender neutral rules and regulations, most courses and employment training are effectively targeted at men rather than women. This is particularly ironic since such training is substantially funded by the EU to facilitate reintegration, on the specific understanding that it will be gender audited. Paradoxically, despite the difficulties, Irish women are moving directly from economic inactivity into paid employment.

Work or family – women as creators of communities

Despite the rhetorical endorsement of the importance of community – at a practical and emotional level very little attention has been paid to those who, in many cases, are the effective creators of such communities not only in Ireland, but throughout Western society, viz. women (Bulmer, 1987). Rossi suggested that:

> The pivotal role women have played in extended kinship ties and the special quality of a woman's culture that characterises the informal networks of female kin or friends whom women so easily transfer into quasi-kin, are extrapolations of the unique bond between mother and daughter (Rossi, 1980: 29-30).

In the US and the UK, in studies of kin relationships, attention came to be focused at an early stage on the content and quality of mother/daughter relationships (e.g. Adams, 1968; Komarovsky, 1967; Young and Wilmott, 1962). In these studies, the mother/daughter relationship was characterised by high frequency of contact, practical help and involvement in each other's lives.

Later work however clearly suggested that the positive quality of mother/daughter ties had been exaggerated. My own London work found (as did Firth *at al*'s 1969; Brannen and Collard's 1982 and Willmott's 1987) that mother-daughter relationships, even when they were identified as being very close, were unlikely to be characterised by intimate confiding. Popping round to see mother was a routine event which indicated concern and fulfilled certain obligations. Even where the mother was identified as 'very close' (and this occurred in the case of only approximately one third of those who had a mother alive), practical help in the sense of helping with shopping, looking after children and giving financial help occurred in only half of these relationships (O'Connor, 1990). Similar trends emerged in, for example, Willmott's (1987) study. Indeed a close reading of the classic Bethnal Green study (Young and Willmott 1962) showed that less than half of the mothers of married women (aged 18-37 years) and whose mothers were alive took care of their homes and children when their daughters were giving birth. The idea that 'your mum is your best friend' was most likely to be prevalent in situations where reliable practical help was essential for survival, and where there were few equally reliable non-kin partners.

We do not know to what extent similar patterns exist in Ireland. However, we do know that 70 per cent of older people receiving care were helped by household members and that in more than three quarters of these households, the carers were women (O'Connor and Ruddle, 1988); with daughters and daughters-in-law making up nearly half of these co-resident carers, as compared with 16 per cent of sons, and no sons-in-law. Thus the picture was one of women providing care to other women across the generations; with men, insofar as they did provide such care, providing it mainly to their wives. O'Connor and Ruddle (1988) also showed that it was married women who were particularly likely to provide such care to their own and their husband's parents. Lynch and McLaughlin (1995) suggested that the provision of such care was assumed by the Social Welfare System and by the Constitution to be the 'natural duty' of married women. They found that gender did not in itself appear to be crucial, since an unmarried 'child' who was providing care to elderly parents was only slightly more likely to be a daughter than a son but that:

> The sex imbalance among married carers, and especially the prevalence of care for their husband's parents by married women, could then be viewed as reflecting the appropriation of married women's labour by their husbands upon marriage (Lynch and McLaughlin 1995:274).

It has been widely recognised that the obligation to provide practical help to immediate kin is being modified in Western society. Indeed two fifths of Finch and Mason's UK sample agreed with the bold statement that 'children have no obligation to look after their parents when they are old' (1990:154). The fragile nature of the negotiated order in very close parent/child relationships has also emerged in my own work (O'Connor, 1994b). It is possible that there is considerable negotiation within families as regards the provision of care in Ireland. Anecdotal evidence would also suggest that there may be considerable tension in mother/daughter relationships where this sort of care is expected by mothers whose family has been their entire world (indeed, the only world which was legitimately open to women in the 1930s, 1940s, 1950s and 1960s in Ireland).

Lynch and McLaughlin (1995) have been particularly concerned with the way in which the demands of paid employment, and the unequal distribution of domestic and care work within the family, reduced the amount of time and energy available to do 'love labour' (Lynch, 1989), and to create a 'female world of love and ritual' (Smith Rosenberg, 1975). This work can include remembering birthdays and organising family celebrations (Communion, Confirmation, seasonal family events, Christmas, Easter, Holidays). Such activities can be seen as part of the very meaning of family. They appear to be overwhelmingly undertaken by married women in Irish society who negotiate with one another as regards the allocation of such work, but with little attempt being made to either re-allocate it to men or reduce the extent or nature of such 'kin keeping' and 'community building'. The work involved in these activities has only begun to be recognised:

> Love labour has been taken as a given – it has been the presumed food on the table of emotional life. Its place has been guaranteed at the table by the efforts of silent people, mostly women (Lynch and McLaughlin, 1995:259).

Such work does not only involve kin. It also involves neighbours and the local community. However, for women, particularly those with young children, whose husbands are away in paid employment all day, the creation of such local communities is extremely important. It may be increasingly difficult where the pool of available women (because of paid employment) is depleted. It is not clear to what extent interaction in such settings effectively creates a local culture, or 'estate style' (Cohen, 1978) which has implications for identity, dress, behaviour, attitudes and values. Important insights into the nature of neighbourly relationships could be derived by focusing on occasions such as children's birthday parties since these are used to symbolically reflect the existence of such communities. These topics have tended to be ignored, possibly because academic research is largely done by people who are not involved in such communities.

Although kin and neighbourhood ties are the traditional bases used by women in the construction of communities, it is clear that new bases are emerging. Thus, the emergence of women's community development groups in working-class areas (Crickley, 1989) has been documented. The phenomenon of local women's groups engaged in self development or voluntary caring activity on behalf of the community has come into sharper focus with its validation by former President Mary Robinson, who has depicted it as a 'quiet revolution'. These kinds of personal and community development activities have in many instances overlapped with local adult education activities. In 1993 Aontas estimated that there were at least 300 local education groups active throughout Ireland. In Dublin such groups emerged in low income communities to meet the social and educational needs of women. For some, participation in such activities provides a wage. Some groups have become closely integrated into the institutional structure through the receipt of (frequently meagre) funding under the auspices of adult education programmes; FÁS return-to-work courses; the EU funded New Opportunities for Women (NOW) Programme; or the community work programmes funded by the Department of Social Welfare, by Combat Poverty and by the Global Fund for Local Development (Connolly, 1996; Daly, 1989; Mulvey, 1991; Kelleher and Whelan, 1992). In working class areas (with 60-70 per cent unemployment), without women's (low) paid and unpaid labour, the direct and indirect costs to the economic system and the state are likely to be very high.

What limited evidence we have suggests that married women are typically involved in a variety of unpaid work within a wide range of organisations. For example, roughly half of those involved in rural community tourism in Ballyhoura (O'Connor, 1995a) were engaged in at least one other aspect of community life (e.g. in the Irish Country-Women's Association; the Gaelic Athletic Association; the Drama Society; the Parents Council/School Board; Tidy Towns; Association for the Mentally Handicapped). A broadly similar picture emerged in the Study for the Fourth Joint Oireachtas Committee on Women and Rural Development (Dorgan *et al*, 1994). The more formally structured adult education arena has been the particular province of middle class women (see Drudy and Lynch, 1993:263). Evidence is limited as regards sports but it appears that women's participation is lower than men's (i.e. 40 per cent as compared with 54 per cent: Henley Centre Ireland, 1991:16). Women participate most in indoor sports, and since facilities for these are often less available, this effectively limits their participation. Here, as in Britain (Green *et al*, 1990) married women, especially those with child care responsibilities and no independent income, have been shown to be less likely to participate than those who are unmarried.

In-depth qualitative studies by Oliker (1989) in America and Gullestad (1984) in Norway, highlighted the fact that women's friendships created and validated their identities as wives and mothers, helped them to deal with the tensions in such identities and through their 'talk' to work out ways of handling these aspects of their lives. Insofar as married women's interaction with other women in an Irish context is of this kind, then it arguably does not challenge the centrality of home and family in their ideas of themselves. However, what we know about this topic in Ireland is limited and dated. Hannan (1979) found that frequency of contact with kin in his study of farm families was affected not only by distance and life stage, but also by class and religion, with Catholics and the higher socio-economic groups having the highest levels of contact with their relatives. He also found that 'the selection of intimates is still predominantly restricted by the ascriptive boundaries of family and kinship relations' (1979:187). When the wives in his study were asked to identify the person who was 'easiest' or 'best' to talk to if they were worried or upset, only 12 per cent chose friends. Although a spouse was most often chosen, siblings or other relatives were also chosen quite frequently (i.e. 27 per cent and 11 per cent of the wives mentioning siblings, and 11 per cent mentioning other relatives). Friends were even less likely to be mentioned as people who were helpful in a practical way; siblings were again most often mentioned, followed by neighbours and their husband's relatives.

What very limited evidence we have would suggest that some women increasingly have purely 'fun' interactions outside their own domestic setting (O'Connor, 1992c). The emergence of phenomena such as the Annual Women's Mini Marathon and the mushrooming of groups of women who run, walk or go out for a 'girls' night out, is notable. The rise in the valuation of female friendships consequent on the women's movement has increased the attractiveness of 'a night out with the girls'. Anecdotal evidence would also suggest that, particularly in the cities, pubs as well as keep fit centres, adult education venues and community centres are becoming increasingly important for married women's interaction with one another. Women may use family based networks as a basis to raise money for community projects; or may be motivated to sit on a school management board because of issues arising in relation to their own children. Similarly ties with kin or friends may motivate or facilitate women's participation in, or their affiliation with other women on a local council or within the more formally defined political arena. What limited evidence is available suggests that women are very active in creating and maintaining 'communities' particularly based on kinship and revolving around personal and community needs.

Typically, women's work in these areas is unpaid. There is often an implicit suggestion that women should be discouraged from competing with men for paid employment; and encouraged to participate in unpaid work in the home, in the 'black economy' and in (unpaid) community and voluntary work. Such attitudes, as the Second Commission on the Status of Women (1993) noted, are unacceptable on the basis of equity, equality and efficiency. Nevertheless where men's earning ability is an important element in their identity and is seen as their core contribution to family life and the basis for their power within the family, such ideas die hard.

How 'happy' are women? which ones?

Within a society where the well-being of the individual is increasingly seen as a criterion for 'good' social arrangements it seems appropriate to look at the implications of social patterns for women, focusing particularly on women's 'happiness' and their psychiatric well-being (although there are of course alternative indicators, such as the level of alcoholism or attempted suicide). It is important to recognise that the question about women's happiness is deceptively simple. It obscures the whole question of what is meant by happiness. The issue is particularly complicated since as suggested by Duncombe and Marsden (1995) many women perform what they call emotional work on themselves to convince themselves that they are 'ever so happy really'. A variety of studies have explored this issue in different ways, and it seems useful to draw them together here.

Whelan looked at respondents' own assessment of their satisfaction/-dissatisfaction 'with their life as a whole these days', and their overall assessment of their level of happiness, 'taking all things together' – the former involving more of a cognitive component and the latter 'having closer links to emotional experiences consequent on immediate or recent events in a person's life' (Whelan, 1992:73). Whelan found that there was no significant difference in men's and women's satisfaction, although there was a tendency for women to be somewhat more likely to indicate that they were very happy. He noted:

> We are confronted with the paradox that being in full-time unpaid home duties is associated with higher life satisfaction and happiness yet that such women are, like other women, more likely than men to experience negative psychological feelings, and are less likely than all others to experience positive psychological feelings. These women are more satisfied with less (Whelan, 1994:203).

This observation vividly highlights the difficulties implicit in the use of satisfaction/dissatisfaction assessments by women within a culture where there is an expectation that if married women are 'normal', they will find motherhood and housewifery satisfying (and where in any case, acceptable cultural alternatives to these elements are generally perceived as unavailable).

Shortall (1991:324) noted that typically Irish studies of family life did not ask: 'Why do women continue subscribing to a system which they frequently appear unhappy with?' In three of the four studies where dissatisfaction was expressed, women were interviewed by women. Messinger (1969) noted that many of the women who confided in his wife said that they were unhappy about being forced to stay at home minding children, doing housework (which they saw as boring) and were resentful of what they saw as their husband's less time-consuming, easier work-load and greater freedom. Yet as Shortall (1991:324) noted, Messinger never asked, 'why the grievances of the women remain secrets to which his wife is privy'. Hannan and Katsiaouni (1977) did note that the wife's satisfaction was greater in families where there was a 'modern' division of labour; although the use of this model obscured the whole question of the nature and source of the wife's dissatisfaction.

Whelan (1994), using the Bradburn Affect Balance Scale, with six items tapping 'positive affect' and six tapping 'negative affect', found that women were more likely than men to have low positive and high negative scores. Furthermore, women who were full-time housewives were in a different position than other married women:

> On each of the items relating to positive psychological experiences, women in full-time unpaid home duties fare worse than other women (Whelan, 1994:203).

The differences were comparatively small, but they were consistent. Thus, for example, 51 per cent of those in full-time home duties had felt 'particularly excited or interested in something', as compared with 66 per cent of other women; 62 per cent had felt that 'things were going their way' as compared with 74 per cent of other women; 63 per cent had felt pleased about having accomplished something, as compared with 73 per cent of the other women. Whelan interpreted this as indicating the unending and repetitive character [of housewifery], and 'the manner in which it can prevent women from pursuing avenues to self development' (1994:203).

My own work (O'Connor, 1992c) has argued that there has been a strong tendency for love relationships (including motherhood and friendship) to become dominated by what Britten (1977:75) has called the 'language of make believe'. The very real costs of creating and maintaining relationships has tended to be ignored, and they have been idealised and mythologised. This type of thinking is particularly inimical to any understanding of the lives of full-time housewives, since their lives are typically rooted in their relationships with others. As such, their lives most certainly have personal meaning. There are costs however. Their relationships with a husband and children, which are the ultimate raison d'être of their lifestyle, may be characterised by conflict and tensions at different points in time. Within an increasingly materialistic culture, their work, given its unpaid, nurturant and frequently symbolic nature, is often seen as not having value, whereas the costs are quantifiable (lack of money; loss of personal independence; frequently restricted lifestyle).

Internationally, it has been noted that women are more likely than men to experience clinical depression. An Irish Health Board study (1991) indicated that the most common reason for psychiatric admission was depression, such admissions making up 28 per cent of all admissions. Furthermore among the women who were admitted for psychiatric care, depression was by far the most common reason for admission, constituting just under two-fifths of all admissions. It has been recognised however that it is necessary to go beyond examining in-patient figures in psychiatric hospitals, since it has been recognised that a good deal of psychiatric illness remains either completely untreated in the community and/or is treated solely by the GP service. Within an Irish context, this in itself poses some difficulties since the Health Research Board's work (and the work of O'Hare and O'Connor, 1987) focused on those treated in psychiatric hospitals and units.

Classic community-based studies of mental health internationally have found high levels of neurosis and/or clinical depression among women, particularly among working-class women; among women who were not in paid employment; who had a young child under 6 years old, who lacked support from husband and/or from close friends (Bernard, 1982; Gove, 1972 and 1978; Dohrenwend *et al*, 1980; Goldberg and Williams, 1988; Brown and Harris, 1978; Brown, 1987). Bernard (1982) and Gaffney (1991) concluded, on the basis of international evidence, that still married females were particularly likely to experience such distress. Whelan *et al*'s work (1991) in Ireland found little difference between men and women; or between the single and married. However, full-time housewives were particularly vulnerable:

> Our own results show a significant positive effect for employment for married women. Less than 1 in 10 married female employees are above the GHQ threshold compared with 1 in 4 who are unemployed and 1 in 5 who are in home duties (Whelan *et al*, 1991:44).

They noted that this score on the General Health Questionnaire (GHQ) could be thought of as providing an estimate of psychiatric disturbance and as enabling one to estimate the proportion of the population 'who would be thought to have a clinically significant psychiatric disturbance if they were interviewed by a clinical psychiatrist' (Whelan *et al*, 1991).

Cleary (1997 and 1986) found that in a random sample study of urban working-class women aged 18-65 years, just under one fifth of the women interviewed had been clinically depressed within the previous year. More than half of the sample had received 'medical help with psychiatric problems' at some stage in their lives (either from their GP or on an in/out patient basis). Furthermore, 40 per cent had taken psychotropic drugs such as tranquillisers or sleeping pills at some stage in their lives and one third were currently taking them (Cleary, 1986). Thus quite clearly at any particular moment in time mental health difficulties were very much a reality for between one fifth and one third of the interviewees. Broadly similar trends emerged in Fitzgerald and

Jeffers' (1994) study of mothers (aged 28-50) of a sub-set of children attending 40 primary schools in West Dublin. They found that just under one third (31 per cent) of these mothers had a formal psychiatric diagnosis of depression. They also found that women whose partners were unemployed; who were in households without a car or a phone; who were dissatisfied with their housing or income; who never had time with friends; and who were dissatisfied with their relationships with relatives, were most likely to be depressed. Similar trends have emerged internationally (Miles, 1988).

It does seem clear then that for Irish married women who are full-time housewives, there are psychological costs which are reflected in the fact that between one fifth and one third of them experience psychological distress (depending on the sample and the measure used). Minturn and Lambert (1964) on the basis of their cross-cultural work, early concluded that the 'normal' situation in which children are reared in Western society, viz. a frequently isolated, dyadic mother/child relationship, was least conducive to women's positive mental health and hence of course unhelpful to the child's well-being. No attention has been paid to the impact of poor mental health of full-time housewives on children in Ireland, though the evidence that is available suggests that poor mental health affects between one in five and one in three of such full-time housewives. It would seem that the major institutional structures are most comfortable with the idea that full-time housewifery is associated with positive mental health, although this is simply not the case.

Summary

In this chapter implicit assumptions concerning the nature of both the family and work have been explored. It is suggested that these assumptions are part of the mechanisms through which patriarchal control is exercised. This is an insidious kind of control since it is effectively part of a taken-for-granted view of the world. The family and work are typically seen as unproblematic realities. The reality is however considerably more complex. Even in purely demographic terms the family has changed dramatically in the recent past, both in Ireland and the rest of Europe. In Ireland perhaps the most striking manifestations of this are the dramatic decline in family size and the dramatic rise in lone parenthood. Fertility per woman has been halved in the past twenty-five years in Ireland; and approximately one in three first time births and one in four of all births are now to lone parents. Since lone parents are overwhelmingly women, such patterns raise fundamental issues about the role of men in the family.

The chapter also implicitly challenges assumptions about family life by looking at the reality of the family as a small group, focusing particularly on the dimension of power. This evidence is incomplete but there is a strong suggestion that men control property; and that violence is used by a sizeable minority of them to maintain their position.

The chapter also raises issues about the way work is defined within a capitalist patriarchal society and the implications this has in relation to the perceived value of women's (unpaid) work. Indeed the very definition of work can be seen as one of the mechanisms through which control is exerted – with women's unpaid work in the home, in the family and in the neighbourhood and community reinforcing their lesser value within a society where economic status is an indicator of worth. Within this context, women devise lifestyles which give them identity and meaning but they do so at a cost to their own mental health. What evidence is available suggests that full-time housewives are particularly vulnerable, with at least one in five having poor mental health.

5

Caring and Coping:
Women Working Full-time in the Home

Introduction

IN many ways, within the existing structural and cultural parameters, women working full-time in the home exemplify the ideal patterns of Irish life. Yet comparatively little attention has been paid to them. These are the women who have 'settled down', who have reared or are rearing children and are homemakers on a full-time basis. In some ways, the equation of adult womanhood with domesticity, service and 'love labour' (Lynch, 1989a) creates a powerful ideological context within which the concept of the full-time housewife fits very comfortably. Yet it is also one which is being challenged in an increasingly individualistic, materialistic society.

This group is decreasing in size in Ireland. In 1996 married/cohabiting couples with a full-time housewife accounted for 63.5 per cent of all couples, whereas they constituted 80 per cent in 1986 (CSO, 1997). This group includes those in two very different situations: full-time housewives with husbands in paid employment and those in households where neither is in paid employment – and it is the former group which has become less common. In 1996 women who were full time in the home and whose husbands were in paid employment constituted 39 per cent of all married or cohabiting couples, whereas in 1986 they constituted 53 per cent of such couples (CSO, 1997).

Typically, given age at marriage, these couples involve women from their mid/late twenties to those over 60 years of age. They include those who were married in the 1950s, the 1960s, 1970s, 1980s and 1990s – a period characterised by dramatic reductions in fertility within marriage. However, although family size has fallen dramatically in the past twenty-five years, in Ireland, more than half (53 per cent) of women aged 35-39 years had three or more children in 1991. This was the highest in the European Community, and approximately twice that of the European average (Rapid Reports, 1993). The experience of motherhood, in the sense of bearing and rearing children, has been very different for these various age cohorts of Irish women. The level of education for women in each decade has also increased (O'Hara, 1987). Women working full-time in the home include those who were excluded from paid employment prior to 1973 by the marriage bar and who are now unable to re-enter the labour force; those who see housewifery and child rearing as more emotionally rewarding than the paid employment currently available to them; those who, in the face of spousal opposition, lack of satisfactory child care arrangements, appropriate job opportunities, or because of the nature of the taxation or welfare systems, have concluded that it simply does not pay them to undertake paid employment; as well as those who married in the expectation of having a male breadwinner, but do not now have one and are unable or unwilling to undertake this role themselves.

In looking at these diverse groups, the chapter draws on published material, although the discussion, at times, will of necessity be speculative. The material here revolves around six main themes. The first focuses on women's emotional power within the family and the second on women's identification with and absorption within the family. The differences between these two are subtle: the former implicitly focuses on women as the key players while the latter explores the subsuming of women under male control, a pattern which is often seen nostalgically as a 'solution' to what are depicted as the problems of marriage and family life today. The third theme highlights an attempt to transform the cultural and structural parameters of marriage and family life by creating a public discourse about such issues and more directly by affecting state legislative activity. The fourth looks specifically at the existence and importance of a feminised concept of love as the context for attempting to understand the dominant pattern of separation Irish style, viz. women's withdrawal from marriage and men's desertion. The fifth revolves around the idea of negotiation and reflects an increased endorsement of individualism within the context of what is portrayed as an equal relationship between the spouses. The sixth raises the issue of poverty and focuses on women who are struggling to survive financially.

The focus is on women who, within the context of marriage and family life, are attempting to deal with the reality of institutional structures which often are not particularly responsive to their needs and interests. It is suggested that although one or more of the above elements may characterise an individual woman's life, these elements will tend to be differentially adopted by women at different life stages; with different levels of education; with different social class backgrounds and with different life options. The chapter suggests that changes and continuities in marriage and family life can be understood by focusing on women, recognising the fact that although they contribute to the making of their own worlds, they do so within a wider structural and cultural reality where power and authority are largely concentrated in the hands of men.

Holding emotional power within the family

Irish women are popularly portrayed as the strong ones within the family. Indeed at times that strength has been depicted as a negative phenomenon, reflected in a kind of manipulative control which thrives on the disempowerment of others in the family (Scheper-Hughes, 1979a, 1979b; Brody, 1973). Irish sociologists have been slow to explore either the nature of such power, or the extent to which its existence is related to the absence of alternative legitimate power arenas. Family-based emotional labour is a key element in the lives and identities of such women. Internationally a good deal of attention has been paid by feminist sociologists to the extent of women's exploitation within the family, e.g. in terms of their non-ownership of land, their disproportionate share of domestic labour, their predominantly economically dependent position and their experience of domestic violence. Such phenomena are very real. Women's emotional power, insofar as it exists, does not negate such experiences and is exercised within legal, economic and other social and cultural parameters constructed by the church and state.

Giddens (1992) argued that with the emergence of the romantic love complex as a basis for marriage, subtle and important changes came about in the area of motherhood and housewifery. He suggested that as women's control over child rearing grew, children increasingly came to be seen as vulnerable and in need of 'long term emotional training', and the household moved from one characterised by 'patriarchal authority to maternal affection' (Giddens, 1992:42). He saw the 'invention of motherhood', i.e. the focus on the home and the changing relations between parents and children, as part of this cultural reconstruction of the family. He suggested that this change, which presupposed the existence of a secure financial basis, occurred in Britain from the late eighteenth century onwards. It is arguable that it occurred considerably later in Ireland where commodified feudalism persisted up to the late nineteenth century, and petty capitalism up to the late twentieth century (Slater and McDonough, 1994), with industrialisation occurring, insofar as it did occur, after 1958.

Hochschild (1983) and James (1989) saw emotional labour as work which was used by women to manage individuals in the public arena, an example being the work of air hostesses. Lee Treweek (1996:119) however suggested that 'emotion work in the domestic sphere is not only about facilitation and nurturance but involves emotionally ordering individuals through a variety of means' – it is a 'means of creating order and a method of control'. Like James (1989:24) Treweek suggested that emotional work can involve a range of 'emotional tools' such as listening, gentle persuasion, firm direction, 'discomforting the person', as well as force. This view of emotional work makes intuitive sense of the depiction of Irish mothers as powerful. It reflects an interior view of the family. Implicit in it is the combining of elements of power and care which are compatible with Foucault's notion of pastoral care (see Smart, 1995). In that context emotional control is exerted and order is created and maintained through kindness, nurturance and knowledge.

Treweek (1996) suggested that force was as much part of emotional work as loving and caring. Certainly this element was very much part of Irish family life in the past. A national sample of Irish adults aged 18-54 years old (IMS, 1993) showed that physical punishment of some kind had been experienced by 86 per cent of those in the study; that 37 per cent had been physically punished with a 'rigid implement' (cane, wooden spoon, etc.). For over 75 per cent of those experiencing physical punishment at home, mothers had been involved in imposing such punishment, inevitably perhaps since they were the people predominantly responsible for child care. Similar trends also emerged in McKenna's (1979) study of over 500 Dublin mothers in the 1970s. McKenna noted that these mothers scored significantly higher than mothers in American studies on a 'control' factor which included items related to intrusiveness, dependency and martyrdom. She noted that the more help a wife received from her husband, the less controlling she was with her children. Hannan and Katsiaouni (1977) also noted that, among the rural families they studied in the 1970s, little help was received, so this 'controlling' pattern was likely to be common. It seems plausible to suggest that relatively large family size and the exclusion of women from paid employment were likely to exacerbate this pattern, the former being important because it increased women's work, and the latter because it increased the relative importance of the family as a power base for women.

Rising educational levels, smaller family size, along with a heightened awareness of psychology, have arguably created a fertile context for a more child-centred style of mothering which relies less on physical punishment than it did in the past. It is not clear to what extent women have retained their position of emotional power in this situation. Indeed the increasing commodification and professionalisation of emotional 'work' (Hearn, 1982) by the caring professions can be perceived as implicitly devaluing the contribution of mothers insofar as it effectively portrays them as 'unskilled carers'.

However, there has been a dramatic change in the proportion of children aged 15-19 years remaining in full time education (from 24.9 per cent in 1961 to 63.1 per cent in 1987: Drudy and Lynch, 1993:141). This, together with the rise in youth unemployment, has implications regarding the effective extension of 'childhood'. Whereas in the early 1960s young people of 17 and 18 tended to be economically independent and treated as adults, by the 1990s they were most likely to be economically dependent and given a considerable degree of financial and emotional support. In many families the ties and cohesiveness of an earlier life stage are being effectively prolonged, as it is emotionally and financially more rewarding for children to remain in the 'nest' than to leave it (Leonard, 1987). This extends the period of 'active' parenting indefinitely, and hence facilitates its persistence as an ongoing source of emotional power, meaning and identity in the lives of many married women.

There has been a growing awareness that married women in Ireland receive minimal reward and status for their labour (Shortall, 1991:311). Indeed, this perception received inadvertent support from the decision of the Supreme Court that the Matrimonial Home Bill (1994) was unconstitutional. This decision made clear that married women, despite 20-30 years of cleaning and cooking for a husband and children, did not have an automatic legal right to joint ownership of the family home because of the responsibility of the state to effectively protect male ownership as the basis for male authority within the family. As noted in Chapter 4, the very definition of what constitutes work undervalues the contribution of women. Nevertheless, Whelan and Fahey (1994) found that 71 per cent of the women in their study felt that being a housewife was just as fulfilling as working for pay, while over half felt that 'a job is all right but what most women want is a home and children'. These trends clearly suggest that a home, a family and care work remain valued activities and life choices despite the increasing acceptance of women's participation in paid employment. Thus, although the contribution of women to family life may confer on them emotional power and although many live fulfilling and emotionally satisfying lives, their power is not underpinned by the wider institutional structures.

Identity absorption within a (gendered) family system

Since divorce only became available in Ireland in 1997, since family ideology is strongly endorsed by church and state and since the majority of Irish married women are not in paid employment (Durkan *et al*, 1995), for many women, marriage and family life are their world. This world is arguably created and maintained by an ideological stress on identification and lack of individuation. Concepts such as oppression make no sense within the context of a discourse of identification: a point recognised by Delphy and Leonard (1992). This has parallels with attitudes in a number of Asian cultures where obligations to support a range of kin are seen as 'natural', 'inevitable' and in no way oppressive, although such responsibilities may reduce an individual to personal penury.

Such a pattern is essentially a culturally-based approach rooted in a non-individualistic tradition. Fahey (1995) has compared this sort of ideology to 'an idealised image of domestic life in farm family households', where the needs of the individual were subordinated to the group. Within that context, he suggests, 'order and stability was achieved through an emphasis on patriarchy and property at the expense of nurturance and emotional fulfilment' (1995, 15:6). This is perhaps to overstate the case since it is possible that many women derive emotional satisfaction from their identification with the status and achievements of the family group as a whole, and the achievements of their children in particular.

The prevalence of this kind of pattern was indicated by replies to the Henley Centre Survey asking women to identify what they saw as the 'best' arrangement in the family. In 1989, almost two fifths of the women felt that the best arrangement was one where the husband had a job and the wife either ran the home or had a less demanding job than her husband and did most of the housework and caring for the children (Henley Centre Report: 1990 pp13, 15). It was noted that the proportion of women endorsing these views had fallen throughout the 1980s. There is a suggestion in the Henley Report (1990:13) that the submergence of women's identity was less on account of the husband than the children. At any rate, only 16 per cent of the women surveyed agreed strongly with the idea that: 'In marriage, it is only right that a man's career should take priority over that of a woman's'.

However, in the European Values Study approximately one third of both women and men perceived men as having 'more right to a job than women when jobs were scarce'. This percentage, which was broadly similar to the European average, was associated with age and educational level (Whelan, 1994). Fine-Davis (1988) noted that similar attitudes had been even more common in the 1970s and to a lesser extent in the 1980s. Almost three fifths of her Dublin sample in 1975 agreed that: 'Women should be more concerned with housekeeping and bringing up their children than with desires for careers', but this fell to under two fifths in 1986. Similarly whereas just over half of those in 1975 agreed that 'if equal job opportunities are opened to women, this will just take away jobs from men who need them more', the proportion endorsing this view had halved by 1986 (Fine-Davis, 1988).

Nevertheless in Ireland in 1997, two fifths of women favoured a situation where the wife had no job – and they were more likely than any other European women to favour this. On the other hand approximately one third (36 per cent) of the women surveyed in Ireland favoured 'equal roles' for men and women. Danish women were most likely to favour this arrangement. The coexistence among Irish women of these two views was unusual in European terms and arguably reflected variation in age and education (Rubery *et al*, 1995:104). Only in Belgium was an even broadly similar situation apparent. It was striking that in Ireland, in contrast to Britain but similar to Greece and Spain, there was little enthusiasm for what one might regard as a 'middle road' i.e. the wife having a secondary job (Eurostat, 1997).

The pattern of women's identity absorption in the family is very much part of the taken-for-granted cultural milieu – and is effectively underpinned by custom and practice, by law and by the state, through for example, its social welfare and taxation policies (Daly, 1989 and Mahon, 1993). Although it is no longer common, for example, as it was even in the 1960s and 1970s for official communications to obliterate the wife's first name, married women still overwhelmingly take their husband's surname on marriage. Within a culture which increasingly endorses individualism for men and women, and simultaneously advocates the submergence of married women's identity within the family, absorption is, in many ways, a potentially fragile strategy. Nevertheless, it is particularly attractive to many women whose sense of meaning and identity is frequently rooted in their relationships with others, especially their children, a phenomenon which can be seen as reflecting and reinforcing their participation in child care (Chodorow, 1978).

The attractiveness of equating one's own well-being with that of the children is enhanced within Irish society in view of the importance of familism in definitions of womanhood and the importance of the family as a mechanism of class placement – its influence being mediated through the educational system (see Chapter 3). Within a cultural tradition which attributes considerable importance to the mother's role in terms of attitudes, support, decisions as regards kind of school, etc., it would not be surprising if a mother saw herself as having considerable importance in ensuring the success of her children in the educational system and hence their ultimate class destination.

Within a society where women are still predominantly defined by their relationship with men, and where they are disproportionately clustered in a small range of poorly paid occupations and/or at their lower echelons (Durkan *et al*, 1995), their best lifestyle opportunities may well lie in identification with their husband. Such an attitude illustrates what Dworkin (1983) has called the 'rationality' of right wing women who see their own and/or their children's best interests as lying with the maintenance of the system. It may offer – especially for middle class women – considerable economic and social possibilities for themselves and their children. It is certainly true that very few full-time housewives, even those with high education and/or professional qualifications, would be able to match the standard of living they enjoy as wives, if they were to find themselves rearing their children on their own, covering child care costs and with the uncertain access to maintenance and the long waiting lists for free legal aid which are widely experienced by women in this situation (Second Commission on the Status of Women, 1993; Fahey and Lyons, 1995).

Fine-Davis (1988) suggested that, overall, women did not see their own interests as sharply as men did. She noted, for example, that women were less likely than men to be concerned with the economic and social consequences of divorce for a same gender spouse (Fine-Davis, 1988:18). In an imaginary situation where a pregnant woman was depicted as suffering from a serious illness, where treatment could save her life, but would result in the death of the unborn, just under one in five of the women (18 per cent) in that study thought that the woman should not have the final say about what should be done (Fine-Davis, 1988:45). My own work (O'Connor, 1995a) has also highlighted women's lack of consciousness of their own interests as an element in consensual control.

O'Hara's work on women on farms (1994b and 1994c) offered further insights into the whole area of identification. O'Hara found that even those women who were heavily involved in farm work, who saw their involvement as very much a partnership, and who talked of the farm in terms of 'ours' were not necessarily joint owners of the family farm. Furthermore, they were usually quite unconcerned about this. O'Hara suggested that insofar as such women had reservations about their own lives, but remained within the accepted parameters because of ties of loyalty, responsibility, financial dependency, etc., their encouragement of their daughters to make different choices could simultaneously vindicate their own identity absorption, and contribute to the creation of a very different world. In this way it was ultimately subversive.

On the basis of the fragmented evidence that we have, women's identification with and absorption within the family context is most likely to be characteristic of older women, women who are not in paid employment, women with young children, middle class women or those in small family enterprises such as farming or shop-keeping. It is a pattern which in many ways is very compatible with the Constitutional position, and indeed with the institutional church's view of the position of women in the home. The benefits of perpetuating class position are likely to be most relevant to middle class women, and the perceived importance of the mother's role in contributing to her children's class placement is likely to be greatest in that situation. Such women may well have most to gain from pinning their hopes on their children, and looking to them to transform the system.

Transforming the parameters of marriage and family life

As previously mentioned, this pattern includes both the creation of a public discourse about marriage and family life and the influencing of state legislative activity.

The creation of a public discourse about marriage and related issues involves the attempt to move issues from the private area into the public domain: specifically to make 'private' marital problems the focus of public debate and, in some cases, legal action. This is a strategy which has been used with extraordinary success by individual married women, by groups of women and by the Council for the Status of Women (now the National Women's Council). It embraces a huge range of activities.

In this section attention will be focused on the use of the media to expose the reality of family life for married women and to confirm the legitimacy of their desire for autonomy.

Through the development of 'talk' shows, particularly Marian Finucane's and Gay Byrne's programmes, 'private' experiences of abuse and marital violence, issues surrounding marital power, sexual experiences, contraception, sterilisation etc. have all been 'exposed' to public view. Issues which, in another context, might be seen as, at best, topics for private negotiation between a wife and husband, or topics for confession to a spiritual advisor, become part of a wider discourse. Indeed, the very fact of publicly exploring such issues undermines the discourse within which they traditionally have been located.

This was vividly illustrated in a series of Marian Finucane programmes in September 93 when a Roman Catholic woman rang in, in distress, because she had been refused absolution in confession on the grounds that she had been sterilised. There was a general feeling among callers to the programme that this was unreasonable since the 'job was done'. This however was followed by a call from a married woman with six children, one of whom was handicapped, who was on the contraceptive pill while waiting for sterilisation. She had sought absolution in an attempt to yield to her son's request for her to receive Communion with him on his First Communion Day. Three of her children were born while she was using 'natural' family planning methods. According to her, the Roman Catholic priest she consulted had suggested a compromise solution, viz. that she attend Confession on the Friday, refrained from the pill that day, and abstained from sexual intercourse until after receiving Communion with her son on the Saturday. In the course of the ensuing programmes the distress of religious, family-oriented, married women who saw themselves as having to alienate themselves from the Sacraments to discharge what they saw as their very real responsibilities towards their husbands and children emerged very clearly. To them, the solution offered was ludicrous. They saw it as 'Jesuitical' hair splitting. They longed for the menopause when they would be able to resume the normal practice of their religious life.

Such 'accounts' are compatible with the dramatic fall-off in weekly confession (Mac Gréil, 1991; MRBI, 1998). Little systematic attention however has been paid to such issues, although they clearly reveal the way in which 'ordinary' married women are struggling to adjust to the changing structural and cultural realities of Irish life. The widespread nature of such feelings is underlined by Drudy's (1993) findings that hurt and/or anger towards the Roman Catholic Church were experienced by 64 per cent of the female respondents in her study.

Issues related to women's attitude to marriage, to sexual fidelity, to marital violence and to the position of men in their lives have also been explored in such chat shows and in more documentary-type radio and TV programmes – including Patrick O'Gorman's *Queuing for a Living*. The fact that such 'personal' topics are explored on the airwaves in itself challenges taken-for-granted assumptions as regards the centrality of the spousal relationship, women's 'natural' lack of interest in sexual relationships, their romantic attitude to marriage, etc. In a sense whether or not the views of particular respondents speaking on the air waves are or are not typical is irrelevant. The important aspect of such programmes is that they provide the opportunity for listeners to compare such views with their own feelings and attitudes about activities, relationships and institutions which, up to very recently, were protected by the boundaries of marital loyalty or the confessional seal. Such programmes are of course highly unlikely to change attitudes or behaviour. They do however implicitly legitimate a wide range of attitudes and patterns of behaviour, if for no other reason, than that they publicly acknowledge their existence.

In a rather different context, the official recognition of separation, as indicated by Census data from 1986, and increasing knowledge about the existence of marital violence, virtually unacknowledged prior to Casey's refuge study in 1987, has arguably affected women's perception of men as trustworthy security figures and, at some level, has increased their feelings of financial and physical vulnerability. The public realisation that violence and abuse can happen has been further underlined by the emergence of a sequence of individual women who have inadvertently shattered the silence surrounding various aspects of male control – legal, sexual, physical, familial and ideological patriarchal control (See Chapter 2). Such women have generated a disquieting awareness of the possibility of an abuse of male power, particularly, and even more disquietingly, by 'respectable' men.

The transformation of structural and cultural parameters also includes legal action: for example the taking of the McGee case questioning the legality of the importation of contraceptives for marital use in 1973 (see Kennedy, 1989 for a discussion of the case). It includes the sensitising of the state to issues relating to women through, for example, the convening of the Joint Oireachtas Committee on Women's Rights; the highlighting of the issue of child sexual abuse and marital violence as public issues, by lobby groups such as the Rape Crisis Centres; the establishment of the Council for the Status of Women (1973) and the First and Second Commissions of the Status of Women (1993); their definition of child care as a state policy issue, etc. It also includes more direct attempts to influence state legislative activity, e.g. in the area of domestic violence, property rights and maintenance. Under pressure from women's groups, and in the wake of the rejection of the first Divorce Referendum in 1986 and rising levels of marital breakdown, the state introduced legislation to provide greater physical and financial protection to married women.

Overall the pattern of activities discussed in this section is somewhat different to those outlined earlier in that they are an attempt to bring private issues into the public domain in a way which validates women's experiences. Inevitably perhaps, middle class, well educated women are most likely to be involved in these activities. However, in many cases the groundwork (whether behaviourally or attitudinally) has been done by a much wider range of women – who individually and collectively have transformed public consciousness about a particular issue, so that legislative change, when it comes, is seen as inevitable.

High expectations – a feminised concept of love and its implications

Within a comparatively short space of time Ireland has moved from being a society where marriage was very much a contractual relationship between families, rooted in economic realities (Arensberg and Kimball, 1940), to one where it is very much a personal relationship rooted in ideas of love, companionship, sexual pleasure and personal fulfilment. In Western society the stress on love as a basis for marriage and as an ongoing characteristic of marital relationships reflects a feminised conception of love, i.e. one characterised by a stress on 'emotional expression and talking about feelings: aspects of love that women prefer and in which women tend to be more skilled than men' (Cancian, 1986). Implicit in this definition of love is an effective devaluation of financial support, practical help and sharing activities – expressions of love with which, at this point in time, in Western society, men feel more comfortable than women. These ideas about male and female styles of loving are supported by a wide variety of British and American literature on friendship (see O'Connor, 1992c).

There are two important implications of this focus on a feminised version of love. Firstly, as noted by Cancian, it implies that if women's need to express their emotions and talk about their feelings is greater than men's, then their need of what we call love is greater. This concept of love thus implicitly underestimates men's dependency on women, and implicitly exaggerates women's dependency on men. Secondly, it suggests that women, by endorsing this concept of love, and building it into their expectations of a spouse, effectively create a position of emotional expertise for themselves within the family. Insofar as men are unable to deal with either the expectations implicit in this type of love or with their wife's position of expertise in this area, they may, especially in an Irish context where, up to 1997, there was no divorce, simply withdraw from the situation, i.e. desert.

In the 1990 European Values Study, both men and women indicated that they saw relational factors as most important in the creation of a successful marriage (Whelan and Fahey, 1994). It is not being argued here that men see different things as important in marriage; clearly this is not so. It is rather that the aspects that both men and women see as being very important reflect a feminised concept of love. Whelan and Fahey (1994) noted that an adequate income and good housing were less likely to be identified as contributing to a successful marriage than personal factors, e.g. 53 per cent and 46 per cent respectively as compared with the 93 per cent mentioning faithfulness and 83 per cent referring to mutual respect and appreciation. If it does not involve these elements, Irish women appear to be increasingly unwilling to remain within what they perceive as an unsatisfactory marriage.

In this respect they appear to be no different from their European counterparts, although in Ireland the picture was less clear-cut owing to the absence of divorce up to 1997. Between 1980 and 1992 the gross divorce rate in the European Community rose from 1.4 to 1.6 per 1,000 inhabitants although it varied widely, with the figures ranging from 2.9 in the UK, and 2.5 in Denmark, to 0.4 in Italy. Fahey (1993:121) argues that both church and state need to recognise that the moral code governing family formation is now centred 'on the values of intimacy, psychological well-being, and emotional fulfilment'. Interestingly, he pins his hopes on the state for what he calls 'a reconstruction of personal relationships' even though he recognises that, with the exception of Manitoba in Canada, no State has even been able to ensure that men pay maintenance.

It has been widely recognised that there has been a dramatic increase in the number of couples experiencing marital breakdown in Ireland – the most recent estimate of those separated/divorced being 95,000 people as compared with 38,000 in 1986 (based on Labour Force Survey figures, Dept. of Equality and Law Reform, 1996). The Labour Force Survey figures have consistently provided lower figures than have the Census results (Fahey and Lyons, 1995). Also, there have been consistent differences in both sources in the numbers of women and men who return their status as separated or divorced. It is unclear why these discrepancies exist. They could indicate that the 'missing' men have left the state or that, for whatever reason, they have returned their status as married (O'Brien, 1995). The Department of Equality and Law Reform in estimating the numbers involved used the Labour Force figures and simply doubled the number of women (the 1991 figure being estimated then at 68,000, and the 1996 figure at 95,000).

In Ireland the dramatic increase in marital breakdown emerged prior to the introduction of divorce; in the context of a very high failure rate for Church applications for nullity and the very long waiting lists for Legal Aid; and the absence to date of effective mechanisms to ensure that maintenance is paid in cases of separation (see Chapter 4). We know comparatively little about the social characteristics of those who returned their marital status as separated. The Census material showed that approximately three fifths of them were between 30 and 49 years old and that they were fairly evenly spread between these age categories. The highest proportions of them were in Dublin County Borough (7.8. per cent), followed by other urban areas such as Limerick, Cork and Galway County Borough.

A sizeable proportion (43 per cent) of those who returned their status as separated in the 1991 Census were deserted. This was particularly likely to be a female experience, since 71 per cent of those who were deserted were women. This pattern, at first glance, sits uneasily with the fact that internationally petitions for divorce are typically brought by women (71 per cent being brought by them in Britain according to Burgoyne *et al*, 1987). It is possible to argue, however, that what is going on here is that women are more likely to be willing to formally end the marriage through petitioning for divorce if it is available. This is perhaps not surprising, since they are more likely to need the protection of the law as regards maintenance. Such a pattern may also reflect the ability of women to deal with emotional problems – an ability rooted in their status as relational experts within a marriage and family context which is constructed on the basis of a feminised concept of love. The high levels of desertion in Ireland, and their predominantly male character, makes sense in this context insofar as it can be seen as reflecting the inability of some men to deal either with what they see as the emotional demands in this situation, or the emotional consequences of its disruption.

This sort of interpretation receives indirect support from Ó Riagáin's (1995) work looking at the characteristics of those who sought the services of AIM over the 1989-93 period. AIM has provided non-directive counselling, legal information, referral and more recently a mediation service to people with marriage and family problems in Dublin. Ó Riagáin found that 80 per cent of the clients were women. This reflects the 'well established international pattern for women to be the primary instigators of separation proceedings'. These women, however, were more likely than the general population to be middle class, in their forties and in paid employment (with only one third of them being full-time housewives). Over 90 per cent of them had at least one child, and about half of them had three or more children. More than three quarters of them had been married for at least 10 years, 42 per cent having been married for at least 20 years. They were thus a 'very married' group.

The marital problems of these women revolved around the areas of communication, personality and incompatibility (mentioned by 47 per cent, 40 per cent and 35 per cent respectively: Ó Riagáin, 1995:32). These problems suggest that the women expected a certain level of intimacy, communication and shared interests from the marriage, a pattern which is compatible with the trends emerging in Whelan and Fahey's study (1994). Furthermore 40 per cent of Ó Riagáin's respondents dated their marital problems from within the first year of their marriage, thereby underlining that one is dealing with basic styles of relating. This pattern is compatible with international evidence on men's greater unwillingness and/or inability to communicate intimately, and women's increasing expectation that communication of this kind will occur within marriage.

Thus what is suggested is that, based on the fragmented evidence we have, the respondent's withdrawal from marriage reflects the strength of a feminised conception of love. In some cases, of course, decisions to leave a marriage are entirely rooted in their experience of violence. However, it is clear that, for women such as those in Ó Riagáin's study, the key issue is the failure of the marriage in relational terms. Paradoxically, separation indicates the importance rather than the unimportance of what Cancian (1986) has called a feminised conception of love.

Evidence from the US and the UK, but not from Catholic South European countries, would suggest that marriage based on a commitment to the ideology of romantic love is highly likely to be unstable (Jackson, 1993). We do not know to what extent this pattern will emerge in Ireland. What is clear however is that in Ireland a sizeable proportion of family units are deviating from the husband-and-wife-and-children model. Insofar as any attempt has been made to explain these trends, attention has focused on the economic dimension. The question as to whether these patterns, like those of desertion, reflect women's endorsement of a feminised concept of love, and their perception of men as unable and/or unwilling to contribute to their emotional well-being within an equal companionate relationship, has not even begun to be discussed.

Negotiating within marriage

Implicit in negotiation is the idea of constructing a social order based on voluntary agreement rather than on traditional patterns of privilege. This is obviously closely related to what has been described by Fahey (1993) and Kennedy (1989) as the rise of individualism. Interestingly, within the context of the family, such individualism is typically denigrated, and is portrayed as a threat to group cohesion. However, it is generally viewed as relatively unproblematic within the context of the state, and is seen as very appropriate within a Christian tradition which places emphasis on individual salvation and moral responsibility (Fahey, 1995). It is therefore difficult to avoid the conclusion that what is peculiarly problematic about individualism within the family is that it necessitates an attenuation of male privileges.

The move to establish a social order based on negotiation is particularly compatible with a concept of marriage as an equal relationship between partners, created on the basis of a love relationship which meets individual needs for personal happiness. However, the assumption that negotiation between spouses is between equals ignores the fact that male power, rooted in economic control inside and outside the family, is still a very important reality: 'Magically the power that is vested in men in all spheres of life is somehow supposed to be neutralised in marriage' (Comer, 1982:180-181). Inevitably, and in contrast to the privatised romantic notion of marriage which we have come to accept, negotiations within marriage do not occur in a vacuum. At the very least the disparity in the visibility of men and women in the public arena will be reflected in wider tendencies to underestimate the importance of women's contributions, thereby further affecting their negotiating ability within individual partnerships.

In this context certain aspects of the relationship between men and women, e.g. men's unearned privileges in the family, will not be seen as problematic and hence will not be negotiable. However, in the past five or six years there have been attempts to deconstruct various aspects of the nature of marriage and family life (Barry, 1986 and 1988; McCullagh, 1991; Mahon, 1987, 1993 and 1994; Gaffney, 1991; Shortall, 1991). These authors do not deal with the extent to which negotiation is actually occurring in Irish marriages, although some are actively encouraging it:

> Living happily ever after has very little to do with fitting into tight glass slippers fashioned by a demanding Prince Charming. It has much more to do with Cinderella becoming one tough bargainer (Gaffney, 1991:22).

The extent of women's responsibilities for child care has been dramatically affected by the decline in family size within marriage. This phenomenon could reflect an increased willingness to use negotiation and/or a greater awareness of the needs of women and their attitudes as regards family size. Changes in family size have occurred in a context where the use of contraceptives among married couples in Ireland is similar to that in other European countries (Nic Ghiolla Phádraig and Clancy, 1991). It has been assumed that the development of the oral contraceptive pill in the 1960s and the legal availability of various kinds of contraceptives since the 1970s have been important in reducing family size. However, Nic Ghiolla Phádraig and Clancy (1995) found that access to contraception did not make an independent contribution to lowering family size, but was rather the conduit through which other factors operated, e.g. age, husband's employment and social class position and wife's work involvement. This trend is supported by international evidence; for example, the average family size arising from marital limitation began to fall in France as early as the 1780s and 1790s, and by the early 1900s, 55 per cent of couples in France had completed families of two children or less (Fahey, 1995). Quite clearly, although the availability of the contraceptive pill is important, the decline in family size needs to be set in a wider context.

Hannan and Katsiaouni (1977) found that there was a clear relationship between the number of children in the family and the husband's power as measured by his having the final say in borrowing money to buy land, being the general boss in financial matters, keeping track of money, etc. They concluded that:

> The greater the number of children in the family, the more power the father has. This result confirms the findings of many earlier studies that the larger the number of children the greater the concentration of power in families (1977:116).

This suggests that a decline in the number of children might well be associated with an actual or desired change in men's power within families. The relevance of this for an understanding of women's negotiating ability within the family has not yet been explored.

In contrast to women's success in effectively reducing the duration of their 'love labour' (Lynch, 1989a) by reducing the number of children, they appear to have had a difficulty in negotiating a reallocation of domestic labour within the home. The tendency to over-estimate men's contribution by concealing a very uneven division of labour within concepts such as 'joint' and/or 'modern' was early identified by Oakley (1974). This phenomenon has been evident in otherwise rigorous Irish studies. For example, Hannan and Katsiaouni (1977:38) noted that between a quarter and one third of the West of Ireland rural families they studied were closer to the 'modern' middle-class model than to the 'traditional' one, on the scales they constructed. The use of such traditional/ modern models effectively concealed the fact that only 1 per cent of the husbands made the beds; 3 per cent cleaned the floor; 7 per cent changed the baby; 14 per cent fed the baby; 16 per cent got the potatoes washed for dinner, etc.

Kiely's (1995) Dublin sample showed that by the late 1980s this pattern had changed little. Only 1 per cent of the fathers were responsible for ironing; 5 per cent for shopping; 5 per cent for doing the dishes; 6 per cent for hoovering; 12 per cent for putting children to bed and 16 per cent for discipline. The only task that most of the fathers were solely responsible for was repairs. On the other hand between half and two thirds of the wives were solely responsible for shopping, ironing, doing the dishes and hoovering. Fathers were marginally more likely to be solely responsible for child care tasks with approximately one in five fathers in that study being responsible for helping with homework, playing with the children and taking them on outings.

In an Irish national survey, the majority of the full-time housewives interviewed felt that shopping, hoovering, taking a sick child to the doctor, getting children ready for bed and making sure that homework was done, should be equally shared between husband and wife, though they felt this ideal was not being achieved (MRBI, 1992:20). We do not know whether Irish men's participation in household tasks increases when they are unemployed. However, studies in Northern Ireland (Leonard, 1992) and in Britain (Pahl, 1984; Morris, 1985) showed that this did not happen.

The patterns in Ireland, although extreme, are somewhat similar to those emerging in Britain, France, Denmark, Sweden, USA, and the former USSR. Coverman, having reviewed a wide range of evidence internationally, concluded that

> wives devote two to four times as many hours as husbands to domestic labour. They perform about three quarters of all the household chores, regardless of wives' employment status, or couple's education, income or sex-role ideology (1989:356).

Other reviews have concluded that 'women consistently undertake more work than men, in terms of hours, whether they are employed outside the home as well or not' (Grint, 1991:35). Eurobarometer findings (1997) showed that according to two thirds of European couples, the woman did most 'of the jobs that need to be done to keep a home running, such as shopping, cooking and cleaning'. In Ireland, among those who were living with a partner, only 30 per cent said that they shared these jobs, half and half (Eurobarometer, 1997). Indeed earlier Eurobarometer findings (1988:vol 34) showed that, in Ireland, among men who did take responsibility for at least one domestic task, the proportion who were willing to cook, clean, shop, or dress children was lower than in any other EC country. It was between a third and a quarter of the EC average on these various tasks (Second Commission on the Status of Women, 1993:118).

Rubery *et al* (1995) noted that the trends were broadly similar when the husband as opposed to the wife was asked about these activities. They found that 84 per cent of the Irish men interviewed said that they did no domestic work, as compared with a European average of 62 per cent. However, in that study only 32 per cent of the Irish wives said that the husbands did no domestic work. The size of the disparity between male and female responses in Ireland was unique, with typically the responses of the husbands and wives varying by no more than 5-6 per cent. It is difficult to interpret this although it may indicate widespread protectiveness on the part of the Irish wives.

A final area of possible negotiation relates to women's access to spending money or to 'time to themselves', or a 'night out'. In Arensberg and Kimball's traditional farm families, the woman usually had access to 'egg money'. In a situation where women are not in paid employment, and do not have access to money-making activities, access to personal spending money becomes more problematic. Rottman (1994a, 1994b) found that in only approximately one third of a random sample of Irish couples did both partners have access to equal amounts of money 'to spend on yourself for your own pleasure or recreation'. Furthermore, when those households in which neither partner had spending money were excluded, equal access to it existed in less than one fifth of the couples. As one might expect, personal spending money was associated with the overall household income level: with 35 per cent of the wives in the bottom quintile having such access, as compared with 85 per cent of those in the top quintile. At each level, however, husbands were more likely than wives to have access to personal spending money (52 per cent as compared with 94 per cent in these quintiles respectively). The typical situation was for the husband's 'share' to exceed that of his wife by, on average, 50 per cent.

It does seem that men continue to enjoy what one might regard as unearned privileges in the family. For example, Rottman found that personal spending money was more available to husbands and that where only one partner had 'an afternoon or an evening out in the last fortnight, for your entertainment, something that cost money', it was most likely to be the husband. Rottman's work also showed that where income in the household was low, Irish women typically controlled it; where it was high, it was controlled by the husband. Thus, even in situations where women ostensibly had access to the household income, their effective span of control was very limited, and they simply ended up with the responsibility for coping on an inadequate income. Similar trends have been documented in Pahl's British study (1991).

Comer (1982) has argued that paid employment increases women's ability to negotiate within marriage. According to Shortall (1991), women with off-farm employment were able to use their financially independent status to increase their authority and involvement in farm decisions. Pahl (1991) also found that, based on her British work, among those couples who pooled their financial resources, the more the wife contributed to the household income and/or the higher her occupational status or educational qualifications, the more likely she was to exert control over finances. The ultimate limits to such negotiation are, however, arguably set by the fact that women usually earn less than men in general, and less than their husband in particular, both in Ireland and in other European countries (Second Report of the Commission on the Status of Women, 1993; Rapid Report, 1993). The implications of these findings for the balance of power within marriage, in a society where the majority of young married women are in paid employment, have not yet been discussed.

There is some evidence that married men, through the process of interaction with their wives, alter their perception of women. Fine-Davis (1988) suggested that although men are still more likely than women to see women as 'inferior' and to think that 'women think less clearly than men', married men, in both her 1975 and 1986 study, were less likely than single men to have this perception. Furthermore, the attitudes of the married men shifted significantly over the 1975-86 period.

We have no evidence on the use of sexual and/or physical resources in counterbalancing access to other resources. We do know that Irish men still typically marry women who are younger than them: so it is possible that married women are able to use their relative youth and/or beauty as a negotiating tool. We know that the majority (71 per cent: Noonan, 1993) of the married respondents in a national representative sample (aged 17-49) had intercourse at least once or twice a week, but we do not know, other than in the realm of folklore, to what extent intercourse is used as a negotiating tool. Equally, we do not know to what extent married women are able to utilise differential emotional dependence within the relationship to create a feeling of powerfulness (O'Connor, 1991).

Schwartz (1994) suggested that the key to marital stability lay in the emergence of what she called peer couples. She saw such couples as being characterised by, firstly, having less than a 60/40 split on household duties and child raising; secondly, each person having equal influence over important and disputed decisions; thirdly, each having equal control over the family economy and reasonably equal access to discretionary funds; and fourthly, each person's work being given equal weight in the couple's life plans. The women in Schwartz's small snowball sample of overwhelmingly middle-class American couples, felt that there was no reason to separate or divorce since their needs as regards respect, interest and equality were being met within a non-hierarchical relationship where child care, domestic work and, for the most part, paid employment were shared. Such patterns seem fairly remote from what we know about Irish marriages.

Just struggling to get by . . .

What Giddens (1992) called 'the invention of motherhood' effectively presupposed the existence of a 'breadwinner' as a secure financial base: an assumption which, as previously mentioned, is unwarranted in the case of approximately a quarter of the married or cohabiting couples in Ireland in 1996 (CSO, 1997:Table 7). In roughly three fifths of these couples both partners were over 55 years, so it was unlikely that either would enter/re-enter the labour force. We know little about the day-to-day lives of such middle-aged couples, although it is not difficult to imagine that if their children are still financially dependent on them, they are under considerable financial pressures. Where the children have already left home, the husband and wife are very much thrown into each other's company, which may be a more or less positive experience. The lives of some of them may be enriched by organisations such as Active Retirement while others, who have seen the rearing of children as the source of meaning in their lives, may experience this as a sad and empty phase.

The National Anti-Poverty Strategy (1997) showed that in 1994 the two largest groups in poverty were households headed by an unemployed person and households headed by those working in the home. It showed that households headed by those working in the home were three and a half times more likely to be at risk of poverty in 1994 than in 1987. It recognised that it was difficult to obtain information on women in poverty since national surveys typically focused on households and assumed that resources were equally distributed within them.

Rottman (1994a and 1994b) showed that although members of families, on average, shared 55 per cent of their income, this sharing was least common at the top and bottom of the disposable income continuum. He particularly noted that households with income derived mainly from social welfare payments typically shared only one third of their incomes, as compared with approximately two thirds in other households. Furthermore he found that the less money there was, the more likely the woman was to be given responsibility for managing it. It was the woman who typically had to deal with 'the constant threat of debt and a feeling of exclusion from the normal standards of living' (National Anti-Poverty Strategy, 1997:57). Inevitably in this situation there were feelings of guilt and inadequacy because she was not able to give the children the things that other children took for granted and which her own children had come to expect.

It has been noted in Chapter 4 that the wife's psychiatric distress is affected by household poverty, a phenomenon which Whelan (1994b) saw as making intuitive sense because the wife is usually the one who tries to meet the family's needs. It has also been shown that women in poor households are likely to have the following characteristics:

shorter life span
higher risk of depression
more health hazards in the home and at work
higher risk of violence
greater risk of illness
more likely to smoke
less informed about preventive health
less access to and choice of contraception
more of their babies die as infants (Daly, 1989:87)

Murphy Lawless (1992) suggested that in a situation where the family was on welfare, the quantity, quality and variety of the food was lower than in families who were not on welfare. In addition, she showed that in this situation the mother typically made do with smaller portions and jeopardised her own nutritional needs. It does not seem unrealistic to suggest that their own and their children's poverty have a very substantial impact on the lifestyles of women in these families, an impact which has been explored in O'Neill's (1992) qualitative depiction of the lives of working-class women, as well as in descriptions of women's experience of poverty (Byrne, 1988 and 1992), and their difficulties in managing on low incomes (Daly and Walsh, 1991; Combat Poverty, 1989).

In low income households, married women may be unable to enter paid employment because of the cost of child care relative to wages. Yet their inability to do so may ironically perpetuate their children's poverty. Callan et al (1996) showed that in 1994 children were at greater risk of poverty than adults; and that children's risk of poverty at that time was greater than it had been in 1973. Indeed Frazer (1991) estimated that 40 per cent of children in the country were in families which were below the poverty line. The National Anti-Poverty Strategy (1997) also noted that approximately one third of the children in the country were dependent on state support. The child benefit that was provided was only roughly three fifths the average cost of rearing a child at a basic minimum level. It is not difficult to see that this is likely to pose difficulties for mothers who are trying to make ends meet.

Rottman noted (1994b) that channelling money through the mother increased the likelihood that it would be spent on the children. However, the logical implication that all social welfare payments should be paid directly to mothers, as a way of tackling children's poverty, has not even been discussed. Many would see this as inflammatory and demeaning to men. Yet the opposite strategy, i.e. channelling resources, other than child benefit, to the men in the household, is not seen as problematic, despite the fact that it is most likely to ensure that the allocation of resources, within already poor households, does not benefit children. At present, in situations where husbands are feckless or irresponsible with money, the state continues to endorse male authority in the family rather than acting as an honest broker in the interests of the well-being of the wife and children. A wife applying for 'split payments' has to have her husband's signature.

For women who have to struggle to provide the basic necessities of food, clothes and heat for their children, the debate about the appropriateness of their participation in paid employment can appear very irrelevant indeed.

Summary

In this chapter attention has been focused on those women who are still seen as the back-bone of Irish society, i.e. married women who are involved in full-time housewifery and child care. Such women are not of course a homogeneous group, being differentiated by husband's occupation and/or income; by the age cohort in which they were reared; by their place of residence and current life cycle stage. They do however share certain characteristics, viz. economic dependence and full-time housewifery. They are living at a time when there is at least a rhetorical recognition of the desirability of women playing a part in the wider society and making choices about their own lives. To a degree which perhaps has not been fully recognised by mainstream institutional structures, these women have taken those possibilities seriously.

The chapter has looked at the changes and continuities in marriage and family life by exploring six themes which, it is suggested, capture important aspects of these women's lives. The first two of these focus on women's emotional power within the family, and women's identification with and absorption within the family. The third involves an attempt to transform the cultural and structural parameters of marriage and family life by creating a public discourse about such issues and, more directly, by affecting state legislative activity. The fourth focuses specifically on the existence and importance of a feminised concept of love as the context for attempting to understand the dominant pattern of separation Irish style, viz. women's withdrawal from marriage and men's desertion.

The fifth pattern focuses on negotiation within the context of what is portrayed as an equal relationship between the spouses; while the sixth deals with poverty and the pressures involved in just struggling to get by financially.

The emergence of some of these patterns has been facilitated by membership of the European Union; by rising levels of education; by the discourses generated by the women's movement and by the media. Obviously there are difficulties in identifying such themes since married women have not been asked about them. Hence they can best be described perhaps as inferential constructs underpinning patterns of behaviour. As such, they are of course open to question. Their usefulness however lies in their ability to 'make sense' of the changes and continuities in marriage and family life. Furthermore, they do this in a way which recognises women as active agents, albeit ones operating within formidable parameters.

6

Young Women –
Just Other Young People?

Introduction

IT is widely recognised that the whole concept of youth is socially created, and that what is defined as 'youth' has changed substantially over the past thirty years (National Youth Policy Committee, 1984; Wallace, 1987a, 1987b). Participation in education has considerably extended the period during which a young person is likely to be financially dependent on the family and the proportion of young people in this situation has increased dramatically. Thus Murphy and Whelan (1995) found that the proportion of second level school leavers who were students doubled between 1980 and 1994, while the proportion who were in paid employment halved. However, with a few notable exceptions (such as Hannan and Ó Riain, 1993) comparatively little attention has been paid to this issue, although it raises questions about identity and about those aspects of a lifestyle which are associated with financial independence, e.g. paid employment, autonomy, and accommodation outside the family home.

In Ireland in 1996 there were 635,300 young people, of whom half were young women, i.e. women aged between 15-24 years old (Labour Force Survey, 1996:1997). Just over two fifths (42 per cent) of young Irish women were in the labour force. Approximately the same proportion was in education; the remainder being classified as 'other non-active', i.e. those who were not actively seeking work or not available for work because of 'home duties'. This is very similar to the pattern across the EU as a whole: 47 per cent of the women aged 15-24 years being in the labour force, 43 per cent in education and the remainder classified as 'non active' (Eurostat, 1994).

In this chapter, we look at young women within the very real limits of the data available. For the most part, research in this area has reflected interests and priorities which could be regarded as stereotypically 'male' insofar as it has been largely concerned with education, training and paid employment. In this chapter we shall look firstly at young women's educational experiences and achievements; secondly at the paid employment area; and thirdly at issues related to unemployment and training.

Wallace (1987a, 1987b) suggested that in Britain girls' roles as young women were reinforced in three ways: firstly materially, by the fact that girls received lower wages; secondly, socially, through expectations regarding appropriate adult behaviour; and thirdly symbolically, by images surrounding concepts of 'nice' girls and 'whores', and the way these were expressed in behaviour and in styles of dress that defined girls as being in one category or the other. What limited evidence we have suggests that similar processes may operate here.

As suggested in Chapter 5, many women in Ireland have implicitly or explicitly taken the possibilities of institutional change seriously. Their daughters, young women born in the 1970s and 1980s, have grown up within a culture which holds out the possibility of a life for women within the public arena – a possibility which is compatible with the needs of the economic system and with the strength of the role models exemplified by their mothers. Yet these possibilities sit uneasily with the continued gendered and subordinate reality of the status and identity of adult women within the public arenas.

In Ireland the educational and occupational structures alternate between treating girls as 'honorary males' and as subordinate women. In this situation their sexual relationships arguably become particularly important in validating their identity as young women. We know very little indeed about their experiences in their families and in the wider community; about the way they manage tensions surrounding heterosexuality or about their attitudes to the structures which define them. These topics will be dealt with in a speculative way in subsequent sections. Given the highly selective nature of the data it is impossible to suggest inferential constructs so as to provide some kind of insight into the sense young women make of their lives. Inevitably then issues related to agency and subjectivity are obscured.

Educational experiences and achievements

In no other area of Irish life has a concern with equality of opportunity been as obvious as in the area of education. However, this has occurred within a context where the full implications of a gendered identity have not been discussed. Thus, even in this area the messages transmitted to young women have been ambiguous. We have little evidence about what sense young women make of this situation or what they see as its implications for their identity – or indeed whether this differs for middle-class and working-class girls.

Traditionally, education for girls, whether working-class or middle-class, was seen as a cultural resource which could be used to increase their marriage prospects. Whelan *et al* (1996) showed that young women have been consistently more likely than young men to complete the Leaving Certificate, although this trend has grown weaker as levels of educational attainment have risen. Nevertheless, in 1994, 87 per cent of the girls and 78 per cent of the boys completed their Leaving Certificate (Lynch and Morgan, 1995). The trends were even more dramatic when the focus turned to those who left school with no qualifications: girls constituting only 25 per cent of this group (Murphy and Whelan, 1995).

Within the formal educational arena there has been an increasing awareness of sexist attitudes and a commitment to promoting gender equality. From the mid 1980s onwards there has been an awareness of gender stereotyping in school books at primary level. In many primary schools boys are being introduced to knitting and sewing and girls to competitive sports, including football. At second level, Hannan *et al*'s classic work (1983) clearly showed the extent to which gender-differentiated patterns existed in terms of the kinds of subjects which were provided for boys and for girls, the kind of real options which were available to them (because of time tabling decisions) and the actual choices that they made. Hannan *et al* concluded that:

> Although there are differences between the sexes in provision and allocation in the subjects we analysed, these differences are ... less than gender differences in the true rate of choice. In other words, the sex difference in pupils' own choices was greater than in either the provision or allocation of subjects to them (1983 :154).

Drudy and Lynch (1993) noted that this generally still held true ten years later. Even when attention was focused on single sex schools, the overall pattern as regards the subjects which were offered to boys and girls was very similar, other than in the areas of technical drawing and home economics. Changes were also occurring in the take-up of subjects, with young women moving out of the Arts and Humanities areas into the Science and Business areas, subjects that would traditionally have been seen as 'male' (Drudy and Lynch, 1993; Gleeson, 1992). On the other hand there was only a small movement by (less able) boys into 'female' subject areas. The two main areas where gendered choices remained strongest at Leaving Certificate level were in the practical-technical areas for boys (particularly technical drawing and construction studies) and the more 'feminine' sciences (biology and social and scientific home economics) for girls. Hannan *et al* (1996:105) concluded that gender imbalance had actually increased since 1980 in quite a few Leaving Certificate subjects. They suggested that insofar as change was occurring, it was reflected in the higher valuation of 'male' areas by girls.

TABLE 6.1
TAKE-UP OF SELECTED SUBJECTS FOR LEAVING CERT 1994, BY GENDER[1]

Subject	% Pupils Taking Subject		Ratio	Log of Ratios	
	M	F	M—F	1994	1980
Home Econ. (Gen)	0	1	.09	-2.39	-4.61
Home Econ. (S&S)	11	56	.20	-1.59	-2.12
Construction Studies	23	1	33.40	3.51	6.89
Engineering	18	1	30.54	3.42	7.51
Technical Drawing	28	1	27.21	3.30	5.39
Higher Maths	17	11	1.58	.46	1.33
Physics	29	9	3.22	1.17	2.11
Chemistry	14	12	1.19	.17	1.04
Biology	33	62	.53	-.63	-.43

[1] Hannan et al (1996: 104).

At Third Level, the trends in subject choice are similarly complex. Women continue to predominate in traditionally 'female' areas (e.g. Social Science and Arts) and men in traditionally 'male' areas (e.g. Engineering and Agricultural Science). However, as at Second Level, there is clear evidence that women are increasingly penetrating what used to be thought of as 'male' areas. Durkan *et al* (1995) showed that women constituted 61 per cent of those entering Medicine; 59 per cent of those entering Law and 52 per cent of those entering Science. One might suggest that these women too have assimilated the implicitly higher valuation of 'male' subjects and career choices.

The whole question of the extent to which the curriculum is patriarchal in content has tended to be ignored. Indeed, implicit in much of the discussions concerning the breaking down of gender differentiated patterns lies the assumption that (traditionally) male dominated subjects are the high status subjects and the 'real' indicators of intelligence and future job prospects. In this context, it is difficult to avoid the conclusion that what is happening is that young girls, particularly middle class girls, are being encouraged to become 'honorary' males at the level of curriculum.

At the same time, however, it was clear from Lynch's (1989b) work that the schools, reflecting the influence of the Roman Catholic Church and/or the wider society, had very different ideas about the appropriate qualities and roles for girls and boys and this was reflected in the ethos of the schools. Lynch found that, in her study, girls' schools, unlike boys' schools, put particular emphasis on developing qualities like caring for others, gentleness, refinement and self-control, attributes which Drudy and Lynch (1993) suggested facilitated women's subordination. They found too that girls' schools gave more time to the teaching of religion, to personal development and pastoral care than boys' schools, and that dress and behaviour codes were stricter in girls' as opposed to boys' schools. There were also differences in extracurricular activities, with aesthetic, moral, religious and socio-personal development having a far greater priority in girls' than in boys' schools, leading them to the con-clusion that:

> While caring for others, being considerate and sensitive are undoubtedly valuable social qualities, they become social millstones for women when men are not socialised into them as well (Drudy and Lynch, 1993: 186).

The distribution of positions of responsibility between men and women at every level within the educational system, and the differential representation of women at First and Third Level also clearly indicate the gendered nature of the educational system. Yet, despite considerable endorsement of the importance of role-models, and the recognition by the Department of Education of the importance of integrating both genders in the management structures (Second Commission on the Status of Women, 1993), little attention has been paid to this issue (see Chapter 8).

We know very little about the implications of these contradictory messages for young women's sense of themselves and their perception of their role in life, their career ambitions etc. McQuillan (1995) did find that in her study of fourth-year secondary school pupils attending mixed schools in Clare, boys were much more likely to take engineering, technical drawing and physics for career reasons than girls were. Both McQuillan's (1995) and O'Donohue's (1995) work implied that, for girls, career options based on such choices were seen as incompatible with their idea of themselves as young women. As one of the young female engineering students explained:

> I was at a stage where I had eliminated all the traditional areas and many subjects and I still wasn't in a position to match my likes and skills with a suitable career (O'Donohue, 1995: 66).

Their concept of a suitable career was 'ultimately informed by gender expectations' (Evetts, 1993), and in Irish society, as these young women perceived them, such expectations led them towards 'caring' ones and away from careers such as engineering.

On the other hand, a variety of studies have shown that girls do better overall than boys in public examinations (Greaney and Kelleghan, 1984; Clancy, 1989; Lynch, 1991; NCCA, 1992; Drudy and Lynch, 1993; Hannan et al, 1996). This is despite the fact that the boys who continue to Leaving Certificate are a relatively select group, since lower ability boys are more likely than lower ability girls to drop out before their Leaving Certificate. Thus, based on their examination of 1994 Leaving Certificate results, Hannan et al concluded that :

> As in the junior cycle, girls significantly outperform boys, with a difference of three quarters of a grade (1996:147).

Hannan et al found that, for example, girls were more likely than boys to get honours in English, French, and Maths at both Higher and Ordinary level; and were as likely as boys to get honours in Physics and Chemistry at Higher and Ordinary Level. They showed that, even in Higher Maths, although girls were marginally less likely to get A1s or A2s, they were marginally more likely than boys to get honours, and marginally less likely to fail. Hence the conclusion that the overall performance of girls in Maths was better than boys. This pattern is particularly interesting since Maths has traditionally been regarded as the 'real' test of intelligence and was the area where boys typically did better than girls at Leaving Certificate level.

As noted by Lynch and Morgan (1995) the fact that girls tend to do better overall than boys at Leaving Certificate level is not a recent phenomenon. In 1980 a slightly higher proportion of girls than boys got an honours grade in those subjects taken by both boys and girls. Indeed it has been noted that girls do better than boys as early as primary school. These patterns have however attracted little explanatory interest among sociologists. This is in stark contrast to attempts to explain class differences in attainment. Lynch and Morgan noted that the traditional 'underperformance' of girls in male areas was seen as a problem by the system while the poor linguistic ability of boys was not seen in the same light. This prompted them to ask whether there was 'some kind of bias in educational thinking' (1995:549). Indeed there is indirect evidence to suggest that these findings have not been taken on board by the girls themselves. Thus, Hannan *et al* (1996) found that, controlling for ability and class position, girls at both Junior and Leaving Certificate level had a poorer academic self image than boys.

Until relatively recently boys' and girls' examination scripts at Leaving Certificate level were in different colours. The elimination of this, and the virtual ending of the practice of giving a double weighting to Higher Maths at Leaving Certificate level for the purposes of admission to University, has begun to create a more level 'playing pitch'. There has however been a tendency for the proportion of A grades awarded in subjects still predominantly taken by boys (e.g. Higher Maths) to be higher than in subjects which are predominantly taken by girls (e.g. Honours French). It remains to be seen to what extent the Commission set up (1997) to review the points system will deal with the issue of gender neutrality in the whole area of assessment.

Traditionally girls have had a lower participation than boys in Third Level. In 1994 this pattern changed, with young women being more likely than their male counterparts to be in full time Third Level Education, 42 per cent of the girls as compared with 36 per cent of the boys being in this position. As one would expect, the daughters of the higher professionals were more likely to be in Third Level than the daughters of the unskilled manual workers (71 per cent versus 16 per cent: Whelan *et al*, 1996). This trend also emerged at second level. Having a mother currently in professional employment made an additional positive impact over and above the effect of social class (Hannan *et al*, 1996). In any case, in each social class, the girls are more likely than the boys to be in Third Level. Thus not only has participation in Third Level increased dramatically overall, but this increase has been particularly marked for women, 14 per cent of the female cohort going on to Third Level in 1979 as compared with 42 per cent in 1994, the comparable male figures being 15 per cent and 36 per cent respectively (Whelan *et al*, 1996). Girls from farming backgrounds, from other non-manual backgrounds (e.g. clerical, sales etc.) and from skilled manual backgrounds in particular were more likely than their male counterparts to enter Third Level.

These patterns emerged in a more muted way when one looked at the gender breakdown of those who were actually in Third Level. Women constituted just under 30 per cent of Third Level students in 1965/66 while they made up approximately half of all undergraduates and postgraduates nationally in 1991, and just over half of those in the universities (Clancy, 1995b; Dept. of Equality and Law Reform, 1994). The extent of their increase at post graduate level was particularly striking. In 1980, women constituted 24.5 per cent of those doing post graduate Degrees, and this had increased to 41 per cent by 1991 (HEA figures; Dept. of Equality and Law Reform, 1994). Men still outnumber women at PhD level. It is possible that this reflects young women's poor academic self image and/or their perception of academic environments as male dominated and unlikely to provide them with paid employment.

The educational system as outlined in this section reflects and reinforces an ambivalence about young women's identity as women. On the one hand, it is committed to treating them 'just the same' as boys; on the other hand, the disproportionate presence of males in positions of authority, its gendered ethos and the differential valuing of 'male' versus 'female' subjects, reflects the gendered nature of Irish society and conveys a rather different message. Nevertheless, despite this context, girls do better academically than boys. There has been little attempt made to explain this. There is evidence to suggest that, reflecting a gendered view of the world, girls have difficulties making career choices in non-traditional areas, although they are increasingly choosing 'male' subjects at Second and Third Level.

Young women's paid employment

Although as the Labour Force Survey 1996 showed, only a minority of the young women aged 15-24 years old were in paid employment, those that were, were overwhelmingly (83 per cent) in regular full-time work (CSO, 1997: 57 and 47). This trend was broadly similar to that emerging among the young men, although they were slightly more likely to be in regular full-time work (87 per cent). Ronayne (1987), drawing on data from the Irish Congress of Trade Unions, showed that nearly three quarters of young workers were low paid. The situation of those on temporary employment schemes was of course considerably worse. Ronayne also showed that the average net income of young men and women in paid employment in various occupations was rarely similar. Young men's net income was typically higher than women's in managerial/professional occupations and in services, areas where women are particularly likely to be employed; while young women's average net income was higher than that of their male counterparts in the skilled/semi-skilled and un-skilled manual areas, where women are not typically employed.

Indeed Durkan *et al* (1995) showed that among those with primary and postgraduate degrees, young women were more likely than young men to be at the low end of the salary continuum. For example in 1992, 15 per cent of young women who were graduates were earning less than £5,000 pa as compared with 9 per cent of the young men. This trend was very similar to the pattern in 1989 (7 per cent and 12 per cent respectively). Furthermore among those with postgraduate degrees, 14 per cent of the young women and 5 per cent of the young men earned such salaries in 1992. As one might expect young men were more likely than young women to be high earners among those both with primary and post primary degrees. It is not clear to what extent this reflects the kinds of occupations they were in and/or a 'gender bonus' for maleness.

The types of occupations held by young women were sharply differentiated from those held by their male counterparts (Labour Force Survey, 1996 [CSO, 1997:37]). The most common occupations held by young women were clerical work (26 per cent), followed by service work (19 per cent), professional and technical work (18 per cent), and commerce, insurance and finance (17 per cent). These four occupational groups in fact accounted for approximately four fifths of those young women who were in paid employment. On the other hand the most common occupational group among the young men was producers, makers and repairers (characteristic of 41 per cent), the remainder of them being distributed across the seven other occupational groups. Thus, young girls' occupations differed considerably from their male counterparts, these patterns reflecting the very restricted range of occupations commonly held by women, regardless of their age (see Chapter 7). Murphy and Whelan (1995) showed that the occupations of young school leavers varied right from the start, depending on whether they were boys or girls. In the early 1980s female school leavers were most likely to be found in clerical occupations, with the balance since then shifting somewhat to service occupations.

The high educational levels of girls were reflected in their disproportionate holding of professional occupations. Thus 21 per cent of the young women, but only 6 per cent of the young men, were in the professional services sector (Labour Force Survey, 1996 [CSO, 1997:32]). The implications of these patterns are likely to be considerable for the participation of married women in the labour force since, as Callan and Farrell (1991) have noted, the participation rate for married women with a university degree was 74 per cent as compared with 34 per cent among those with Leaving Certificate only.

Reilly (1995) has been one of the few to have looked at the extent and impact of union membership on wage rates. He found that in the YEA/ESRI follow-up survey of school leavers in 1987, although young workers were less likely than adult workers to be union members, 44 per cent of the young women were union members. Rather surprisingly, this was higher than the comparable male figure (33 per cent), although it was lower than the adult union density estimated by Roche (1992). Reilly also showed that although union membership did not have any significant effect on young men's wages, it raised the wages of young women workers by over 22 per cent. Thus he concluded that unions played an important role in reducing the gender gap between young women's and young men's wages. The importance was greatest among small employers, a trend which also emerged in British studies. Interestingly, Reilly also noted that kin ties (in the sense of working for relatives) had a very different effect on wages, with young women, like young men, earning approximately 24 per cent less if they were working for relatives.

What evidence there is suggests that the types of occupations young women are in are characterised by a high concentration of women, with the wages of young men in these areas being higher than those of young women. We know very little about the experiences of young women in what were traditionally 'male' professional areas, or indeed about the making or breaking of such young women's professional identities. The disproportionate presence of women in such areas has, potentially, considerable social and cultural implications.

Unemployment and training

Rubery et al (1996) noted that in the 1990s youth unemployment rates for both men and women rose on average across the EU. In Ireland, in contrast to most other EU countries, unemployment rates among young women were lower than among young men in 1990 and they remained so – the typical EU pattern being for young women's rates to be higher in 1990 (by 6 per cent) and to be more or less similar to young men's in 1994 (whether including 12 or 15 countries; Rubery et al, 1996). It is not clear however to what extent women's lower level of unemployment in Ireland rests on their willingness to 'trade down', i.e. to accept employment which is below their educational level and hence below the income level that they might expect to obtain, although there are occasional explicit or implicit tantalising references to such 'trading down' (Breen, 1984b; Hannan and Ó Riain, 1993; Sexton *et al*, 1991; Callan and Wren, 1994).

Wallace (1986) suggested that among the young women she studied, paid employment was important insofar as it provided young people with money, and hence with the possibility of independent accommodation and freedom from parental surveillance. It offered them an alternative, and short-term, definition of adulthood. This was particularly important since their expectations of domestic life were in Wallace's terms (1986:101) characterised by 'critical ambiguity'. Wallace (1986) also suggested that in Britain in the 1980s youth unemployment reached such levels that it was no longer possible to see a transition to employment as the 'normal' route through which adult identity was established. The trends emerging in Ireland were not dissimilar. Hannan and Ó Riain (1993) noted that unemployment had increased dramatically (from 9 per cent in 1979 to 26 per cent in 1987, when the overall unemployment rate rose from 6 per cent to 18 per cent over that period) At that time the gap between youth unemployment and overall unemployment was no different in Ireland than in the average EU situation, but the level of youth unemployment was extremely high, because our adult rate was so high. By 1995, the youth unemployment rate was 19 per cent in Ireland, as compared with an overall unemployment rate of 12 per cent (the comparable figures across the 15 EU countries being 21 per cent and 10.7 per cent: Eurostat, 1996).

Such overall rates conceal very wide disparities since youth unemployment has been shown to be very strongly associated with working-class background and educational level, this effect being mediated through the likelihood of finding a job in the first place, and through the likelihood of obtaining a job with greater job security, better promotional prospects, better pay, pension rights, training conditions etc. (Breen, 1985). These patterns have persisted (Kennedy, 1993).

Hannan and Ó Riain (1993: 49) found in their study that, although overall unemployment rates for men and women within the five years after they left school were very similar, and were in both cases strongly associated with educational qualifications, the unemployment rate for women with no qualifications (at 50 per cent) did not change the longer they had been out of school. On the other hand, the unemployment rate for men with no qualifications fell from 67 per cent to 37 per cent over

the five-year period. Breen's (1991: 37) study of unqualified school
leavers showed that, around five years after leaving secondary school,
women who lacked educational qualifications had only a very small
likelihood of entering training schemes.

> The experiences of this cohort of school leavers suggest that many of those
> who appear to most need some form of intervention in the labour market are
> unlikely to get it. Our results ... point to unqualified female school leavers
> being one notable such group (Breen, 1991:84).

Breen noted that this failure of labour market programmes to provide
for unqualified female leavers also emerged in other studies of training
and temporary employment. One might argue that what is effectively
happening is that the state through its procedures and practices is acting
very much in a gendered way and thus maintaining male privilege.

European Social Fund resources can be seen as particularly important
in this context insofar as they could significantly alter the job
opportunities of women with no qualifications who were unemployed.
These funds are required to be gender audited. Among the under-25s in
1994, women made up 40 per cent of those in training, and 50 per cent
of those in employment schemes (FÁS, 1994:24). However, direct
expenditure disproportionately went to men both on the training and
employment schemes (women accessing 38 per cent and 32 per cent of
this expenditure respectively: FÁS, 1994:25). There was no evidence
that these trends were changing (Dept. of Enterprise and Employment,
1994: Appendix 2).

Furthermore, the higher the level of training, the lower the
proportion of women benefiting. Women made up only just over one
third (35 per cent) of those following courses in the post-foundation
skills area, although they were equally represented with men in basic or
foundation courses. Insofar as training for women was provided beyond
the basic foundation level it was mainly in areas which were predicted to
have a poor economic outlook (e.g. clothing and clerical occupations).
Women were under-represented in those areas which had a favourable
outlook (e.g. skilled production work and electronics). Even those
agencies (such as FÁS) which did have a positive action programme
seemed to be particularly concerned with increasing the proportion of
women apprentices, a declining area of employment. Only 14 per cent
of those benefiting from management development measures
administered by the various agencies were women. Thus despite the
European Union's commitment to gender proofing, expenditure was
disproportionately skewed in favour of young men.

One would expect that in the face of long-term unemployment young women with low education may simply move into 'home duties'. There was indeed indirect support for this insofar as young women were less likely than their male counterparts to be unemployed for a year or more (Labour Force Survey, 1996 [CSO, 1997:61]). Emigration is also of course one of the responses to youth unemployment. The NESC Report (1991) noted that, in general, it has been predominantly young people, under 24 years of age, who have emigrated. The balance of men and women who have emigrated has fluctuated considerably over time. However, since 1980, when net emigration re-emerged, the outflow has been predominantly male (the ratio of females per 1,000 males being 736). Sexton *et al* (1991) suggest that this was related to the dramatic decline in male employment over the 1981 to 1988 period (by nearly 70,000 at a time when the number of women in paid employment increased by 14,000). Thus quite clearly emigration cannot explain the under-representation of women among the long-term unemployed.

In some ways, unemployed young women face similar problems as regards income and housing as those who are students. In both cases, state payments are set at a level which makes it difficult for them to acquire year round accommodation and so there is a tendency for students to remain at home or to return home during the holiday period, and for the unemployed to remain living at home. There are, however, important differences. For the girl in higher education, the acquisition of 'cultural capital' (Bourdieu, 1977) can be seen as an element in the definition of an adult status. Furthermore, the acquisition of such capital carries with it the expectation of financial return. For the (typically working-class) girl who is unemployed, the position can be rather different, involving the possibility of continued financial dependence on an already impoverished household, where as Wallace has noted :

> Lack of a job . . . condemned her to the status of a junior within the home, and it was more likely that she would be given domestic chores to do as well (1986:109).

We know almost nothing about the ways in which girls' unemployment is handled within families (e.g. the extent to which it is used to ensure continued affectional involvement as suggested by Leonard's 1987 work on spoiling and 'keeping close'). It is possible that tensions will revolve around autonomy and, given the evidence that young people are more likely to be sexually permissive and less approving of the church as an institution (Whelan, 1994), conflict may revolve around bringing home occasional sexual partners and/or more long term cohabitation within the family home.

We know that unemployment has a negative effect on the mental health of young people. McCarthy and Ronayne's work (1984) found that between half and two thirds of unemployed young people were less confident, more confused, more depressed, more anxious and less happy than their counterparts in paid employment. Furthermore, Hannan and Ó Riain's work (1993) showed that the implications of unemployment in terms of psychological distress had an equal impact on young women and young men.

The role of the state in the context of youth unemployment is particularly interesting since, with the exception of lone parents, its intervention in this area is unrelated to child care issues, return to work questions, etc. It does however occur within the context of patterns which favour males over females.

Home and wider community: still a man's world

The overall tenor of the evidence we have, tenuous though it is, suggests that young women, particularly working-class young women with no qualifications, are in various ways treated as 'less valuable' than their male counterparts.

Hannan and Ó Riain (1993) found that young women were less likely than young men to be living at home, a pattern which they saw as related to various factors including their higher levels of education. They also noted that children of highly educated mothers, as well as farmer's daughters, were particularly likely to leave the parental home, although these patterns too were mainly explained in terms of a girl's own educational level. As previously mentioned Wallace's (1987a) study explained similar patterns among employed young men and women in very different terms i.e. in terms of the lower expectations that young men would contribute to domestic work, and the greater personal freedom they enjoyed while they were living at home:

> As many informed me, they would be mad to leave. Where else could they have their clothes washed and ironed and food provided for between £10 and £15 per week? (Wallace, 1987a:158).

Anecdotal evidence would suggest that such phenomena are very much a reality in Irish families and that they are not peculiar to young men who are unemployed. We have no systematic evidence about them however; nor about their effects on girls' evaluation of themselves; on their emotional independence or on their decisions as regards accommodation.

Hannan *et al* (1996) found that in their study both the Junior and Leaving Certificate girls were more likely than the boys to make their own beds, use the vacuum cleaner, set and clear the table, prepare meals, do the ironing, etc. They also found that these patterns did not vary by social class. Such trends are broadly similar to those emerging in the UK. Both Lees (1993) and McRobbie (1978) found that many of the 14-16 year olds in their studies were spending approximately 15 hours per week helping their mothers with housework. Lees (1993) found in her study that, although there was some evidence that boys as well as girls were participating in housework, it was clear that the girls still tended to do most; while Brannen (1995) found, in her study of British 16 year olds, that family care as opposed to self care tasks were most likely to be carried out by young women.

Within the wider community – in a club or organisational context – what evidence we have suggests that the group who were best catered for were young men at Senior Cycle in the educational system; with working-class girls with no educational qualifications being least catered for (Ronayne, 1992). Many of the organisations were sport oriented, mainly to team-based sports, and as such they were more attractive to young men than to young women. Young women preferred non-team-based forms of sports provision, as well as music, arts and drama and these were typically less developed in the clubs. Thus although roughly one in five of the young people in Ronayne's study rated the provision of facilities as poor or very poor, more than two fifths (i.e. 43 per cent) of young women with no qualifications assessed them in this way. Ronayne concluded that in the case of this group, the evidence was 'overwhelming', as regards:

> the extent to which inequalities in the education-labour market are reinforced by patterns of participation in youth provision (1992: 18).

Although, overall, 23 per cent of young people aged 15-24 years were members of a youth club or organisation, only 7 per cent of young women with no qualifications were members; as compared with 54 per cent of young men with no qualifications. Ronayne noted that:

> . . . there is evidence that young men with no qualifications are being catered for by both sports and non-sports related provision. This is not the case with respect to young women (1992:12).

There have been attempts by some organisations to deal with the situation. The National Youth Council of Ireland (NYCI) set up a working group to look at the participation of young women at club/group level, and at the issue of the relative absence of women at senior levels within these organisations. Their research data was based on responses from 60 per cent of the 51 organisations affiliated to the NYCI, the NYCI itself and Foróige (an unaffiliated organisation). Although four fifths of these organisations had a female membership of 50 per cent or more, women were severely under-represented in senior positions. It was found that, overall, 73 per cent of the chairpersons were male. In addition the majority of formal positions on the management boards in these youth organisations were held by boys and the bigger the organisation, and the higher its profile within youth work, the less likely girls were to be in the top positions. The position which was held in the majority of cases by girls on these boards was that of secretary. Clearly, there are issues around the perceived appropriateness of women in positions of power on management boards, since the majority (74 per cent) of the members of these management boards were elected (NYCI, 1990).

Similarly, when the NYCI examined those youth organisations which had employees (54 per cent of those in the study), positions of power (i.e. director/chief executive or assistant director/second executive) were predominantly held by boys (64-71 per cent). This Report also looked at the extent to which women were appropriately represented on the standing committees of the National Youth Council, given the membership of these organisations. Again more than half of them sent fewer women than men to these committees (anything from none to half), and chairpersons of these committees had all been men since 1988. The Report recommended reserved seats and quotas on management boards both in the NYCI and in the affiliated organisations, as well as in-service managerial training for women in youth organisations. It is perhaps not coincidental then that whereas at the 1988 Assembly, the NYCI executive was entirely composed of men, by 1992-93, 40 per cent of its members were women.

The Report thus clearly showed that, even in organisations which had a high membership of young women, for whom issues related to maternity leave, child bearing and child rearing are less relevant than among older women, positions of power at all levels were overwhelmingly held by men. The majority of the organisations were little interested in changing this pattern. The Report found that, although the NYCI had produced a policy statement on equal opportunity, only 13 per cent of the organisations had discussed it. Furthermore, it found that although more than half of these organisations did have special programmes for young women, there was no clear idea as to what such programmes might involve, and in fact they ranged from 'traditional' girls' activity days, to public meetings on women in politics. Since then a resource book for working with girls and young women, and a two year Women in Management Certificate Course for employed/youth workers (Mulkeen 1994) have been introduced. It remains to be seen what effect they will have.

Overall then, what limited evidence is available suggests that young women carry a disproportionate responsibility for domestic work within the home, a pattern which reflects and reinforces their culturally perceived servicing and subordinate role in relation to men. Within local organisations the message that young women, particularly those with low levels of education, receive is that their needs are not important. Power in such organisations remains overwhelmingly in the hands of young men.

The tensions surrounding heterosexuality

For young women, tensions can revolve around their own evaluation of themselves as sexual beings. They can experience pressure to be heterosexual and to 'prove' this by being heterosexually active, within an increasingly sexually permissive but overtly degendered society where abortion is stigmatised, where attitudes to 'taking precautions' are ambivalent and where the availability of the contraceptive pill can be used to erode any attempt by them to say no.

The sexual element in young women's identity and the processes involved in its control have been virtually ignored in research. Hannan *et al* (1996) did find in their study, that girls in second level education were consistently less likely than their male counterparts to see themselves as physically attractive. Hannan *et al* suggested that these attitudes reflected an underlying poor sense of self esteem, which was related to 'general cultural messages/evaluations' (1996:174). It is not clear whether such attitudes were affected by the increased availability of pornography and the commodification of women's bodies. However, the authors noted that among girls, as indeed among boys, having a boy/girl friend was associated with a more positive view, although even in this situation girls were significantly more likely than boys to have poor body images.

Hanafin's (1992) study of Leaving Certificate pupils was suggestive as regards the kinds of processes which might reinforce these perceptions. That study showed that, at a stage when young women were coming to terms with their sexual identity, a sizeable proportion, even within the highly structured, theoretically asexual classroom situation, experienced what can only be described as sexual harassment. Hanafin found that half of the girls from the mixed schools in her study reported that remarks about their bodies had been made in their hearing by boys at school; a quarter (28 per cent) said that remarks of a sexual nature which they found offensive had been made to them. Two fifths of them had personally experienced 'playful' pinching or slaps on the buttocks, often accompanied by equally 'playful' comments of a sexually suggestive nature with which they felt uncomfortable. Just under one in four had been 'touched up' or 'groped' by the boys in the school. These activities can be seen as an attempt to reflect and reinforce boys' sexual domination. The (implicit) acceptance of this by the school would seem to reinforce the view that it was 'natural' for girls to be intimidated by boys. We do not know to what extent similar processes exist in other settings.

The Second Commission on the Status of Women (1993) clearly recognised the need for courses in the sex and relationship areas for both boys and girls, embracing not only issues related to parenting, childcare, budgeting, the legal and financial aspects of family life, but also those related to prejudice, equality, and the issue of sexual identity. It remains to be seen to what extent these will be tackled within the relationships and sexuality programme which is being introduced under the aegis of the Minister for Education at primary and second level, and what the effect of this intervention will be.

Other than at an anecdotal level (Egan, 1997) we do not know to what extent young Irish women become involved in heterosexual relationships as a way of avoiding being seen as 'lessies' (lesbians). The limited evidence available does suggest that lesbianism is perceived as a stigmatised identity. Two fifths of those in a non-random sample of lesbians and gay men, half of whom were under 30 years old, had been threatened with violence because they were assumed to be gay. The overwhelming majority (84 per cent) knew someone who had been verbally harassed, threatened with violence or physically attacked because they were assumed to be lesbian or gay; with a similar proportion (81 per cent) saying that the possibility of such harassment had affected their own behaviour (Gay and Lesbian Equality Network,

1995). Similar themes have emerged in the very limited number of publications about lesbianism among women of any age in Ireland (Crone, 1989; O'Carroll, 1994; Dublin Lesbian and Gay Society, 1986).

In Ireland as indeed elsewhere in Europe the uncoupling of marriage and sexual activity has meant that marriage is no longer seen as a necessary prelude to sexual intercourse. We do not have systematic evidence about the attitudes of young Irish women to virginity, sexual reputation, etc. However, there is some evidence that the median age for first sexual intercourse is between 20-21 years for young women (and between 19-20 years for young men), with just over half of them having their first sexual experience when they were aged less than 21 years (see Inglis, 1994). This was considerably older than in Britain where the median age for both young women and young men was 18 years. However there is also evidence to suggest (IMS, 1996) that approximately half of the 16-17 year olds felt that it was 'okay' for a young unmarried person to start having intercourse before the age of eighteen. The IMS study also suggested that, according to themselves, a sizeable minority (22 per cent) of the 16-17 year olds were sexually active.

Active heterosexuality inevitably includes the possibility of unwanted pregnancies. The British Population Census figures (see Riddick, 1993) indicated that since 1970, 72,000 Irish women have travelled to Britain for abortions (Mahon and Conlon, 1996). Obviously, abortion is not an issue which arises solely in the case of young single women. The available statistics on the proportion of those having abortions who were single are not clear (Fahey, 1993: 120), although it has been suggested that roughly three quarters of those who had abortions in 1992 were single (Mahon and Conlon, 1996). Just over two thirds of the single people in Noonan's (1993) national sample aged 17-49 years were sexually active, with over half reporting having sex at least once a month. This was considerably higher than the trends emerging in Wiley and Merriman's (1996) study. If we accept Noonan's figures, it is possible to estimate that 600-650 out of every 1,000 single women were sexually active, with approximately 500 having sex at least once a month. Fahey (1993) estimated that there was one recorded abortion in Britain on a woman from Ireland for every two non-marital births here. This suggests that there were approximately 33 non-marital conceptions per 1,000 women, in a context where there was a birth rate of 22.8 per 1,000 single women in 1991 (McCashin, 1993).

It is estimated that ten women in a thousand will become pregnant annually using reliable methods of contraception such as the combined pill and the progesterone-only pill (IFPA, 1994). And this is with careful use. With less careful use, it has been estimated that 30-40 per 1,000 women will become pregnant. These methods of contraception are the most popular ones among single women (Wiley and Merriman, 1996; Noonan, 1993). The range is greater in the case of other methods, e.g. 20-150 where the male partner uses condoms and 20-200 per 1,000 where 'natural' methods are used. Given the levels of sexual activity among single women, the levels of conception are not incompatible with known levels of failure in contraceptives. Indeed there was indirect evidence for the significance of such contraceptive failure insofar as just under half of those who sought abortion, became pregnant at that time because of contraceptive failure (Dean, 1984).

Of course not all women use contraception all the time. The IFPA Report (1994) showed that within a context where two thirds of its respondents were single, and just under half were under 25 years old, approximately one fifth of the first visits which involved a medical consultation were for the 'morning after' pill. Hyde (1996a, 1996b) also showed that among her sample of young Irish women, there was a feeling of invulnerability to pregnancy; an acceptance of the idea that intercourse should be open to the possibility of conception; that 'being prepared', in terms of carrying condoms, was 'loose' and cast aspersions on their respectability – all of which created a context where the use of contraception was problematic. Furthermore, what evidence we have suggests that access to family planning services is uneven nationwide (Wiley and Merriman, 1996). In this context there is considerable pressure on young women to be heterosexually active but little acceptance of the need to locate conception in the wider context of social responsibility. Such a context Porter suggested would take on board the idea that 'firstly, moral societies have a responsibility to cope humanely in crisis situations and secondly, they have a responsibility to care for society's carers' (1996:294). Porter suggested that such a context was only likely to emerge when the reality and complexity of individual women's reactions were addressed. Fletcher in one of the very few attempts to do this highlighted the subtlety and complexity of such feelings and suggested that:

> Irish society's negative view of abortion, which has developed without listening to women's words, now inhibits Irish women from voicing their experiences of abortion (1995:63).

Conlon's work (1994a, 1994b) focused on those who attended the Irish Family Planning Association's pregnancy counselling service. The majority (70 per cent) were single and half were under 24 years of age (but only around one fifth of the total sample were aged 19 years or less). Almost three quarters of them had partners whom they had told about their pregnancy, and almost four fifths of these were supportive. Nevertheless almost one third of those who attended for pregnancy counselling had told no one. Approximately half of the total sample had no previous pregnancy. Where information was available, the total cost of the abortion in the majority of cases was £350-£600 in 1992-93 figures. This publicly stigmatised and secret route was most likely to be taken by young women who could raise such funds.

There is some evidence to suggest that the overwhelming majority of women who go to Britain for abortions do not consult with any medical professional, either their own GP or at a pregnancy advice agency (Dept. of Health, 1995). They rely on friends, family, acquaintances and magazines for their information and make the arrangements themselves. We have very little information about such women or their experiences.

Equally we do not know what young Irish women think about marriage. Lees (1993) and Wallace (1987a and b) found that among the girls they studied in Britain, deferral of marriage was one way of dealing with the tension implicit in their perception of it as an institutional arrangement where they were unequal and subordinate. They were aware of the power relationships within marriage and were adamant that they would not put up with 'being bossed around'. They assumed that they would marry but they wanted to put it off for a while – to have 'a bit of a life', a level of independence and freedom. They were aware of the romantic happy-ever-after image of marriage and were critical of it. In their own day-to-day experience they saw the amount of housework and child care that it was 'normal' for married women to do. They did not accept that this was a woman's role within marriage and yet they saw that this was the way things were. Interestingly, they saw marriage as the legitimate place for the expression of female sexuality. Marriage was an appropriate validation of their identity as 'good' women and the inevitable pinnacle of what they could hope for in life. They resolved the tension by hoping to put off marriage until, as they said, they had 'had their lives'. At this point in time, we do not have the qualitative evidence, but it is possible that the attitudes of young women in Ireland to marriage may be similar to those in these studies.

Friendships with other young women potentially provide a way of managing the tensions surrounding heterosexuality:

> Talking for girls and women is not relaxation, but managing contradictions and its centrality to girls' activity is no surprise. They see talking as positive, sorting out problems with friends, establishing their own space and time, but it is always overdetermined by boys (McCabe, 1981:12).

What evidence there is internationally strongly suggests that female friendships are highly beneficial in psychological terms and are seen as providing high levels of intimacy and acceptance (Rose, 1985; Caldwell and Peplau, 1982, O'Connor 1992c). Griffin's (1985) qualitative work on working-class young women in Britain vividly highlighted the strength and reality of their friendships:

> These best friendships were typified by young women going everywhere together, walking along arm-in-arm, wearing exactly the same clothes, shoes, hairstyles, even jewellery (Griffin, 1985: 61).

Griffin's work clearly showed that these friendships were long term and embedded in a network of other friendships (in contrast to the typical focus on dyadic best friends among young women; see O'Connor 1992c). Furthermore she found that they were a source of resistance to the established structures, whether this was the teacher's authority in the school or the male culture in the engineering industry. 'Resistance' was reflected and reinforced in their depiction of themselves as a group with its own culture and lifestyle, and captured in the phrase 'us girls together'. Indeed it can be suggested that for young women in Ireland such friendships provide one of the few positive sources of validation of their identity as gendered young women. The National Youth Council study (1998) showed that friends were mentioned by half of the young women in that study as the first place they would seek support if they had a serious emotional problem. We know almost nothing about such relationships however, although Lynch's (1989a) work has drawn attention to the scarcity of time young people have to create any 'solidary relationships'.

Friendships are typically rooted in similar identities and lifestyles. In this respect friendships between young women are vulnerable to change as they move from school to college; from their own home area to a bigger town or city; from singleness to coupleness. Very little attempt has been made to spell out the factors which facilitate or constrain the development of such friendships, e.g. money, transport, the availability of 'similar' others, cultural attitudes which make it easy and worthwhile for women to spend time with other women, and a network through which new contacts can be made (O'Connor, 1992c and 1998). We do not know to what extent, if at all, such friendships are affected by the perceived sexualisation of all relationships which is seen as characteristic of Western society today (Faderman, 1981).

It is obvious that we know relatively little about how young women deal with the tensions surrounding heterosexuality in Irish society. In particular it is unclear to what extent the shape of their lives is dictated by the need to be seen to have a sexual relationship with a man, within a society where the attitude to contraception appears to be ambivalent but where abortion is highly stigmatised. Nor indeed is it clear whether tensions surrounding heterosexuality are managed through friendship and talk with other young women.

Young women's attitudes to the wider institutional structures

In looking at the attitudes of young people, it is difficult to say to what extent one is looking at a cohort or life stage phenomenon. Steinem (1993) has been among those who have suggested that older women, because of their experiences with men, are likely to be more radical than young women. Lees has suggested that feminism can appear threatening to young women who are trying to forge their identity in a society where being a woman is clearly associated with being subordinate to men. Feminists in this situation may sometimes be seen as 'extreme, though what they really mean is that they conflict with conventional subordination' (1993: 294).

The 1990 European Values study does provide some insights into the attitudes of young Irish women to specific areas. Just over one third of those aged 18-29 years in that study disapproved of a woman who wanted to have a child as a single parent when she did not have a stable relationship with a man, as compared with approximately two thirds of all Irish women (Whelan and Fahey, 1994c). Similarly only 12 per cent of those aged 18-29 years agreed that 'men had more of a right to a job than women when jobs are scarce', as compared with 35 per cent of Irish women and 31 per cent of European women (Whelan, 1994c). This can be regarded as not unrelated to the impact of the women's movement and other social changes, the overall trends being very similar across Europe.

The attitudes of young Irish women to a mother's participation in paid employment were not very much different from that of other Irish women. More than three quarters of those aged 18-29 years thought that a working mother 'could establish just as warm and secure a relationship with her children as a mother who does not work' as compared with around two thirds of all Irish women. The young people's views were similar to those of married women in paid employment (79 per cent of women in paid employment, 56 per cent of women in 'home duties', and 59 per cent of the men in the study endorsing these views: Whelan and Fahey, 1994:56). Less than two in five of the 18-29 year olds agreed that 'a pre-school child is likely to suffer if his or her mother works' as compared with 46 per cent of Irish women overall (and just over one third of those in paid employment and 58 per cent of those in 'home duties').

Whelan and Fahey noted that even among the youngest age groups, men were almost twice as likely as women to think that pre-school child would suffer if her mother worked and that it was more difficult for a mother who was in paid employment to achieve a warm and secure relationship with her children (1994: 57). These trends were also obvious in Fine-Davis's studies (1983 and 1988).

Young people in their study were different, but not dramatically so, from the rest of the population in the area of religious practice. In the MRBI (1998) study, 38 per cent of Catholics aged 18-24 years attended mass weekly or more often, as compared with 58 per cent of all Catholics. Levels of participation were higher in the European Values Study amongst both, with 71 per cent of those aged 18-26 years old attending mass weekly or more often, as compared with 81 per cent of the total population (Hornsby-Smith and Whelan, 1994). In that study young people differed little from the rest of the population, but were different to their European counterparts, in terms of a belief in God; life after death; a soul; and the existence of heaven and sin (1994:33).

Fine-Davis (1988) showed that young people were more likely to have positive attitudes to divorce; they felt that children suffered greater psychological damage by living with two parents who were in constant conflict than by living with one divorced parent in a stable home. Younger people were also more likely to see divorce as a way of society showing compassion for those suffering from marital breakdown, and as a way of protecting minority rights and facilitating reconciliation with Northern Ireland (Fine-Davis, 1988). Interestingly, they were less likely than their older counterparts to focus on the social and economic effects of divorce on the wife. Younger respondents were somewhat more likely than older respondents to approve of abortion when the mother's health was threatened by pregnancy (Whelan and Fahey, 1994; Fine-Davis, 1988). However, the attitudes of all age groups grew more positive between the 1981 survey and the 1990s so that one is dealing with both a change over time as well as with a youth effect.

Whelan and Fahey (1994) showed that, as one might expect, the younger age group were more in favour of complete sexual freedom, with roughly one third of them in 1990 (as indeed in 1981) being in favour of this, as compared with 17 per cent of the Irish population as a whole. However, there was some suggestion that views about permissive sexual conduct were not maintained as they aged (Whelan and Fahey, 1994). Furthermore, even among the under-35 year olds, radical attitudes (e.g. the idea that marriage is an outdated institution) were still only characteristic of a very small minority (15 per cent) and it was the under-35 year old urban men in manual occupations who were most likely to express such attitudes (Whelan and Fahey, 1994: 75).

Interestingly, and compatible with the high status of the family in Ireland as an area for women's activity, just over half of those aged 18-29 years felt that 'being a housewife is just as fulfilling as working for pay', as compared with almost three quarters of the women overall (Whelan and Fahey, 1994). Even among those women with at least Leaving Certificate and aged 18-29 years, more than half still felt that being a housewife was just as fulfilling as working for pay (See Table 11, Whelan and Fahey, 1994). Indeed just over four out of ten of these young people (18-29 years) agreed that 'a job is all right but what most women really want is a home and children'. Their views were in fact broadly similar to those among married women who were in paid employment, although differing from those of the housewives (44 per cent of the 18-29 year olds as compared to 66 per cent of the housewives agreeing with that view).

When Hannan *et al* (1996) asked Leaving Certificate students to choose from five alternative arrangements as regards combining paid work and family in their own and a spouse's life, the two most popular were (i) that they would work part-time and their spouse would work full-time (chosen by 37 per cent of Leaving Certificate girls) and (ii) that they would work full-time and pay someone to mind the children (chosen by 53 per cent of Leaving Certificate girls). Thus it is clear that the majority envisaged continuing paid work, whether on a full-time or part-time basis.

We do not know to what extent young women see themselves as having separate and/or different interests from young men. Indeed it would perhaps be surprising if they thought of themselves in this way since so much of their experience is in institutions which purport to be gender neutral. However, a National Youth Council Survey (1998) of young people aged 15-24 years found that just under one third of the young women (32 per cent) and more than half of the young men (52 per cent) felt that equal opportunities existed. What limited evidence is available suggests that their attitudes differ relatively little from those of other women, especially women in paid employment. They have positive attitudes to married women's participation in paid employment, and for the most part do not see such participation as making it difficult for a woman to establish a warm and secure relationship with a child, or as negatively affecting a pre-school child. Nevertheless half of them see being a housewife as just as fulfilling as paid employment. Indeed it may well be that they have absorbed the idea that a family setting offers greater possibilities as regards power and/or self expression than they can expect within the world of paid employment. However, they expect to be in such employment, whether on a full-time or part-time basis.

Summary

The evidence in this chapter is uneven and to varying degrees incomplete. However, it has suggested that young Irish women are growing up in a society which has ambivalent and inconsistent attitudes to them as young women. On the one hand, in the educational and occupational areas, they are ostensibly treated as just other young people. On the other hand, gender is very much a reality in these situations. It is reflected in the very different ethos of girls' and boys' schools. It is also reflected in the very different kinds of occupations held by young men and young women and the different wages they receive. Young women are attractive to the market, not least because of their cheapness, although unions act to some extent as a check on the gender gap in wages. Yet girls outperform boys in the educational system and they are disproportionately represented in the professional and service sectors.

In training schemes and in organisations within the wider community there was evidence to suggest that the priorities of these structures were boys, particularly middle-class boys, and that the state colluded with such prioritising. It is difficult to avoid the feeling that in such organisations, middle-class girls were catered for only insofar as they became 'token' middle-class males, adopting and hence implicitly validating those activities which were of particular interest to young middle-class men. Nevertheless according to a survey conducted by the National Youth Council of Ireland, young women were very much under-represented in positions of authority in such organisations. Within a society where women's lack of occupancy of positions of authority within the public arena has been attributed to their marital status and family responsibilities, these patterns are provocative. Yet there is no evidence to suggest that these young women, who are by far the most highly educated cohort, have come to terms with the gendered reality in such organisations.

For many young women, sexuality is arguably a key element in their identity. Indeed one might suggest that there is now considerable pressure on young people to be sexually active as a way of validating that identity. We do not know to what extent young Irish women's sexuality is controlled at a symbolic level in a similar way to that which was described by Lees (1993), i.e. by negative labelling of active sexuality, and by the legitimatisation of sexual activity in a steady relationship with one boyfriend. However, what evidence there is does suggest that sexual harassment is a reality in the lives of a sizeable minority of second level schoolgirls.

It is arguable that tensions are generated within young women by the failure of the institutional structures to deal positively with their reality as young women. In this situation, 'talk' and friendship relationships between young women potentially play an important part in managing these contradictions. We know virtually nothing about these relationships. Indeed, it is true to say that we know very little about the experience of being a young woman in a society where structures are typically created by and for men.

7

Women and Paid Employment: Facing up to the Issues

Introduction

THE dramatic increase in the participation of married women, particularly young married women, in paid employment is one of the most striking changes to have occurred in Irish society over the past twenty-five years. Within a context where the service sector is the main and expanding area of employment, and where jobs are gendered, women are attractive to the market. In Ireland and across the rest of the EU, women account for most of the recent increase in employment. We do not know to what extent the sheer numerical presence of women in the labour force has changed the nature of that place; women's relationships with each other; their definitions of themselves or their relationships with men. However, the feminisation of the labour force, potentially at least, creates a tension between a patriarchal ethos which is comfortable with women being financially dependent on a male breadwinner and a capitalist economy which is interested in recruiting cheap labour. The extent of this tension can be exaggerated given the tendency for the majority of these women to be employed in low paid, 'dead-end', predominantly female occupations.

This chapter will firstly briefly describe the changes in the labour force, including the feminisation phenomenon. Secondly, it will explore the extent to which women are engaged in part-time employment within a context where paid work is still based on the male as the norm, despite the increasing feminisation of the labour force. It will be shown that the majority of young Irish married women have adjusted to the (male) model, and in stark contrast to their British counterparts, they overwhelmingly work full time. Thirdly, the chapter will look briefly at the issue of pay. Implicit in many of the discussions about women's employment lies the assumption that flexible, (low-paid) work is what women 'want', since this is most compatible with their family

188

responsibilities. It is difficult to envisage a situation where women's preferences would be for low-paid employment. It is however easy to see that women's disproportionate allocation to such work is very much in men's interests. The question as to whether such arrangements are what men 'want' is usually not asked.

Fourthly, the chapter will look at the extent to which women are clustered into a small range of predominantly female occupations. It will also include a series of brief case studies of different kinds of low paid/low status work, so as to suggest the kinds of processes through which the position of women employed in such work is maintained. Fifthly, some of the factors which have been put forward to explain the dramatic increase in the participation of married women in paid employment will be briefly discussed, focusing particularly on children, education, individual choice and attitudes to such participation.

As outlined in Chapter 2, up to the 1970s the participation of Irish married women in paid employment was extremely low. Increases in such participation have occurred despite, rather than because of, any encouragement by the institutional church or the state. Although belatedly encouraging the service sector, state policies regarding taxation, child care, etc. have for the most part continued to effectively inhibit the participation of married women in paid employment. Nevertheless it has increased dramatically. Unsupported by the state, women, particularly young married women, have made their own arrangements as regards child care, and reconciled paid work and family as best they can. We know very little indeed about how they do it, or what implications this has in relation to the shape of these worlds.

The existence of opportunities for paid employment has offered women choices, but in many cases these have been highly constrained. The kinds of jobs that are available to many of them are poorly paid and characterised by low possibilities as regards promotion. Thus, the 'solution' at an individual woman's level (i.e. paid employment) reflects and reinforces the overall problem, viz. a highly gendered system of paid employment where wages, benefits and other privileges are disproportionately obtained by those who 'fit' best within the system – men, particularly well-educated men.

The labour force: its measurement and composition

In this section we will look briefly at methodological difficulties and describe the main patterns in women's participation, focusing particularly on the feminisation of the labour force.

There are methodological difficulties involved in measuring women's participation in paid employment. Firstly, as Fahey (1990, 1993) suggested, the apparent increase in the participation of Irish married women in paid employment might reflect a changing balance between agricultural and non-agricultural sectors; and in particular it might reflect married women's movement from unpaid and invisible agricultural work to visible paid work. We have no way of knowing the extent to which this is so.

Secondly, prior to 1991 the practice in both the Census and Labour Force Surveys was to use the respondents' own description of their principal economic status (Fahey, 1990). This is still the only measure available in the case of some variables. Using this measure the proportion of women who were economically active rose from just over 27 per cent in 1971 to just under 38 per cent in 1996 (O'Connor and Shortall, 1998). Inevitably perhaps, within a society where women are defined in terms of family identities, women who were in part-time paid employment or working in the family business returned their main occupation as 'housewife', thereby under-estimating women's level of paid employment, and indeed also their level of unemployment. The ILO measure on the other hand takes into account whether or not the respondents have worked for at least one hour for payment or profit (including work on the family farm or business) in the past week. The use of this measure as opposed to principal economic status increases the proportion of those who were economically active in 1996 to 41 per cent. Using the ILO measure in 1996 then, 576,200 women and 918,200 men were economically active, with 88 per cent of these women and men being in paid employment (Labour Force Survey, 1996 [CSO, 1997:53]). It is a more accurate, internationally comparable measure but is not available for the earlier years. Thus to compare the current Irish situation with that existing in 1971, it is necessary to use the principal economic status measure which underestimates women's economic activity.

With a small number of notable exceptions (e.g. Walsh, 1993; Fitzgerald and Hughes 1994; O'Connell, 1996; Smyth, 1997; CSO, 1997), until very recently little attention was paid to the feminisation of the labour market. Yet the patterns are very striking. Using principal economic status as a measure, the labour force participation rate of men had fallen steadily from 82 per cent in 1971 to 69 per cent in 1996. On the other hand, the labour force participation rate of women had risen steadily from 28 per cent in 1971 to just under 39 per cent in 1996, the most dramatic increases in the case of women being in the early 1990s.

References to Ireland as a 'Celtic tiger' are misleading (O'Connell, 1996) since 90 per cent of the increase in employment between 1971 and 1996 was in women's employment (CSO, 1997: see Table 7.1). Furthermore, these trends cannot be simply accounted for in terms of an increasing number registering as available for work since the actual numbers of women in (paid) work has risen steadily and consistently over the period (see Table 7.I).

TABLE 7.1

NUMBERS AT WORK, UNEMPLOYED AND LABOUR FORCE PARTICIPATION RATES BY GENDER 1971-1996 (ROUNDING Ns AND %s)

	At Work 000s	Unemployed 000s	Labour Force 000s	Labour Force Partic Rate (%)
Women				
1971	276	14	290	28%
1981	329	30	359	30%
1991	386	53	439	33%
1996	488	52	540	39%
Men				
1971	774	62	836	82%
1981	809	104	913	77%
1991	747	156	903	71%
1996	797	138	935	69%
TOTAL				
1971	1050	76	1126	55%
1981	1138	134	1272	53%
1991	1133	209	1342	52%
1996	1285	190	1475	54%

Derived from CSO 1997: Table 1

These trends are not peculiar to Ireland. They began in the 1970s and intensified in the 1980s right across Europe. Rubery and Fagan (1993:1) noted that, over the 1980s, 'women have taken up most of the new jobs created in the Community'. Between 1983 and 1989, two thirds of the jobs created in the European Community were filled by women. Throughout the 12 countries in the EU, women's average annual increase in employment was 1.8 per cent with a range of from 5.3 per cent to 8 per cent – the latter being in Ireland (Maruani, 1992:3). Indeed Maruani (1992) suggested that:

The feminisation of the working population, especially in white-collar jobs, is one of the most important social developments of the late twentieth century, and one that will leave its imprint on the ongoing construction of Europe (1992:1).

However, despite the increase in the participation of Irish women in the labour force, particularly married women, the proportion of Irish women in the labour force is still below the EU average, 41.1 per cent of Irish women aged 15 years and over being in the labour force, as compared with an EU average of 45.3 per cent (Eurostat, 1997).

Marauni (1992) argued that women's increased levels of economic activity across Europe reflected the fact that the demand for labour occurred in areas which were already characterised by high concentrations of women:

the continuation of this concentration is an indicator of persistent segregation at the same time as it helps explain the growth in female employment (Maruani, 1992: 12).

In 1995, right across the EU, the main area of employment, and of employment growth, was in services; 65 per cent of all EU employment being in this sector, compared with 60 per cent in Ireland (Eurostat, 1996:4). Just under 80 per cent of women across the EU (and in Ireland) were in the service sector. In Ireland, up to the late 1980s, the state effectively disregarded the service sector. Nevertheless it has continued to grow. Indeed over 87 per cent of the increase in women's employment over the 1971-96 period was in that sector (CSO, 1997). To have any real picture of women's experiences in paid employment, it is necessary to focus on that sector. In fact little research attention has as yet been paid to it, even at the basic level of mapping wages and working conditions.

Maruani (1992) suggested that it made sense to think of women's participation in paid employment in terms of three models.

- a single left-hand peak indicating that participation in paid employment was mainly a characteristic of young women (aged 20-25 years) who were predominantly single, and who stopped working after marriage or childbirth

- a bimodal pattern indicating that women stopped working from 25-40 years in order to rear their children and then returned to paid employment when their children were 'off hand'

- an inverted U indicating continuous participation in paid employment throughout the life cycle, and being broadly similar to the male pattern.

In the early 1970s prior to the removal of the marriage bar in Ireland, Ireland would have been typical of the first pattern. In the early 1970s, 7.5 per cent of married women were in the labour force. The United Kingdom and the Netherlands would be seen as exemplifying the second pattern, with Denmark and the former GDR exemplifying the third pattern (Rubery *et al*, 1995). Now, however, in Ireland the picture has become more complex, with the older generations conforming to the first pattern, and the younger ones (as in e.g. Spain, Portugal), conforming to the third model.

Thus attempts to explain variation in the labour force in Ireland need to take into account the fact that it is inversely related to age, i.e. 37 per cent of Irish married women overall were in paid employment but 58 per cent of those aged 25-34 years were in this position (1996 Labour Force Survey [CSO, 1997], using the measure of principal economic status). The percentages were slightly higher when the ILO definition was used. In 1996, using this measure, 63 per cent of married women aged 25-34 years were in the labour force as compared with 52 per cent of those aged 35-44 years, 37 per cent of those aged 45-54 years, and 25 per cent of those aged 55-59 years (Labour Force Survey, 1996 [CSO, 1997:55]).

TABLE 7.2

WOMEN'S PARTICIPATION IN PAID EMPLOYMENT BY AGE GROUP AND
MARITAL STATUS (I.L.O. DEFINITION)

	15-19 years	20-24 years	25-34 years	35-44 years	45-54 years	55-59 years	60-64 years	65 years	Total
Single	18%	68%	85%	80%	73%	55%	36%	6%	50%
Married	26%	57%	63%	52%	37%	25%	14%	3%	41%
Separated	–	50%	59%	59%	57%	44%	24%	3%	53%
Widowed	–	–	48%	53%	41%	28%	16%	2%	9%
TOTAL	18%	67%	71%	56%	42%	29%	17%	3%	41%

Labour Force Survey 1996(1997):55 (rounding off %)

On average across the EU the unemployment rate for women is higher than that for men (Rubery *et al*, 1996). In Ireland, using principal economic status, the unemployment rate for women appeared to be much lower than men's in 1996. Women's unemployment rate was 9.7 per cent as compared with a male unemployment rate of 14.7 per cent. However, using the ILO measure, the unemployment rate for women and men was virtually identical, at around 12 per cent, the overall EU pattern being for women's unemployment rate to be higher than men's (both in EU 12 and 15; Rubery *et al*, 1996; Fig 2).

Part-time employment

In Ireland, approximately four fifths of women who are in paid employment are in full-time employment. This is somewhat higher than the EU average (72 per cent: Rapid Reports, 1993:9). Even using the ILO's broad definition of paid employment (Labour Force Survey, 1996 [CSO, 1997]), just over 22 per cent of the 508,000 women who were in paid employment in 1996 were in part-time employment (CSO, 1997:2). Maruani (1992) noted that part-time employment was generally characteristic of Northern Europe, with part-time work being particularly common in the UK and the Netherlands, and being very much less common in Southern European countries such as Greece or Spain. In 1994, part-time work made up 11 per cent of the total share of employment in Ireland, as compared with 5 per cent in Greece, 7 per cent in Spain, 24 per cent in the UK and 36 per cent in the Netherlands (the EU average across 15 countries being 15 per cent: NESF, 1996).

Overall, however, in Ireland its share of total employment almost doubled between 1985 and 1994 (from 6 per cent in 1985 to just under 11 per cent in 1994: NESF, 1996). It decreased slightly between 1995 and 1996, but overall increased by 56,900 between 1991 and 1995 (Labour Force Survey, 1996 [CSO, 1997]). Although the trend is towards an increase in part-time paid work, the. pattern is less developed here than in other North European countries. Connell *et al* (1996b) noted that virtually all of the increase in part-time employment occurred in the service sector. It is difficult to know to what extent the reliance on part-time workers in this sector reflects weak unionisation or the nature of the sector.

The Irish Labour Force Survey 1996 (1997) showed that just under three quarters (73 per cent) of those who were in part-time employment were women, and the majority of these were married and aged 25-44 years. This pattern is typical of other European countries. It also showed that the majority of these part-time jobs were regular rather than occasional and thus can arguably be seen as part of a restructuring of the labour force. Only one group of men seemed to be more likely than women to be in part-time work, viz. young men. A third of the men but only 15 per cent of the women undertaking part-time work were under 25 years.

Barry and Jackson (1988) are very critical of the depiction of part-time work as meeting the needs of married women across Europe without referring to the fact that part-time paid employment was particularly popular in the Netherlands where hourly earnings for part timers were the same as for those working full time. In many countries part-time paid employment for women can be seen as compatible with the needs of the market for a flexible cheap labour force. It can be simplistically presented as reflecting an adjustment between (women's) family demands and economic responsibilities. However, the three EU countries (including Ireland) with the lowest level of publicly funded child care have very different proportions of women in part-time employment. Furthermore there is evidence that the presence of dependent children was not universally associated with high levels of part-time employment among women (O'Connor and Shortall, 1998; Bulletin on Women and Employment, 1994).

At a more general level, implicit in the idea of the compatibility of a 'handy' little job with women's domestic and family responsibilities is the idea that such work is less stressful than more career oriented types of employment. Such assumptions are highly questionable. In Fine-Davis's (1983) study, women in different kinds of settings, e.g. offices, factories, shops, reported that they experienced stress from having to do the same work over and over again, having a high degree of responsibility for people, etc. Such features are likely to characterise what is typically known as 'women's employment'. Furthermore, working conditions, including holiday times and rates of pay, are considerably less satisfactory for lower paid, lower status workers than for their more highly paid counterparts.

Pay

There are considerable difficulties involved in looking at pay levels. Barry (1996) noted that although there was no comprehensive data on pay in Ireland, a variety of studies had shown that women were one of the groups who were particularly vulnerable to low pay. It has also been shown that although the likelihood of being low paid was affected by gender, it also reflected the incidence of low pay in a particular country (which in turn partly reflected the absence of minimum wage levels), and the sector and organisation in which the employee worked.

The highest incidence of low pay occurred in Ireland, the UK and Spain and the first two of these had partial minimum wage levels or none at all (Bulletin on Women in Employment, 1994: Table 3; Barry, 1996). Because women are concentrated at the bottom of the pay hierarchy, the more dispersed the rates of pay are, the more likely they are to penalise women. Centralised and integrated collective bargaining systems in which women were involved were seen as key in reducing women's disproportionate representation among the low paid (Bulletin on Women and Employment in the EU, October 1994).

In Ireland and in Britain there is a selective wage minimum system but this covers only approximately 10 per cent of the labour force. Barry noted that the collective bargaining system with its focus on pay differentials did little to improve the position of the low paid. The situation was compounded by women's over-representation in particular sectors, e.g. the retail sector; hotels, catering etc., many of which were not covered by collective bargaining.

The Report of the Second Commission on the Status of Women (1993) noted that ICTU research found that low pay in Ireland was most common in areas of traditional female employment, e.g. in textile, clothing, footwear, cleaning and at the lower levels of the civil service. It also estimated (1993:104) that approximately 90,000 women in full-time employment were low paid, with a further 40,000 of those who were in part-time employment being identified as low paid. This calculation was based on Nolan's (1991) work. He found that 24 per cent of all employees were low paid, and that women made up 62 per cent of those in this position. In a situation where women made up 23 per cent of full-time employees but 56 per cent of those full-time employees with low pay (Nolan, 1991) there are issues around the type of work which is seen as appropriate for women and the level of payment for such work (Second Commission on the Status of Women, 1993:102). Furthermore, since age did not improve the prospects of women who were on low pay, there are issues around women's occupancy of jobs which have no promotional prospects.

These patterns are not peculiar to Ireland. Women were equally or over-represented among the full-time low paid workers in every member state in the EU (see Table 7.3). These figures underestimate the real extent of low pay among women since they typically exclude two groups, part-time workers and workers in the informal economy, both of whom are particularly likely to be women, and particularly likely to be low paid.

In Ireland, there are difficulties in comparing men's and women's wages since the only data which is systematically collected focuses on industrial workers in manufacturing industries, and women are predominantly employed in the service sector. The average hourly rate for women industrial workers in the manufacturing area in Ireland has remained substantially lower than the male rate. In 1971 it was 56 per cent of that received by men and by 1996, it was 74 per cent, the differences in weekly earnings being even greater, viz. 48 per cent and 65 per cent respectively (CSO, 1997:2). To a considerable extent the difference in hourly earnings reflects the fact that women in the manufacturing area are grouped into a small number of industries where male comparators are limited and where 'women's work' is less highly valued.

TABLE 7.3

THE PERCENTAGE OF LOW PAID FULL-TIME WORKERS WHO ARE FEMALE
IN THE EUROPEAN UNION

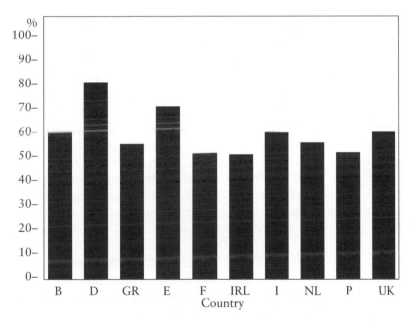

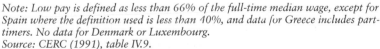

Note: *Low pay is defined as less than 66% of the full-time median wage, except for Spain where the definition used is less than 40%, and data for Greece includes part-timers. No data for Denmark or Luxembourg.*
Source: *CERC (1991), table IV.9.*

It is widely recognised then that, overall, women's low pay is related to their concentration in occupational groups which are predominantly female, defined as low skilled and poorly paid. Treiman and Hartmann (1981) in a wide ranging review found that, overwhelmingly, studies showed that the crucial factor was job segregation by sex, i.e. the more feminised an occupation was, the more likely it was to be poorly paid.

This has implications as regards women's wages across all occupations because of the fact that women are overwhelmingly concentrated into areas of predominantly female employment. In these occupations the absence of male comparators means that pay rates are not subject to equal pay legislation (Rubery and Fagan, 1993:2; EOC, 1996; Smyth, 1996).

Callan and Wren (1994) found in their study that women's hourly earnings across all kinds of paid employment was 80 per cent of men's, half of that difference being explained by what they called 'productivity related characteristics', mostly labour market experience. There was an 'unexplained' difference of approximately 10 per cent in hourly earnings which could not be accounted for by specific attributes such as length of labour market experience, educational level, etc. It is not impossible that this might reflect the existence of a 'gender bonus' for maleness.

What evidence is available suggests that, in various occupations, men tend to have better contracts and working conditions (Breathnach, 1992). A number of studies have also suggested that women's educational levels need to be higher in order to 'compensate' for their gender. For example Callan and Wren (1994:45) noted that 'non married females would be expected to earn higher wages than their male counterparts . . . [since] they tend on average to have higher qualifications'. Since they do not earn such higher salaries, 'discrimination could still be a problem in the younger age groups'. In other studies such as Ruane and Dobson's (1990) study of academics and Garavan's (1994) study of bank managers, there was also evidence of a differential pay-off for educational qualifications among men and women. Similarly, Maruani's (1992:20) examination of women in the labour market across Europe led her to conclude that 'in many cases, women are more qualified than the positions that they fill require', thereby suggesting that they were being paid less than their male counterparts with similar educational credentials.

As noted in Chapter 2, this raises issues about the relative value of men and women, and the valuation of 'male' and 'female' work within what is still a highly segregated labour market. This is a fundamental issue in closing the wage gap between men and women. Despite some attempt at EU level to encourage countries to look at this issue, it has been virtually ignored in Ireland.

What kinds of paid employment do women have?

It has been noted that throughout the EU women are concentrated into a small number of areas such as domestic services, health, footwear and clothing, education and the retail trade (Employment in Europe, 1996). The Labour Force Survey (1996) showed that more than four fifths of the women who were in paid employment, as indicated by their principal economic status, were either clerical workers, professional and technical workers, service workers or workers in commerce, insurance and finance. Thus 25.7 per cent of the women in paid employment were clerical workers, 25.7 per cent were professional and technical workers, 17.6 per cent were service workers and 14 per cent were commerce, insurance or finance workers. This pattern is surprisingly similar to that found in Belgium and the Netherlands (Rubery and Fagan, 1993).

It has also been noted that women tend to work mainly with other women (Rubery and Fagan, 1993:2). The Labour Force Survey, 1996 (CSO, 1997:13) showed that clerical, service and professional and technical occupations were feminised occupational groups in the sense that more than half of those employed in them were women. The most feminised was clerical work, with 77 per cent of clerical workers being women. Contrary to what one might expect, 53 per cent of those in professional and technical occupations were women. Indeed using the Labour Force Survey's sectional categories (Table 14), 65 per cent of those in the professional services sector and 62 per cent of those in the personal services sector were women. Rubery and Fagan (1993:9) suggest that these trends are typical of those in the more northern European countries. It is clear then that not all women's work is low paid (see Chapter 8).

We will look more closely at a small number of in-depth studies so as to get some insight into the processes through which the position of women in low paid employment is perpetuated. Within the machinery of the state itself (i.e. the civil service) the existence of a strata of 'unpromotable women' (Crompton and Jones, 1984:248) is a crucial element in facilitating the existence of men's career paths within the service. The lack of male comparators in these areas, and indeed also in manufacturing, has limited the effectiveness of equality legislation. This sort of structure was virtually institutionalised in the civil service until comparatively recently since women were traditionally recruited as clerk typists to the clerical assistant grade, whereas men (without typing) typically began at the clerical officer grade. Daly's (1985) work highlights a very different sort of process, viz. women's effective collusion with low paid exploitative work, partly because of their economic need for this work, and partly because they did not perceive it in employer/employee terms.

Clerical work

As previously mentioned, approximately a quarter of the women in paid employment in Ireland were classified, on the basis of their principal occupational status, as being clerical workers and this is a highly feminised occupation. Rubery and Fagan (1993:6) noted that clerical work seems to become such a feminised occupation with economic development, and that in the 1980s it was an important source of job growth and particularly female job growth across the EU as a whole. In Ireland, it was particularly important as a source of total female employment growth in the late 1980s – and this is likely to continue (Fitzgerald and Hughes, 1994).

Nevertheless we know relatively little about clerical work. Mahon's work (1991a) provides an insight into the experiences of women in the lowest grades in the civil service, viz. clerical assistant and clerical officer. These were included among the low paid (Blackwell, 1989). They were, and indeed still are, predominantly female occupations, with women constituting 82 per cent of those at clerical assistant level, and 79 per cent of those at clerical officer level in 1995 (Co-ordinating Group of Secretaries, 1996). Typically, people in these grades have little possibility of promotion; minimum opportunity for on-the-job training; few fringe benefits and little possibility of an increase in their earnings. Of the women in these grades interviewed in Mahon's study, three quarters had not been promoted since they joined the civil service and more than half of them had been there for between twelve and nineteen years. Where there were internal competitions, the chances of promotion were limited and were largely allocated on the basis of a system in which school leavers and those actually in posts competed in an examination system. This inevitably favoured school leavers.

The overwhelming majority (91 per cent) of the women in Mahon's study had children under eight years of age. Nevertheless, despite these family responsibilities and the unhelpful nature of their career structure, 61 per cent were interested in promotion. Mahon described them as 'an under class in the system'. She suggested that they continued in these occupations partly because of financial necessity and partly because of the lack of alternative equally secure employment. However, she also found that in her study half of those who were at this level said that they enjoyed the intrinsic aspects of their jobs. Not too surprisingly perhaps in view of the low level of pay, short holidays and a dependence on mothers and mothers-in-law for free child care, such posts traditionally have had a high level of turnover. It is not clear what the impact of an increasing reliance on two wages to cover mortgage costs has had on this turnover.

It is interesting to note that even in O'Broin and Farren's (1978) study of civil service typists in 1972 the majority of the typists perceived the promotional system in itself as unfair and saw few promotional outlets. The majority of these women, who were interviewed before the marriage bar was lifted in 1973, were under twenty-five years of age. At that time Geary and Ó Muircheartaigh (1974), on examining the issue of equalisation of opportunity in Ireland, noted that 'on average, men have by far the better jobs, whether "better" be adjudged by pay or by skill required to practise, or both', even though they also pointed out that the women were better educated. Interestingly however they go on to note:

> it remains to be seen if this situation is unfair to women . . . in an unemployment situation it may be judged expedient to sacrifice efficiency in the interest of what is judged a more equitable distribution of paid jobs.

The clear implication is that the allocation of paid work to men is 'equitable', even when this involves the 'sacrifice of efficiency'. It is difficult not to see this as a defence of male privilege. Twenty-five years later the restructuring of the lower grades in the civil service and in particular the abolition of the grade of clerical assistant and its fusion with the next grade, viz. clerical officer, is the first structural attempt to deal with this problem.

Service work

The services area encompasses a variety of occupations including, for example, those in the catering area (cooks, waiters, bar tenders etc.) as well as hairdressers, beauticians, launderers, maids, cleaners, caretakers. In Ireland, this occupational group is highly feminised and in the 1983-90 period, service work was the second most important area of female employment growth in Ireland (Fitzgerald and Hughes, 1994). The pattern emerging in this area is similar to that in Spain and France (see Rubery and Fagan, 1993). The whole service area has the highest proportion of part-time jobs, with 21 per cent of those employed in this area being involved on this basis (Corcoran *et al*, 1993:43). There is a gender difference however insofar as just over 27 per cent of the women were involved in this sector work on a part-time basis, as compared with 6 per cent of the men. In Ireland, we have comparatively little detailed knowledge of women's employment in this area, with the exception of catering (Breathnach, 1992) and cleaning (Daly, 1985).

Rubery and Fagan (1993) showed that women made up the majority of those employed in the catering area across the EU as a whole. They noted that within the catering area, various jobs were predominantly female and others predominantly male, but that these differed between different countries. They also noted that across Europe men were more likely to be qualified cooks, and to work in high class restaurants and hotels, and women were more likely to be found in small businesses, fast food and institutional catering, and were more likely to be asked to combine cooking with other tasks.

In Ireland women now make up 55 per cent of catering trainees (Rubery and Fagan, 1993:103). The catering area has become increasingly important in Ireland in the context of tourism, which over the 1985-1990 period contributed 37 per cent of the net employment growth in the economy, with an investment of £625 million, half of it from the EU. Interestingly, with a few notable exceptions (e.g. Breathnach, 1992), very little attention has been paid to the female/male breakdown of these jobs. Breathnach (1992), drawing on detailed surveys carried out by the Council for Education, Recruitment and Training, found that women made up 54 per cent of the 57,000 people who were directly engaged in providing tourism services, and that if one excluded what he called the male intensive transport sector (mainly concerned with bringing tourists into the country) women made up 60 per cent of those in tourism employment. This led him to conclude that tourism 'was an atypical sector in the Irish economy, in that is characterised by a predominantly female labour force'.

Breathnach (1992) showed that as one might perhaps expect, even within the accommodation sector, and specifically within the hotel sector, women were less likely than men to have full-time permanent jobs. For example, they made up 59 per cent of full-time permanent employees, as compared with 88 per cent of part-time seasonal employees. This same pattern reappeared in what Breathnach called the 'miscellaneous' tourism sector including golf, craft centres, car hire, language centres and historic houses. It is perhaps worth noting that the two of these areas which have particularly benefited from lottery funding, viz. golf courses and car hire, are largely, according to Breathnach, areas of male employment.

Breathnach's (1992) work shows how even within areas of predominantly female employment, particular jobs become identified as male and female, and although the jobs vary cross-culturally, those which are seen as 'women's work' typically have poorer pay and working conditions. Furthermore there is some suggestion that the state and the market ensure that within any service area the 'better' jobs are allocated to men.

Thus it is not surprising that women right across the EU have a high share of the cleaning jobs. Daly's study (1985) is one of the very few which has looked at the 'lived experiences' of a sample of women part-time cleaners in the mid-west area of Ireland, locating these within the context of an understanding of the structure of the cleaning industry. The picture she presented clearly underlined the informal nature of these women's relationship with the market. Only 6 per cent of them had a contract of employment, and the overwhelming majority even of these did not know its terms and conditions. Informal practices, which benefited the employer, were commonplace. For example, 60 per cent of the respondents said that in the event of a colleague missing work for a week, they would cover for her without pay. They implicitly accepted an 'unfair' relationship with an employer. The majority (80 per cent) believed that they should give a week's notice to their employer, but only half of that number felt that an employer should give an employee a week's notice and a similar proportion believed that an employer was not required to give any notice.

Three quarters of those working for a contract cleaning company (which constituted the majority of the respondents) had been recruited through relatives, neighbours and friends. Their relationship with the world of paid employment was mediated through an informal network. More than four fifths of them knew their co-workers before they joined the company. Work teams were organised in such a way as to make it difficult to have contact with colleagues on other sites. They saw the paid work area as very much an extension of their neighbourhood and family area. Daly noted that:

> These women's lack of consciousness of their disadvantage relative to other specific workgroups, and indeed the workforce in general, is striking. Failing to adopt an economistic approach to their work, they rarely compare inter-colleague workloads and terms of employment (1985:66).

On the one hand, their attitudes to their jobs were highly instrumental, with more than half of them using most of their wages for basic necessities such as rent, food and clothes; and more than half saying that they stayed in their present job because of the money. On the other hand, they had little awareness of their employment rights; and were largely unaware of the ways in which their labour could be exploited, or indeed little knowledge of the whole dynamics of employee/employer relationships. The level of union membership among these part-time cleaners (at 13 per cent) was very low.

Typically, part-time cleaning work is done by married women, and this was also typical of the trends emerging in Daly's (1985) work. Furthermore, Daly found that, in relation to the women in her study, participation in paid employment occurred in addition to their performance of household tasks. The majority always washed and cleaned, made the beds and paid the bills at home although the husbands of approximately half of those interviewed had some involvement in cooking meals, feeding and changing the baby, and shopping. Just over two thirds of the women said that their husbands helped at least 'a fair amount'. Despite the generally low level of household income and the use of the wife's income for basic necessities, only a quarter of the husbands approved strongly of it. Nevertheless, this level of low pay could be assimilated within a model of male economic power within the household. The major part of the household work still fell on the woman, a pattern which was reflected in and reinforced by the anti-social hours worked.

Daly perceptively noted that the attitudes her respondents brought to the workplace appeared to reflect their perception of themselves as housewives rather than paid workers. When they were asked what qualities were necessary to be a good cleaner, they overwhelmingly referred to personal qualities, such as personal cleanliness and capacity for hard work. Less than one in twenty even referred to the importance of experience. The aspects they saw as important in their job, apart from the pay, were: a nice supervisor or boss, good friendly workers and convenient hours. They had little awareness of their own value or their identity as paid employees.

Daly asked these women why most part-time cleaners were women. Nearly half of them said it was 'because men wouldn't do it'. Others said it was partly because of the low wages, and partly because men perceived it as women's work. Approximately a quarter noted that women's main responsibilities were in the domestic and family area, and thus they concluded that the hours suited women and also that women had no other choice of job. Daly noted that none of those interviewed saw that there might be a connection between gender and disadvantage in paid employment.

This study on part-time cleaners showed that women in the sector were very lowly paid; that only a tiny proportion of them had contracts of employment; that they implicitly accepted an unfair relationship with management; that they were generally not unionised, were unaware of their rights, isolated from workers on other sites, and bound together by informal ties with those in their own site. They saw themselves basically as housewives, and saw their skills as personal, indeed often female, characteristics. They effectively colluded with the devaluation of their work.

Manufacturing

The Labour Force Survey (1996) showed that only a minority of women were employed in manufacturing industries. Roughly one third of these were employed in the metals, metal products, mechanical, electrical and instrument engineering industries. Indeed this area, together with employment in the chemical, rubber and plastic products, accounted for almost half of all female employment in the manufacturing area. Traditional areas of female employment such as textiles, clothing, footwear and leather employed just under one in five of the women in the manufacturing area. Pyle's work (1990) suggests that women's share of the labour force in these (predominantly indigenous) areas has decreased.

Jackson and Barry (1988) noted that in the early 1980s multinational companies tended to recruit young employees and/or those who had no experience of industry. In 1983 women made up 51 per cent of the employees in foreign electronics companies but only 28 per cent of the overall manufacturing workforce. Jackson and Barry also noted that, at that time, just over three quarters of all women in the electronics industry were in unskilled production jobs, and virtually none were in the skilled grades. These jobs were relatively poorly paid, and this was associated with low levels of unionisation in these multinational companies. We do not know to what extent these trends have persisted. Jackson and Barry (1988) also noted that indigenous manufacturing companies tended to employ men rather than women; a practice whose cost in terms of productivity and competitiveness has never been examined.

Explanations for married women's participation in paid employment

Explanations which suggested that women were a reserve army of labour which could be drawn on in times of scarcity have been shown to be inconsistent with overall trends (Smyth, 1997). Thus, in Ireland female employment continued to rise during the recession in the 1980s, while male employment continued to fall. These same patterns appeared in the 1930s depression in the USA; and in the 1980s in Britain (Walby, 1990). More specific explanations have focused on factors related either to the demand for labour or to its supply (Smyth, 1997; O'Connor and Shortall, 1998). The most convincing of these explanations appears to relate to the expansion of the service sector and hence, within a gendered market, to a demand for female labour. Nevertheless differences in the labour force participation rates of older and younger women suggest that the supply of labour is differentially affected by the wider context.

As outlined in Chapters 2 and 4, state policies in the taxation and welfare areas in Ireland, effectively discourage the participation of married women in paid employment, and are particularly unhelpful as regards the re-integration of married women into the workforce. The social security system is by and large organised around the principle of a breadwinner among married/cohabiting couples. Female breadwinners, with partners who are not in paid employment, are rare, constituting 4.4 per cent of all couples (CSO, 1997). In Ireland, and indeed right across the EU, women are much more likely to be pulled into unemployment by the unemployment of their spouse, than *vice versa*: the unemployment rate for wives with unemployed husbands is 38 per cent, as compared with an overall unemployment rate of 17.4 per cent for women (the comparable EU figures being 33.2 per cent and 9.8 per cent: Eurostat, 1993:83). Furthermore, the effect of the taxation and social welfare systems is such as to particularly discourage medium to low earning wives, and these are likely to be among the less educated.

It has been noted that no single factor can explain the increase in the participation of married women in employment and that it is:

> as likely to have involved many influences, including the changing structure of employment demand, and attitudinal and institutional factors (such as equality legislation). Various studies have suggested further causes such as increased female earnings, declining fertility and smaller family sizes and improvements in the level of educational attainment. It is difficult however to determine to what extent any one factor influenced the position (Connell *et al*, 1996b).

Here we are particularly concerned with evaluating the evidence on the importance of a number of 'supply' factors which are commonly put forward. They include explanations involving children and child care, educational level, rational choice and attitudes to paid employment.

Children and child care

In Ireland the presence of children has been widely seen as central to an explanation of the extent of married women's participation in the labour force (e.g. Callan and Farrell, 1991; and Walsh, 1993). However, it is increasingly recognised that there is no direct correlation between total number of children, or even the number of dependent children, and such participation (Maruani, 1992; Bulletin on Women and Employment, 1994). Thus it has been noted that:

> The female activity rates are influenced less by the number of children or availability of childcare than by the strategies for coping with family obligations. This is where the European countries exhibit the greatest diversity (Maruani, 1992:9).

The *Bulletin on Women and Employment in the EU* (1995:6) clearly showed that, focusing on mothers aged 20-39 years, with a dependent child aged 14 years or less, there was a very wide range of variation in both full-time and part-time participation in the labour force across the EU: total participation, ranging from 76 per cent in Denmark to 32 per cent in Ireland (see Table 7.4, Col. 3).

TABLE 7.4
THE EMPLOYMENT RATE OF MOTHERS[1] AGED 20-39, 1991

Countries	Full time %	Part time %	TOTAL %
Portugal	66%	5%	71%
Denmark	49%	27%	76%
France	44%	17%	61%
Belgium	39%	23%	62%
Greece	39%	3%	42%
Italy	38%	5%	43%
Spain	30%	5%	35%
Luxembourg	27%	13%	40%
Ireland	23%	9%	32%
Germany	20%	28%	48%
Britain	18%	35%	53%
Netherlands	5%	36%	41%
Europe 12	31%	20%	51%

[1] Mothers are defined as women with a dependent child aged 14 years or less. *Bulletin on Women and Employment in the EU* (1995) April: 8.

The impact of bearing and rearing children is mediated by the state, through the structure of the labour market; and it is affected by women's educational levels, in the context of social norms and practices concerning women's participation in the labour force. In Denmark, for example, the overwhelming majority of women, with or without children, were in paid employment (motherhood effect = +2). In Ireland, the effect of motherhood on women's participation was the most highly negative in the EU (at -51) with the UK being in an intermediate position (at -34).

Being a mother thus had very different implications in various EU countries. This tells us more about the way in which motherhood is constructed in particular societies than it does about the presence/absence of children. Furthermore these patterns did not reflect a country's degree of economic development or indeed state provision for child care, since the employment rate for mothers in Portugal (at 71 per cent) was very similar to Denmark (at 76 per cent), despite their very different patterns of part-time work, stages of economic development and child care provisions (United Nations, 1995).

In Ireland, since the 1960s, the most dramatic changes have occurred in the participation of married women in the 25-34 year age group, with 4.8 per cent of them being in the labour force in 1961, as compared with 39 per cent in 1989 and 58 per cent in 1996 (Working Group on Child Care Facilities for Working Parents, 1994 and Labour Force Survey, 1996). Indeed there was evidence that in 1991 mothers with children under three years were more likely than mothers with children aged 3-9 years to be in paid employment in Ireland. In 1996 although the labour force participation rate of mothers with three or more dependent children (33 per cent) was lower than the average for all mothers (37 per cent), the participation rate of mothers with one or two dependent children (43 per cent) was higher than the average (CSO, 1997). These patterns challenge simplistic notions that the participation of mothers simply reflects age or number of children.

This dramatic increase in the participation of young mothers in the labour force in Ireland has occurred in a context where state provision and/or funding of child care is one of the lowest in Europe, and where the participation of husbands in domestic activity is extraordinarily low (see Chapter 5). Workplace child care was actively promoted by the Irish Congress of Trade Unions in the 1980s, with Congress showing, in 1989, that there were economic benefits for employers who provided child care facilities. However, there has been very little development of such facilities (Working Group on Child Care Facilities for Working Parents, 1983 and 1994).

Furthermore, although much attention at EU level from the 1980s onwards has been paid to the whole area of job sharing, flexitime, career breaks, etc. as ways of combining paid work with family responsibilities, this has evoked little interest in Ireland. For example, it has been estimated that only 1 per cent of the workforce in the private sector job shares. Job sharing is technically available in two fifths of the state-sponsored bodies studied by the Department of Equality and Law Reform (1994) and in 90 per cent of the local authorities, as well as in the civil service. It has been estimated, however, that in the public sector job sharing involves only 8,000 people, mainly women (Fisher, 1996). The model of employment based on a full-time (male) employee is still seen as very much the norm in Ireland and evidence from the US and the UK that the arrangements cited above are associated with greater productivity have been ignored.

Education

In every EU country the level of education had an effect on the participation of women in the labour force, although the strength of this effect varied even among young women with dependent children. For example, the impact of education was modest in Denmark (a pattern which one might suggest reflected the high levels of state-funded child care there as well as the whole normative context supporting women's participation in paid employment). The effect of education was stronger in Portugal, and greater still in Ireland where there was a difference of 38 per cent in the economic activity rates of mothers with compulsory and graduate education (see Table 7.5).

In Ireland it is not clear to what extent these patterns reflect the greater economic return that such women can expect, their different attitudes as regards the importance of mothers being at home full-time, or their smaller family size (*Bulletin on Women and Employment in the EU*, 1995, 6:8). In any case 68 per cent of women with graduate education, as compared with 29 per cent of those with compulsory education, aged 20-39, and with at least one dependent child, were economically active in Ireland. Highly educated women are more likely to have continuous careers, and to work full-time (Maruani, 1992). In some countries, such as Ireland, the effect of education was greater among women aged 25-39 years than among those aged 40-59 years. This is not surprising in view of the fact that the latter were affected by the 'marriage bar' in the early 1970s and, as noted in Chapter 4, their re-entry to the labour force has not been facilitated.

TABLE 7.5
THE ACTIVITY RATES FOR WOMEN AGED 20-39 BY EDUCATIONAL ATTAINMENT AND MATERNAL STATUS, 1991[1]

	Women without dependent children				Mothers				Mother-hood effect
	Compulsory	Post-compulsory	Graduate	All	Compulsory	Post-compulsory	Graduate	All	
B	72.1	88.8	94.6	83.9	58.2	76.9	86.1	70.3	−16
DK	75.9	85.3	94.2	85.6	82.4	89.4	95.2	87.6	+2
D	77.4	86.7	92.9	85.4	44.8	53.9	61.8	51.9	−39
GR	50.6	70.9	89.5	61.1	37.4	47.7	81.2	47.4	−22
E	62.2	81.0	92.2	73.7	39.1	61.2	83.9	46.8	−37
F	na	na	na	84.3	na	na	na	69.9	−17
IRL	71.9	84.3	91.1	82.7	29.5	46.8	68.1	40.7	−51
I	64.9	83.5	94.6	73.9	42.4	67.4	88.6	51.6	−30
L	78.5	95.1	93.4	83.2	41.0	48.9	68.6	43.5	−48
NL	76.1	84.0	93.1	84.0	36.3	53.9	69.5	48.1	−43
P	78.7	80.0	98.1	81.7	73.7	86.8	96.2	76.9	−6
UK	89.2	89.8	94.4	90.3	56.0	64.3	74.0	59.2	−34
EUR12	77.1	85.9	93.6	83.7	48.3	60.0	76.2	57.8	−31

Note: Comparable education data are not available for France. Data relate to women who are the household head, either individually or as part of a couple. Mothers are defined as women with a dependent child aged 14 years or less.
Motherhood effect = (activity rate of mothers − activity rate of women without dependent children)/activity rate of women without dependent children x 100.
Bulletin on Women and Employment in the EU (1995) April: 8.

Thus it is clear that women's education has an effect on their participation in paid employment, although the nature and extent of this effect varies depending on the wider context.

Rational choice

Hakim (1991) suggested that women typically see paid employment as less important than men; that they choose to put domestic and family responsibilities to the fore, thereby choosing to engage in part-time and/or low paid employment:

> Expectations and aspirations are focused on what has been called the 'marriage career' with paid employment taking a back seat (1991:105).

However, Whelan (1994) showed that in the European Values Study there was relatively little difference in the importance attached by Irish men (72 per cent) and women (60 per cent) to paid employment. Indeed, the importance attached to paid employment varied little between single and married; and between full-time and part-time employees. Similarly the importance of good pay and security varied little across gender and marital status categories. Neither was there any real difference between the importance attached by married men, married women and single men to personal development; responsibility; opportunity to achieve something; to use initiative etc. in a work setting (Whelan, 1994: 88). There was no real difference in the proportion of men and women in that study saying that they 'take a great deal of pride in their work'; that they 'enjoy working but don't let it interfere with the rest of their life' or indeed that 'work was the most important thing in their life'. Differences between married and single people were more complex, with a slightly larger proportion of both married men and married women taking a great deal of pride in their work; although the proportion of single men and women who saw work as the most important thing in life was considerably larger than the comparable proportion among the married.

Whelan found that women were somewhat more likely than men to say that they 'wouldn't work if they didn't have to'. These trends appeared both in the case of single and married respondents. This may reflect the greater compatibility of financial dependence with definitions of womanhood. Such trends may also be related to the fact that although it is increasingly accepted that women have the right to 'choose' to seek paid work, the popular perception is that men 'ought' to seek paid work (Callan and Wren, 1994). Women are seen as ultimately responsible for child care and so it is they who must consider how to combine child-rearing and domestic work with paid work.

Hakim (1991, 1995, 1996) argued that women choose to be either home-centred (uncommitted workers), or committed workers. At first glance, rational choice arguments make a great deal of sense when one focuses on the participation of married women in paid employment, within a particular society. However, they implicitly discourage an explanation of the context within which women make such choices (Bruegel, 1996). This context involves the variety of factors which were outlined in Chapter 2, including the cost of child care (insofar as it is not provided by the state or the family); the wages available to women; taxation arrangements; the structure of the labour market; the legal situation, etc. As noted by Smyth (1997) the rational choice perspective tends to take for granted women's child care responsibilities, rather than seeing them as something which, as in Denmark, might be shared by the state. It tends to assume that the labour market is such that men and women get equal returns for their education and training, something which has been shown not to be so (Callan and Farrell, 1991; Durkan *et al*, 1995; Callan and Wren, 1994). It ignores the wider legal context which, prior to 1973, meant that regardless of their rational choices, married women in a variety of occupations could not participate in paid employment. It ignores the fact that, because of such factors, a wife's wages relative to her husband's may be reduced, even among those with identical preferences and similar capabilities (O'Connor and Shortall, 1998). It ignores the fact that in some cases, sheer economic necessity will preclude any element of choice.

Overall then, the studies found that there was virtually no support for any suggestion that women in general, or married women in particular, saw paid employment as less important or as something which had a different meaning in their lives than in those of their male counterparts. Arguments which focus on rational choice can appear intuitively attractive in explaining the decision of a particular married woman, in a particular situation, at a particular moment in time. However, they effectively obscure a great number of questions and issues.

Attitudes to participation

Fine-Davis (1988) clearly showed that by the mid 1980s there was still some ambivalence about the participation of mothers in paid employment, although attitudes were changing. In 1975, 68 per cent of her respondents agreed that 'it is bad for young children if their mothers go out to work, even if they are well taken care of by another adult'; by 1986, the proportion endorsing such views had fallen to 46 per cent. Whelan and Fahey (1994) showed that in the 1990 European Values Study the trends were very similar, 46 per cent of the women in their study agreeing that 'a pre-school child is likely to suffer if his/her mother works'.

Positive attitudes were consistently more likely to be expressed by the highly educated and by married women who themselves were in paid employment. However, the majority of both men and women in the 1990 European Values Study, whether in paid employment or not, agreed that a working mother could establish just as warm and secure a relationship with her children as a mother who does not work (79 per cent of women in paid employment, 56 per cent of women in 'home duties', and 59 per cent of the men: Whelan and Fahey's study, 1994:56).

The majority of each of the three groups in Whelan and Fahey's study felt that 'having a job is the best way for a woman to be an independent person'; and they agreed that 'both the husband and wife should contribute to household income'. In both Fine-Davis's (1983 and 1988) and Whelan and Fahey's (1994c) studies, the general pattern was for men's views to be more similar to those of housewives than to those of women in paid employment. Men were more likely to see the role of women as being in the home; they were more likely to see women as dependent, and to see the wife and mother role as the most fulfilling one for women. Inevitably, this raises questions about the extent to which the meaning and significance of 'difference' was being defined by men for women; and the extent to which such men, in their present or future capacity as policy makers, will be willing to take on board the reality of women's diversity, as opposed to relying on their own perception of what women should want.

The attitudes emerging in the Irish sample as a whole were surprisingly similar to the European average, with such differences as existed not always being in the expected direction. For example, Irish women were less likely than the overall European average to feel that a pre-school child was likely to suffer if his/her mother worked (46 per cent versus 68 per cent; Whelan and Fahey, 1994c). Irish women were also somewhat more likely than the European average to feel that being a housewife was just as fulfilling as working for pay (71 per cent versus 57 per cent); and they were less likely to see a job as the best way for a woman to be an independent person (59 per cent versus 74 per cent). One might speculate that this reflects a greater acceptance of children's emotional independence, combined with Irish women's greater valuing of the lifestyle and possibilities for independence involved in full-time housewifery.

Fine-Davis (1983) suggested that for women in lower socio-economic occupations, housewifery could offer a better opportunity than paid employment to use their skills and talents. However, the housewives in her study were acutely aware of a lack of appreciation of their work, and felt a sense of isolation and a lack of opportunity to meet people. The picture which emerged in her study as regards the extent of physical and nervous stress among housewives 'due to the nature and pace of the work' (1983:198) was confirmed in Whelan *et al* (1991). Thus, full-time housewifery still exacts a cost in terms of mental health. Nevertheless, family size has been dramatically altered and women's day-to-day power within the family seems to have substantially increased. It may be that women are less optimistic about effecting a similar transformation in the world of paid work, and that this is what lies behind their feeling that being a housewife is just as fulfilling as working for pay. Despite such attitudes there is every indication that their participation in paid employment is likely to increase.

Summary

In this chapter we have been concerned with describing the overall extent and nature of the participation of Irish women in the labour force. In Ireland as elsewhere in Europe the labour force is becoming increasingly feminised. This fact is most vividly captured by noting that 90 per cent of the increase in employment since 1971 has been in women's employment. This increase has been facilitated by the expansion of the service sector, where women's employment is predominantly concentrated. Thus it is clear that it is necessary to study the pay and working conditions of those in this area in order to have some insight into women's experiences in paid employment.

In fact, however, the most systematic national wage data is available on industrial workers in the manufacturing sector. Women's hourly wages in this area were 74 per cent of men's in 1996 (CSO, 1997). Callan and Wren (1994) found that women's hourly wages were 80 per cent of the men's in their study, and that only 10 per cent of the remainder could be explained by labour market experience, education, etc. Indeed there was some evidence that women's 'return' on their educational qualifications was less than men's (Garavan, 1994, Callan and Farrell, 1991) and that they needed to be more highly educated to 'compensate' for their gender.

The evidence, such as it is, suggests that as Maruani (1992:1) noted, the increased participation of women in paid employment does not mean that 'women have won occupational equality'. This is because women are congregated into areas of predominantly female employment, in a situation where there is a low valuation of work predominantly done by women. In the absence of male comparators equal pay legislation is ineffective. In this context it is perhaps not surprising that women are disproportionately represented among the low paid in Ireland and elsewhere in Europe.

Nevertheless this chapter has shown that despite this and despite the lack of state encouragement, the participation of married women, and particularly of young mothers, in paid employment has increased dramatically. This is perhaps one of the most striking changes in Irish society in general, and in married women's lives in particular over the past twenty-five years. This trend has of course been compatible with the demands of the market for cheaper labour. It has also been facilitated by women's high levels of education. We do not know to what extent and in what ways this dramatic change in the participation of young mothers in paid employment has altered the nature of the workplace, the family and the relationships between men and women. It is difficult however to believe that it has had no effect.

8

Women and Top Jobs:
Getting In but Not Getting On

Introduction

THERE is an increasing realisation at EU level that the problem is not simply one of women being unwilling or unable to participate in paid employment, but of their continued virtual absence from decision-making positions in the main institutional structures, including the paid employment area. This chapter will be mainly concerned with women within two broad categories of 'top jobs', viz. managerial and professional occupations. It has been suggested (EOC, 1997) that the proportion of women in these occupations constitutes a central indicator of progress:

> The hierarchical order of work organisations with disproportionate numbers of women at the bottom and disproportionate numbers of men at the top is also an expression of gender. This order preserves traditional power relations between women and men and confirms the symbolic association of masculinity with leadership and femininity with supportiveness (Acker, 1988:482).

The whole question of women's under-representation in 'top jobs' raises two main issues. Firstly, it raises the question of women's access to positions of authority. Across the EU as a whole, women are considerably more successful in acquiring what Savage (1992) has called positions of 'expertise' rather than 'authority'. Thus in 1990, in the EU countries, women held 23 per cent of the administrative and management positions, but they constituted 45 per cent of the professional, technical and related workers (Bulletin on Women and Employment in the EU, 1994:1). Secondly, in the case of women who are involved in professional occupations, it again raises the whole question of the value of women's work within an occupational structure which is characterised by the clustering of women into particular areas, which are then less highly paid.

Of course, it is recognised that a focus on 'top jobs' effectively excludes working-class women. Typically there is a great deal of discomfort around this; and indeed the concerns of 'well heeled articulate women' are frequently derided and castigated both by left-wing women and middle-class men. However, the Social Action Programme which was adopted by the European Commission stressed that social policy, including equal opportunities, 'is a productive factor facilitating economic growth, rather than a burden on the economy or an obstacle to growth' (EC, 1997:1):

> Women's lower rates of participation in paid employment in the EU is a large factor in militating against the competitiveness of EU versus non-EU countries (particularly given women's generally higher educational attainments) (EU, 1994:41).

It is popularly assumed that women's under-representation in management positions in Ireland reflects the impact of the marriage bar, the presence of children or a particular stage of economic development. These explanations are increasingly seen as questionable in view of the international evidence. For example, the proportion of women in senior positions in the civil service in the UK is much the same as in Ireland, although the marriage bar was removed there in the 1940s. Furthermore, although the proportion of women in administrative and management positions varies considerably across Europe, it is very similar in Denmark and Ireland (14.4 per cent and 15.1 per cent respectively), despite their very different levels of state support for child care (United Nations, 1995:84). Variation also appears to be unrelated to stage of economic development, with, for example, women constituting 58 per cent of administrators and managers in Hungary which was rated 50th on the United Nations human development index, as compared with 15 per cent in Ireland which was rated 19th on the same index (United Nations, 1995). Indeed Norris (1987:75) suggested that, politics *does* matter, compared with other factors such as the level of economic development or economic growth. She suggested that the presence of women in such positions was most likely to be associated with socialist/left-wing governments. However, although this seems plausible in terms of the proportion of women in such positions in Sweden or Hungary (39 per cent and 58 per cent respectively: United Nations, 1995:84), it is obviously not a sufficient explanation since the proportion of women who were administrators or managers was approximately the same in the USA as in Sweden.

This chapter first explores the issue of whether women are or are not in 'top jobs'. Secondly, it 'highlights the structural, cultural, procedural and individual barriers' (Liff and Dale, 1994) which serve to perpetuate this situation, focusing on career structures; organisational culture; organisational procedures; the failure to reconcile work and family life; as well as women's own characteristics including their lack of confidence, organisational naiveté, etc. There appears to be little ideological support for women's occupancy of positions of authority in the area of paid employment. It remains to be seen to what extent, individually or collectively, they will be able to challenge what Lynch (1994) has called 'a hegemonic belief' that it is natural for men to be leaders. Within the limits of the data available it is impossible to identify inferential constructs through which women might make sense of their lives so that issues related to agency are likely to be obscured.

Women in top jobs: aren't they there?

There are technical difficulties in assessing how many people are in what have been defined as 'top jobs', viz. those in the managerial and professional areas. These difficulties partly arise because of variation in the level of jobs which are identified as managerial, and the tendency for women, insofar as they are in managerial positions, to be at the lower levels of the hierarchy. There are also some difficulties as regards the definition of professional activities, particularly insofar as distinctions are or are not made between these and associated professional and other technical occupations.

The proportion of women in administrative, executive and managerial occupations in Ireland has increased over the past twenty-five years. In 1971 women constituted 5 per cent of those in such occupations, as compared with 24 per cent (15,400 women) in 1996 (Irish Labour Force Survey, [CSO, 1997:35]). Thus within a context where employment in this area increased by 27 per cent over the 1987-94 period, the growth in female employment was almost double that of male employment (by 43 versus 22 per cent: Barry, 1996:32). Very little academic attention has been paid to these trends or to their cultural and social implications.

What limited evidence we have also suggests that women constitute the highest proportion of those in management positions in areas which would be regarded as of lesser status/pay, e.g. in the hotel trade and the cultural sector, where 'the rewards for these higher level jobs may again be linked to women's pay levels' (Rubery and Fagan, 1993: xiii). This trend is evident across Europe (EU, 1997), although it has also been noted that even in such areas 'their presence is not yet reflected at senior levels'. Thus, Breathnach showed that women constituted two thirds of all of those employed in hotels; 40 per cent of those in managerial positions within that area and less than one per cent of those at managing director/general manager level.

There are difficulties in making international comparisons as regards the proportion of women in managerial positions (see Rubery and Fagan 1993). The British Equal Opportunities Commission (1997, using a broad definition of management and administrative positions, found that in 1996 women constituted 33 per cent of those in such positions in Great Britain (as compared with 23 per cent in the UK according to the United Nations Report, 1995). It appeared that there was a 'gender bonus' insofar as women directors in that study earned 81 per cent of the salaries of their male counterparts, and women managers 88 per cent of the salaries of their male counterparts (EOC, 1997). They noted that there had been a dramatic increase in the proportion of women who were corporate managers and administrators in the UK since the 1980s. Nevertheless, women still only constituted 3 per cent of directors and 13 per cent of senior and middle managers (EOC, 1997). Similarly, Eurostat (1987) showed that women constituted only a very small proportion of those in top management positions: 3 per cent in Ireland and 2 per cent in Denmark, West Germany and Italy.

Women tend to be congregated into a small range of professions which are typically seen as of lower status and are paid less (Eurostat, 1995). In Ireland, as elsewhere in Europe, education and health are key areas for women's employment in professional occupations. In Ireland women constituted 65 per cent of the 239,000 in this sector (Labour Force Survey, 1996, CSO:30). Over the 1987-1993 period the number of women employed in this area increased by over 14 per cent while the number of men declined by under 2 per cent (Durkan *et al*, 1995; Barry, 1996). These areas of employment, and women's share of them, are likely to continue to increase (Fitzgerald and Hughes, 1994:41 and 44). Indeed professional and related jobs provided the main source of employment growth in the 1980s not only in Ireland, but also in Belgium, Greece and the Netherlands; and the second most important area of employment growth in France, Spain, Portugal and Germany. In six of these eight countries, these sectors accounted for at least one third of all net female growth in employment (Rubery and Fagan, 1993:10). Indeed according to Eurostat figures (1995) the proportion of professional women in Ireland was considerably above the EU average in 1992.

It has been noted that although internationally, in both industrial and developing countries, the participation of women in both managerial and professional occupations generally increased since 1970, women were more under-represented in the former than in the latter (i.e. in positions of authority as opposed to expertise: Savage, 1992). The United Nations Report (1995), using slightly different definitions of professional and management positions, showed that women made up 47 per cent of the professional and technical workers in Ireland as compared to 15 per cent of the administrators and managers. Thus it is clear that, for the most part:

> the increasing numbers of 'expert' women in the labour market should not be seen as evidence that women are moving into positions of organisational authority, but rather that, as organisations restructure, there is increased room for women in specialised niches subordinate to senior management although enjoying a degree of autonomy from direct control (Savage, 1992:147).

For example, in Sweden, women constituted 63 per cent of the professional and technical workers, but 39 per cent of administrators and managers; while in Denmark the pattern was even more extreme, viz. 63 per cent and 15 per cent respectively (United Nations, 1995: 84). In a small number of countries women's educational expertise seemed to be more than proportionately reflected in their access to positions of authority. For example, women constituted 24 per cent of the professional and technical workers in Australia, but 41 per cent of the administrators and managers (United Nations, 1995). It is not clear what accounts for these very different patterns.

Thus although the figures differ somewhat, depending on the classification schema used, it is clear that professional services constitute an increasingly important sector of women's employment, and that in Ireland, the proportion of women in such occupations has increased. Women now constitute two thirds of those in such positions, even though they are rarely at the highest levels or in what are perceived as the more prestigious occupations. Attention will now be specifically focused on the position of women in one management (civil service) and one professional area (teaching) as well as on self employment, before looking more analytically at the factors which are associated with the position of women in these areas. These specific areas have been chosen largely on pragmatic grounds because of the availability of the relevant data.

Civil service

Since the mid 1980s, there has been an awareness of equality issues in the civil service structure and a series of annual reports monitoring this. Nevertheless in 1995 women constituted only 7 per cent of those at senior management level, i.e. at the level of secretary or assistant secretary in the civil service (Department of Finance, Tabular Statement, 1997: Table 1). Men constituted the overwhelming majority of those at middle and senior management levels in 1995, just as in 1987 (Second Report of the Co-ordinating Group of Secretaries, 1996:48). Indeed it was only at higher executive officer level (a supervisory grade) that the proportion of women exceeded the token level of 30 per cent in 1995 and this had already been reached in 1987. On the other hand the proportion of women in what is popularly seen as the 'fast track' graduate recruitment grade (i.e. administrative officer) had, depending on the measure used, either fallen or remained much the same since 1987. This had occurred despite the fact that since the 1980s there has been ongoing concern with the mechanisms for recruitment at this level (The First Report of the Third Joint Oireachtas Committee on Women's Rights, 1991; Co-ordinating Group of Secretaries, 1996).

TABLE 8.1

PROPORTION OF WOMEN EMPLOYEES AT EACH GRADE IN THE CIVIL
SERVICE (GENERAL SERVICE GRADES) 1987 AND 1995

Grades	Women 1987	Women 1995
Secretary	0%	4% (1)
Assistant Secretary	1%	6% (5)
Principal Officer	5%	13% (43)
Assistant Principal	23%	23% (227)
Administrative Officer	26%	21% (18)
Higher Executive Officer	34%	37% (697)
Executive Officer	44%	51% (1,220)
Staff Officer	67%	75% (772)
Clerical Officer	68%	79% (3,526)
Clerical Assistant	83%	82% (3,837)

From Co-ordinating Group of Secretaries (1996): 48 (rounding up figures)

The total proportion of women in administrative and executive occupations in the civil service increased, from 14 per cent in 1971, to

28 per cent in 1981 and to 33 per cent in 1993. Similarly the proportion of women in professional occupations in the civil service had increased, from 7 per cent in 1970 and 1981, to 16 per cent in 1993 (Durkan *et al*, 1995). The timing of these changes does not suggest that the 1980s monitoring process has been particularly effective in bringing about change. Indeed it has been suggested that the approach adopted by the civil service to date has been weakened by the fact that it did not identify targets but simply focused on 'analysis and monitoring to resolve problems' (Callan and Wren, 1994:88). The civil service's own Strategic Management Initiative has suggested that there is a need to adopt a more proactive policy with:

> a requirement on each Department to draw up an individual plan covering its proposals for action on gender issues, with particular reference to the gender balance of grades employed in that Department (Co-ordinating Group of Secretaries, 1996:49).

There is indirect evidence that receptivity to such ideas varies between Government Departments, being considerably higher, for example, in the Department of Social Welfare than in the Department of Finance (Department of Equality and Law Reform, 1997).

The under-representation of women in senior management positions in the civil service is not peculiar to Ireland. Similar trends emerged in the British and Canadian civil service. Equally Levinson *et al* (1992) noted that in the US civil service although women constituted 48 per cent of the employees, only 11 per cent of the senior executive service jobs were held by women. They noted that men were promoted at a rate 44 per cent greater than women in grades that constituted a 'gateway' to these higher jobs. They estimated that if these trends persisted, women would hold less than one third of these senior executive jobs in twenty-five years time. The consistency of the picture across widely different cultures and economic systems challenges popular explanations that the under-representation of women in these structures is solely due to idiosyncratic Irish factors such as the late removal of the marriage bar.

It is provocative that Portugal has by far the highest proportion of women at management level in the civil service at just over 30 per cent, followed by Spain at just under 20 per cent. Denmark, whose state-funded child care facilities are very extensive (Jorgensen, 1991) came third as regards the proportion of women at management level in the civil service. These patterns may reflect the low status of civil service. Alternatively, it is possible that they reflect the fact that in the 1980s the

Portuguese and Spanish governments embarked on positive action programmes to move women into decision-making positions and introduced fines for discriminatory practices (Rubery and Fagan, 1993:113). It is also possible in these societies that such patterns reflect the triumph of class over gender.

In Ireland the under-representation of women in senior management positions is not peculiar to the civil service. Women constituted only 3 per cent of those at senior management grades in the local authorities in 1995 (Mahon and Dillon, 1996). Similarly although women constituted 71 per cent of health board employees nationally, they occupied 7 per cent of the management positions and none of those at senior management level (Department of Equality and Law Reform, 1994). Only 2 per cent of those at senior management level in state-sponsored bodies are women (Second Monitoring Committee, 1996). There seems to be little support for assumptions that the pattern is changing in a positive direction. Indeed, McCarthy (1986) noted that in 1983 the proportion of women at senior management level in the semi-state bodies was 11 per cent.

There are conflicting opinions about whether these patterns are most likely to change first in the private or in the public sector (Kanter, 1991 and Maruani, 1992 respectively). The limited evidence that is available in Ireland suggests that similar difficulties exist in both areas. For example, women accountants in both professional practice and industry were failing to 'break through the glass ceiling', with none of the top fifty organisations in Ireland having a woman finance director, despite the fact that women were admitted to the Institute in 1924 and constituted 42 per cent of those entering it in 1993/94 (Barker and Monks, 1994).

Teaching

Teaching is a particularly interesting example insofar as it exemplifies a profession where women are concentrated into particular areas, e.g. primary teaching, and where they are absent from the higher levels within each area. In Ireland, the proportion of women teachers declines dramatically from first to third level: women constituting 77 per cent of those at primary level, 53 per cent of all those at second level, and 21 per cent of those in the universities. These trends are inversely related to pay levels.

Furthermore, although women make up 77 per cent of teachers at primary level, they hold 48 per cent of the principalships (Lynch and

Morgan, 1995). So whereas women in primary level have approximately a one in ten chance of becoming a principal, men have an approximately four times better chance (12 per cent of female teachers at primary level as compared with 41 per cent of the male teachers being principals). This structural bias towards the appointment of males as principals is reflected in the fact that the average period between qualifying and first appointment as a principal is nine and a half years for women but five years for men (Second Report of the Third Joint Oireachtas Committee on Women's Rights, 1992).

In the 1980s a number of initiatives were taken by the Irish National Teachers' Organisation to promote gender equality through the endorsement of a policy on it (1984); the appointment of an Equality Officer (1985) and an Equality Committee (1987); the taking of a number of successful cases to the Labour Court; the provision of Gender Equality Modules in all INTO training courses (1991); and attempts to change women's perception of themselves, through the dissemination of pamphlets such as *Why don't you apply for a principalship?* and of research on gender inequalities in 1985 and 1990 respectively. These initiatives were associated with a dramatic increase in the proportion of women applying for and getting principalships. Thus, whereas women made up 29 per cent of the applicants in 1983/84, they made up 51 per cent in 1991/92. Over this period women's likelihood of being appointed also virtually doubled, with women who did apply for promotion being more likely than men to be successful (Lynch, 1994).

Coolahan (1994) and the Second Commission on the Status of Women (1993:27) noted that without measures to address 'imbalances arising from past discrimination', equal opportunity legislation will simply offer an 'equal chance to become unequal' (Coolahan 1994:118). Interestingly, however, the Department of Education perceived its status as an equal opportunity employer as effectively precluding such action, depicting it as a breach of a (narrowly defined) principle of equality, rather than as an attempt to generate equality at an outcome level (Coolahan, 1994). Indeed in its own review of its contribution to the promotion of equality (Second Co-ordinated Report, 1992), the Department of Education made no reference whatsoever to the issue of the under-representation of women in senior positions, such as the fact that, for example, 96 per cent of the senior inspector posts were held by men (Lynch, 1994). Equally there was no reference to the fact that despite the importance of role models, at second level even in girls schools, where principals were traditionally female religious, men had been almost twice as successful as lay women in getting principalships when a lay person was appointed (ASTI, 1991).

As previously mentioned, women now make up 21 per cent of full-time academic staff in the Irish university sector (Smyth, 1996; O'Connor, 1998). The proportion of women in such positions has changed relatively little. In the 1980s women made up 15 per cent of such full-time staff in the universities, and 18 per cent in other designated institutions (HEA, 1987). Some of these designated institutions (such as Dublin City University, where women now constitute 29 per cent of its academic staff) have since become universities, thereby accounting for at least part of the increase. The proportion of women who are at (full) professorial level within the universities nationally, at 4 per cent, is particularly low. Indeed, it has been shown that it is around the same as it was in the mid 1970s. The proportion of women at this level actually fell in the mid 1980s, thereby creating the impression in the late 1990s that things had improved over time (O'Connor, 1998). It is not difficult to see the implicit message which is being given to the young women who now constitute approximately half of those at undergraduate and postgraduate level.

The under-representation of women academics in the university sector is remarkably consistent across Europe, with Portugal being the country with the highest proportion of such women. Broadly similar patterns emerged in Stiver Lie and O'Leary's (1990) review of the position of academic women in higher education in a variety of countries including Turkey, Netherlands, USA, Norway, United Kingdom, West Germany, Jordan and Israel. Of those countries, the one where women made up the highest proportion of academic staff (32 per cent) and the highest proportion of those in (full) professorial posts (20 per cent) was in Turkey (Acar, 1990). Rubery and Fagan (1993:62) noted that women's share of such posts was not related to the overall participation of women in paid employment; to improvements in the general educational level; in overall economic well being, or in state intervention. These trends are reminiscent of those emerging as regards the proportion of women in senior positions in the civil service. They raise issues about the relationship between class and gender and, at the very least, challenge naïve assumptions that women's access to such positions increases with 'modernisation'.

Women as employers or self employed

Obviously although women can have access to a position of authority through promotion, they can also acquire it by becoming self employed or employers. It has been estimated that women entrepreneurs own approximately 25-30 per cent of all small enterprises across Europe. The Local Employment Initiatives Network has estimated that women now account for about one in three new enterprises in Denmark; one in four in the UK; and one in five in Ireland, Greece and Spain (MacDevitt, 1996). In the USA women are increasingly moving outside the corporate hierarchy and starting new businesses at five times the rate of men; and they now own 25 per cent of all small businesses there (Grint, 1991).

In 1994 employers and self employed made up a very high proportion (21 per cent) of all of those in paid employment in Ireland (Employment in Europe, 1995). However, this pattern was predominantly a male one: self-employed women making up less than 9 per cent of all women in employment in Ireland, as compared with 29 per cent among the men. Female self employment has fallen over the past twenty years from 16 per cent of all women in paid employment in 1975, to 9 per cent in 1994 (Employment in Europe, 1995). An attempt has been made to facilitate women's self employment through the EU funded New Opportunities for Women programme and the Local Employment Initiative. However, as the Fourth Joint Committee (1996) noted, these initiatives are temporary and low budget.

Right across Europe women's businesses tend to be concentrated in the service sector, an area which has expanded enormously in Ireland. It is however a sector which is highly competitive, and moreover one which in Ireland 'falls outside the ambit of state agencies which focus mainly on manufacturing industries' (MacDevitt, 1996:17). One of the biggest difficulties women face is access to credit. Securing a business loan typically demands a minimum level of capital, and this creates problems since women are less likely than men to own property. Furthermore they are often perceived as less credible by financial institutions; and their ideas for business development, which are typically in the service sector, are seen as less attractive in business investment terms. MacDevitt noted that women's business ideas and plans often did not fit with the criteria set out by more mainstream financing bodies, since they were interested in starting out small, and growing slowly.

Almost no research has been done on Irish women who are employed or self employed. One study examined a small sample of women who had been approved for feasibility grants to develop enterprises within the manufacturing area. It found that these women embarked on an entrepreneurial career either because they saw no possibility of promotion within their current job or because they felt that being a housewife and mother was not fulfilling enough (O'Connor, 1987). Typically they were in their thirties, with just over half being married (and the majority of these with children). Their lack of a financial track record and/or limited business experience posed difficulties for them at the outset. Many of them felt that although they had a relatively high level of education, they were discriminated against by the traditional banking system; with some perceiving 'a lack of respect and credibility for businesswomen among bank officials' and others seeing themselves as lacking the informal contacts which they considered vital (O'Connor, 1987:31).

Although self employment constitutes a potential alternative avenue, it is one which is difficult for women to access because of their typically low level of independent resources; difficulties surrounding access to credit and the perceived 'unattractiveness' of the sort of small scale services enterprises which they are typically interested in establishing.

Why aren't women in top jobs?

In attempting to understand why women are under-represented in management positions, either in administrative areas or at the top of professional hierarchies, attention is focused on a series of factors including the career structure in organisations; organisational culture; organisational procedures; the failure to reconcile work and family life; women's lack of confidence, etc. There are also issues around the valuing of women's work within the professional services area. As outlined in Chapter 2, this has begun to be recognised at EU level and is in fact the focus of an ongoing legal battle in the UK concerning the salaries paid to speech therapists, who are predominantly female, and psychologists, who are predominantly male (Lester, 1997). Hence a very brief discussion of the resourcing of predominantly female areas of employment is included here.

Career structures

It is suggested that three types of phenomena are important in this area, viz. the narrowness of the 'channel' from which managers in predominantly male areas of employment are recruited; the low ratio of promotional to basic posts in predominantly female areas of employment, e.g. nursing; and the remoteness of predominantly female career structures from centres of decision making about resources.

The first kind of pattern is very evident in local authorities. Mahon and Dillon (1996) noted that the proportion of women who reached the higher end of the supervisory grades was quite low (24 per cent). The proportion who reached what is regarded as middle management was even lower: women making up only 14 per cent of those at the first rung of middle management (administrative officer) and only 4 per cent of those at the next level of middle management, viz. senior administrative officer. The predominant pattern was one of reliance on recruitment from the level below so that the possibility that men would be appointed at senior management level was effectively maximised. Of the top managers in the local authorities, 80 per cent had entered as clerical officers, i.e. almost at the bottom of the hierarchy, which was even more extreme than in 1966 when 60 per cent had entered at this level.

In this situation men who enter at clerical officer level have a very high possibility indeed of being promoted. This was very obvious in my own study of the health boards (O'Connor, 1995b, 1996a) where a similar sort of structure existed. Men at Grade 3 had a better than one in two chance of being promoted to at least supervisory level. Women at the same level had a one in eight chance. If one assumes that the men and women who were recruited at Grade 3 were of a similar calibre, it is obvious that there is a statistical possibility that the women who reach supervisory level or above will be of a higher calibre than their male counterparts. Typically, however, they will not reach senior management level (Department of Equality and Law Reform, 1994b). Thus what appears to be a very fair system is in fact drawing on a very narrow and increasingly male pool, and is giving a disproportionately high possibility of promotion to men at the lower levels.

The career structures in areas of predominantly female employment, such as nursing, are very different, although even in these structures men have a greater possibility of promotion (14 to 1 versus 28 to 1 respectively: O'Connor, 1995b). These patterns were not peculiar to the selected health boards. The Department of Equality and Law Reform concluded that nationally in general nursing, in psychiatric nursing and in mental handicap nursing, 'women appear to do somewhat worse than men insofar as career advancement is concerned' (1993:46). Evidence in Britain suggested that on average a female nurse who took no career breaks took 14.5 years to reach her first promotional post, as compared with an average of 8.4 years for men.

If one assumes that in Ireland those completing a nursing qualification are as intellectually able as those entering the civil service at clerical officer level, it is obvious that the male clerical officers, with a better than one in two chance of promotion to a broadly similar if not better salaried position, are in a very different position from women nurses with a 28 to 1 possibility of promotion to matron/assistant matron positions. This difference partly reflects the low ratio of promotional posts within nursing (O'Connor, 1995b, 1996a).

There were similar differences in male and female possibilities of promotion in what the health boards refer to as the 'paramedic' professions (such as physiotherapy, occupational therapy, environmental health officers, radiography, social work, psychology, speech therapy, pharmacy, etc.). Thus nationally women had a one in twenty chance of being at senior/supervisory level in their own professional hierarchy in these professions as compared with a roughly one on ten chance among the men (Department of Equality and Law Reform, 1994b).

There is some evidence to suggest that predominantly female areas of employment tend to be remote from decision-making structures, a pattern which in itself has implications as regards women's access to managerial positions. In some cases this arises because of the effective downgrading of those at the top of the professional hierarchy. For example, respondents in the Midland and Mid-Western Health Board study noted that matrons used to have an input into budgets, but that since the insertion of (typically male) lay managers and lay hospital administrators between them and the health board management team, matrons were only responsible for salaries. The development of these posts had blocked their opportunities as nurses, and had diminished the status of nursing ('Haven't the men won out?'). In the UK, women with a nursing background now constitute 20 per cent of those in management positions (NHS Management Executive. Employees' Guide, 1992 and Proctor and Jackson, 1992). As part of an initiative of the Office of Health Management it has been suggested that time specific targets and positive action programmes should be devised (Dixon and Baker, 1996). A start has been made by funding leadership programmes so as to select 'candidates who will lead the health and personal social services in the twenty-first century' (Office for Health Management, 1997 3:2). It remains to be seen what impact such initiatives will have on the proportion of women in senior positions in the health boards.

Organisational culture

A variety of studies have highlighted the existence and importance of a complicated fabric of management myths and values that legitimise women's positions at the lower levels of the hierarchy; portray managerial jobs as primarily masculine; define women as unfit for managerial positions etc. (Clarke 1992; Garavan, 1994). The Hansard Society Commission (1990), in identifying four 'general and pervasive' barriers, referred specifically to 'outmoded attitudes about the role of women', such as scepticism about their abilities and stereotyped assumptions about their character and their 'natural' role, as well as 'subtle assumptions, attitudes and stereotypes which affect how managers sometimes view women's potential for advancement' (1992:10). The same phenomenon was noted in reports on the British (Walters, 1987), American (Levinson, 1992), and Canadian (1990) public service. These prejudices are seen as an important barrier to women's promotion internationally (Davidson and Cooper, 1992 and 1993; Robinson, 1996). Cockburn (1991) suggests that they become visible when women seek to move out of their 'proper' place:

> Men reward women for sexual difference when they are in their proper place, penalise them for it once they step into men's place.

Cockburn (1991) suggested that when they do this women are given the message that they are 'out of place', a phenomenon which can be compared with a Northern Ireland organisational culture that 'chills out' the minority group in that setting. This is particularly likely to occur in predominantly male managerial and administrative structures. There, 'men are found to be culturally active in creating an environment in which women don't flourish' (Cockburn, 1991:65). The culture in these areas has been described as one which 'opens itself to women and yet squeezes them out, which integrates them, yet marginalises them' (Walters, 1987:14).

Comparatively little attention has been paid to organisational culture in Ireland although Lynch (1993:74) has identified it as 'one of the factors which poses an obstacle for women's progression in their career structures'. Furthermore, its existence was very obvious indeed from a close reading of both Mahon's (1991a, 1991b, 1991c) work on the civil service and Barker and Monks' (1994) study on female and male accountancy careers. It also emerged very clearly in my own study of the Midland and Mid-Western Health Boards (O'Connor, 1995b, 1996a). As the majority of the women at middle and senior level in these health boards perceived it, the organisational culture was not conducive to the promotion of women: 'You get the impression of so many cliques and black suits . . . The Board has to work at creating an entity, fitting you in, making people feel they belong; at present the women are outside it.' Yet women made up the majority of health board employees. They felt that prejudice existed; that 'mediocre men are in a position of power; you can only get to a certain level'; that it was 'assumed that a man will go further'; that the route to promotion was shorter for men than for women. They felt that women were taken 'less seriously' by management and that 'there are jobs for the boys – years in advance you know that they are going to get that job'. The respondents noted that there were frequently informal 'routes' to senior positions whereby a man was selected, without interview, as an assistant to the person in the senior post. Such a move was commonly seen as a signal that this was to be the next senior position holder ('men cloning the clones'). They saw men as 'having the problem' and there was a good deal of pessimism about how this could be changed. Some felt that there was another generation coming up; that the generation that had been accustomed to 'male domination' would be gone within ten years. Others were less optimistic and noted that such people were still influential and set a tone with 'humorous' comments (like asking 'when is this equality business going to end?').

The respondents drew attention to the subtle ways in which, as they saw it, management 'up and down' put them under pressure to prove themselves, e.g. by drawing attention to any mistake they made with derogatory remarks such as 'what do you expect? It was a woman who did that.' They noted that when a woman stepped into a job that had 'always' been done by a man, there were attempts to undermine her by those so-called 'humorous' comments. There was a general feeling that a woman would have to be twice as good to have any chance of the job and that management were more 'comfortable' with trusting a senior appointment to a man.

The respondents felt that men at senior level still had very traditional views about women, and saw employing them as a 'total hassle'. If women were married, management anticipated the costs and inconveniences of maternity leave, and if they were not, they wondered 'what was wrong with her'. Those who had been in management settings noted that typically they were the only women there, and were very excluded from the male network.

Targets were seen as part of the solution. The women in this study saw such measures as 'the structural stuff that gives women confidence'; that would 'boost women's confidence'; 'make them encourage women' and so reduce the chance that women would be 'squeezed out'. A few were anxious that in that situation women would be seen as getting the jobs 'because they are women', a view that was challenged by others who noted that, as it was, competent women were being passed over. Some were uncomfortable with what they saw as any 'special treatment' of women on the grounds that it would be resented by men. On the other hand they were pessimistic about the extent to which 'a level playing pitch' could be brought about without such strategies since 'It's not in management anywhere in the world'. Their ambivalence was summed up by one participant who said: 'I'd like to compete equally with men if we got a fair shot'.

The TUI (1990) study of a random sample of union members who were teaching mainly at second level showed that although the women's level of education was significantly higher than that of their male counterparts, around three fifths of both the men and the women thought that being a man was a positive factor in achieving promotion, while only a tiny minority (3 per cent) thought that being a woman was advantageous. The report also showed that one in three male vice-principals or principals had prejudicial attitudes towards women, a pattern which is obviously likely to have implications as regards women's promotion. One in four of the women interviewed felt that they had been asked sex-discriminatory questions at interviews. Broadly similar trends also emerged in the Higher Education Study, with 60 per cent of the women in that study, but only 24 per cent of the men, believing that promotions were influenced by a candidate's sex (HEA Report, 1987). Similarly there was 'a very widespread perception of gender bias' in a study of second level teachers in Ireland, the majority of whom thought that 'being male was important in reality in obtaining a principalship' (ASTI, 1991:19). Similar trends emerged in Mahon's (1991a: 30, 31) study of women in the civil service in Ireland; in Rosenberg et al's study (1995) of women lawyers in the US; in Corcoran et al's study (1995) of women in non-traditional occupations in the UK; and Hicks's (1990) study of managers of hotel chains in Britain.

It is important to note that in some cases women effectively colluded with the situation. In the health board study, despite the fact that men were approximately four times more likely to be promoted from the lower to the senior end of the administrative hierarchy, a minority of women said that 'there are no barriers; haven't we got promoted?' Similarly in Mahon's study of the civil service, 82 per cent of women in the higher grades (Mahon, 1991a:56) as compared with more than half (52 per cent) of those at the middle grades thought that women had the same promotional opportunities as men. Obviously this trend can be interpreted in many ways, although the possibility that it indicates a tendency to promote women who endorse the status quo cannot be eliminated.

Male prejudice was particularly relevant for those in predominantly male structures, or in those parts of the structures, e.g. at senior level, where men predominated. These phenomena raise challenging issues as regards the creation of organisational cultures which positively value difference and the creation of an environment where 'opportunities exist to enable all staff to be employed at the top of their capacity' (Doherty, 1997).

Organisational procedures: interviewing, profiling and training

Weber's (1947) model of a bureaucracy was characterised by a specialised division of labour, a hierarchy of authority with a clearly demarcated system of command and responsibilities, and a formal set of rules and procedures. There has been increasing criticism of the assumption that those in the hierarchy are depersonalised automatons. It has been argued that once we accept:

> that staff bring their personal interests into organisations and that these shape the way they discharge their functions, we must also accept that gendered perceptions, practices and attitudes will be present too (Halford, 1992:172).

Within this context, the assumption that all male interviewing boards are acceptable is highly questionable. Nevertheless, they persist in a sizeable number of cases in the civil service, both in competitions run within Departments and those run by the Civil Service Commission and the Top Level Appointments Committee. In 1994, 38 per cent of boards interviewing for positions at senior management level (i.e. assistant secretary level or above) were all male, as were 20 per cent in 1995 (Department of Finance, 1997, Tabular Presentation:5a and 6a).

There is evidence that even where women were present on interviewing boards they were typically in a minority position. In the open recruitment competitions, even in that minority of cases where there was more than one woman on the board (9 per cent in 1994; and 21 per cent in 1995: Department of Finance, 1997, Tabular Statement) the impact of this was potentially reduced by an increase in the size of the board. It is difficult to see why equal representation was possible in only 2 out of 68 competitions, particularly since the over-representation of men in senior management positions has been described as a 'grave and profoundly disturbing pattern of inequality' (Department of Equality and Law Reform, 1994b).

These trends were not peculiar to the civil service. Mahon and Dillon (1996) found that overwhelmingly in 1994/95 interview boards organised by the Local Appointments Commission for the appointment of city/county managers and assistant managers were all male. A woman had been included on approximately half of the interview boards for finance officers, and on all interview boards for county secretary competitions in 1993/94. On the other hand, between 90-100 per cent of the competitions at middle management level (where the board is put together by the local authority) involved all-male boards. There was evidence that this pattern did not simply reflect the absence of 'suitable' women, since survey data in the study showed that men were more likely than women to have been asked to sit on interview boards.

The pattern of predominantly male interviewing boards, and the importance of gender in influencing promotion, also emerged in the education area (TUI, 1990; HEA, 1987). The difficulty of accessing information on the gender composition of interview boards has also been widely noted (e.g. see Gleeson 1992:201 as regards the educational area; and Department of Equality and Law Reform, 1994 as regards semi-state organisations). Even in the Eighth Annual Report on the Civil Service it was noted that the data was incomplete since:

> . . . many Departments did not use departmental competitions as a selection method for promotion and . . . other Departments had difficulty in producing meaningful figures on participation rates (Department of Finance, 1997:23).

Mahon and Dillon (1996) and myself (O'Connor, 1995b) also highlighted the fact that boards were typically chaired by a man who himself was often a retired public sector employee. Such men would have grown up and worked in a society where the marriage bar existed, and where the participation of married women in paid employment was both extremely rare and socially sanctioned. Their presence is not conducive to the appointment of women to senior positions.

The Hansard Society Commission (1990) noted that where marking schemes were quite loose, men were more likely than women to be appointed. Walters' (1987) work showed that in her study of the barriers to women's promotion in the British civil service, although senior management (which was predominantly male) scored males and females similarly on their abilities, when they were assessing them for senior management posts they took into account 'overall style and approach' and, on these criteria, the males were perceived as 'more suitable'. In the marking scheme used in local authorities, only 15-25 per cent went for qualifications; 20-25 per cent of the marks were allocated on the basis of the board's assessment of the personality and personal attributes necessary for the job, with 50-60 per cent of the marks going for general competence (Mahon and Dillon, 1996). It has been shown that the more subjective and informal the criteria, as in this case, the more likely it is to favour men (Goss and Brown, 1991).

Much was made in Mahon's (1991b) study of the civil service and in my own study of the health boards (O'Connor's, 1995b) of the importance of women being assigned high profile work which would enable them to achieve visibility, and so effectively increase their chance of being seen as appropriate people for promotion. Mahon noted that the more visible, high status 'plum jobs' were typically given out by (male) superiors and tended to flow along male lines. The women in the health boards also highlighted the importance of getting a wide variety of job experiences; having access to 'acting-up' jobs and to 'influential male sponsors', and equally the importance of not 'getting stuck' in low profile areas, where their very competence militated against their transfer/promotion. In both the local authorities and the health boards women felt effectively excluded by the male networks inside and outside the workplace, networks which it was recognised typically enabled men to make contacts, get to hear about promotional opportunities, and generally to become visible. In some cases, this meant that male candidates, but not female candidates, knew those on the interviewing board.

The provision of training opportunities reflects the organisation's perception of the worth of the employee and its willingness to invest in him/her. It is by no means clear that such opportunities are equally available to men and women. McCarthy (1986) noted that, in the companies she studied, the majority of managers felt that women's lack of confidence was the main factor which inhibited their promotion. Yet, as she noted:

> Where self-development was mentioned as being an important training goal, it referred to those on the managerial staff, and to a large extent excluded female employees (1986:22).

Hence, they were caught in a 'Catch 22' situation in which, on the one hand, their lack of confidence was seen as inhibiting their promotional prospects; and on the other hand, in order to gain access to self development courses, they needed to be promoted to managerial level. The women employed in the health boards stressed the need for more training, particularly management workshops and assertiveness courses for women at all levels (O'Connor, 1995b). Access to more expensive high profile career oriented courses, and cover to attend them, was seen as being disproportionately available to men.

It is widely accepted that indirect discrimination is very common although it has been very difficult to prove under existing legislation (see Chapter 2). It may be reflected not only in criteria, e.g. age limits, which are disproportionately more likely to affect women than men; but also in the idea that men 'need' promotion more; in the practice of giving men rather than women experiences which are likely to facilitate promotion, e.g. giving male primary teachers experience of teaching senior classes; in permitting men to skip steps on the career ladder, but expecting women to complete each one; operating from a position where there is a reliance on qualitative indicators of a candidate's 'style'; and attaching differential importance to management experience in the case of men and women. It is increasingly accepted that without change in the organisational culture it is impossible to devise procedures which will eliminate such practices.

Reconciliation of work and family life

Perhaps the most common explanation for the under-representation of women in positions of authority are the conflicting demands of paid work and family life. It is increasingly recognised that it is not motherhood itself, but the way in which it is socially and culturally constructed, which is the crucial factor. It was shown that the effect of motherhood on women's participation in paid employment in Ireland was the most negative in the EU; whereas in Denmark motherhood actually had a small positive effect on such participation (see Chapter 7). Perhaps not surprisingly then a number of studies have shown that in Ireland, even today, women in senior posts in the civil service (Mahon, 1991), in banking (Garavan, 1994), in the academy (O'Connor, 1998), and in accountancy (Barker and Monks, 1994) were more likely to be single, and less likely to have children than their male counterparts. This kind of 'reconciliation' of work and family is one which exacts a very high personal cost indeed.

Overwhelmingly, the women in the Midland and Mid-Western Health Boards study (O'Connor, 1995b) did not see the barriers to women's promotion as lying in the area of domestic and family responsibilities, although the failure to facilitate these was seen as symbolic of the health board's lack of concern for them as women. This may well reflect the fact that the study focused on women who were already one step up from the basic grade. Within the context of Irish society, it is arguable that only those who have found some way to reconcile paid work and family responsibilities are likely to have been able to reach this position in the first place.

At a more general level, much has been made of the extent to which the whole work setting is premised on the perceived normality of a male career and lifestyle and thus ignores the fact that women continue to bear most responsibility for child care (Mahon, 1991a). Indeed in Barker and Monks' (1994) study, of those who had children, nearly half of the men had a spouse/partner who took care of the children but this was true of none of the women. In this type of context a stress on long hours, fixed schedules etc. (which are assumed to be associated with productivity), constitutes a strategy for potentially excluding women. Such assumptions are not supported by research. Rather, such work has shown that actual output increases as people are given autonomy (Barker and Monks, 1994).

Maternity leave is a very basic element indeed in facilitating the reconciliation of paid work and family life. However, even after it was legally introduced in 1981, McCarthy (1986) noted that among the companies she studied it was often regarded as highly contentious, with the managers being hostile to maternity legislation and its operation. The ongoing practice of not replacing women on maternity leave (and expecting their colleagues to carry their tasks) has played an important part in fuelling hostility towards the employment of women at any level, but particularly in senior posts in the civil service (Mahon, 1991) and in sections of the health boards (O'Connor, 1995b). Under pressure from Europe, it is proposed to provide parental leave, i.e. a minimum of three months non-transferable leave for each parent in the case of each child who is under eight years. The EU Directive on this must be put into effect in June 1998. At this stage it appears that it will be unpaid in Ireland. It is difficult to anticipate what the take-up will be like.

There is a good deal of resistance to job sharing at management level. McCarthy and Drew (1994) noted that, in their study of private and public organisations in Dublin, although job-sharing existed in more than half of these organisations, it was by no means always available to senior staff. A similar pattern emerged in the health boards (O'Connor, 1995b). Furthermore, even when job sharing, flexibility and career breaks were provided, they were typically taken by women; such take-up was seen as indicative of a lower level of commitment, thereby further reducing women's possibilities as regards promotion.

Individual characteristics

A variety of phenomena have been identified here including women's lack of interest in promotion; their lack of confidence; their organisational naiveté and/or their lack of interest in the kind of management which they see as the norm.

Perhaps the most common of these explanations twenty years ago was that women were not really interested in promotion. As McCarthy (1986:39) noted, such explanations 'pointed directly to the women themselves'. This kind of explanation had the 'virtue' of effectively blaming the women themselves for their under-representation in senior positions within organisations. It was very much part of a taken-for-granted reality at that time. It reflected a stereotypical view of all women and was reinforced by the marriage bar, the absence of maternity leave, different wage scales for men and women, etc. In such a context, beliefs about women's lack of interest in promotion could easily be maintained.

Such explanations are still advanced today. They ignore the fact that high levels of commitment to paid employment have been consistently shown to be related to educational level, to the nature of the work being undertaken, and to the expected 'pay off', of education, investment in training, etc., factors which, as previously mentioned, have been shown to be gender related. In this situation some women will decide not to apply for senior posts because they are unwilling to undertake the differential investment in education and training necessary for promotion in the case of women.

Certainly studies have shown that, even when they are qualified to do so, women are less likely than men to apply for promotion. Kelleghan *et al*'s (1985) study found that only 16 per cent of female primary teachers who were in a position to apply for promotion intended to do so, as compared with 50 per cent of the men. Similarly, at second level, women teachers were less likely than their male counterparts to aspire to and/or to apply for a principalship (ASTI, 1991). The low participation rates of women in promotion competitions, particularly at senior management level in the civil service, have also been noted. Furthermore, as in teaching, it has been noted that women who did apply for such positions had a relatively high success rate (Co-Ordinating Group of Secretaries, 1996). Assumptions that these patterns reflect deep-seated differences between men and women are implicitly challenged by the fact that the proportion of women applicants for the post of principal in primary schools changed dramatically over a very short period (Lynch, 1994).

It is certainly true that women's typically low levels of self-confidence are not helpful. The implications of this lack of confidence are very real. In the health board study, those in the nursing sector saw women as poor at presenting themselves and at taking credit for their achievements, particularly in an interview setting. It was a skill where they saw men as 'having the edge', as better 'talkers'. A low level of confidence also affected women's willingness to apply and re-apply for jobs: 'If you go for it (i.e. promotion) once and don't get it, you are not going to go again' (O'Connor, 1996a).

These low levels of confidence can be seen as reflecting a wider cultural evaluation of women. Hannan *et al* (1996) found that even among Junior and Leaving Certificate students, girls were more likely than boys to have a low level of self esteem. It is possible to suggest that where the face of authority is overwhelmingly male; where women's work is seen as less valuable than men's; where women are paid less; where there are very few powerful female role models within the public arena; and where there is a belief that men's power and authority is 'natural', inevitable and appropriate, women's low levels of self confidence can be seen as reflecting an 'androcentric' cultural reality (Lynch, 1994).

In some cases women's lack of self confidence was exacerbated by a kind of organisational naiveté. Mahon noted that the women she studied in the civil service tended to work hard at the jobs they had and noticed career 'routes' much later than did their male counterparts. They 'assumed' that their hard work would be noticed and that this was the basis for promotion. Similarly, among those in the health board study (O'Connor, 1995b) there was a general naiveté as regards the reasons why people are actually promoted within organisations. Women thought of promotion in terms of recognition and reward for discharging existing responsibilities well. The whole question as to why an organisation would promote people who had shown that they were willing to discharge higher level responsibilities at a low salary simply did not occur to them. Similarly Barker and Monks (1994) showed that the women accountants in their study were just as interested in career progression as the men. However, they were less likely to get involved in office politics; and more likely to want to get on with their jobs rather than 'trumpeting their successes around the office and, particularly, in the key promotion ears' (Barker and Monks, 1994:40).

In the health board study it was clear that the net effect of organisational naiveté and lack of confidence was that it did not even occur to many of the women at middle and senior level to consider a career in management ('Is it possible?' 'You get the feeling you have to be an incredibly high-flier'). This was exacerbated by their perception of that structure as a very male area. Some even seemed to be waiting to be 'asked': 'Nobody said it to me'. They noted that 'Women wait to be asked, they are waiting for someone to spot talent'.

It was striking how often those in the nursing hierarchy in the Midland and Mid-Western Health Board study did not even 'notice' where the centres of decision-making were in relation to resources. It has been suggested that this reflects a kind of 'consensual control' (O'Connor 1995a) involving the obscuring of gendered power, so that the women did not 'notice' which structures had power, or that women were under-represented in such structures.

Some of those in the health board study were very ambivalent about the kind of management they experienced. They described it as 'money management' rather than 'a more person oriented style of management'. There was a feeling that 'line management' was 'too hierarchical', 'too rigid'; they felt that they would like to see more of a 'team based' approach. The existing rigid male style was perceived as 'intimidating' and defensive, with very little communication 'from the bottom to the top'. This sort of management was not seen as attractive. There was also a strong feeling that management would be a lot more attractive, 'if there were enough females there to give you back-up; you'd have more confidence if more were in the same boat'.

Nevertheless despite low levels of self confidence, in many areas women were very interested in promotion, and extremely frustrated by what they saw as the low possibilities of achieving it. For example, some of those in the nursing sector in the health board study saw themselves as 'the last of a generation', people with a vocation, who would not go on strike, and they both admired and were critical of what they saw as the more militant attitudes of a new generation of nurses. There was a strong feeling of anger and frustration as they adjusted their expectations down in the face of a (realistic) assessment of their low possibilities of promotion: 'If you started off being really ambitious, and, if, after a set number of years, you haven't moved, you aren't going to keep on'. Ironically, the pressure to 'give up' was exacerbated by the fact that financially they could be better off without promotion, so 'you may as well be happy as a staff nurse'.

Resourcing of predominantly female areas

As elsewhere in Europe, women are very strongly represented in the professional services sector in Ireland. The figures vary depending on how the category is defined although in Ireland, as across the rest of the EU, professional women are concentrated in the health and education areas. For example in Ireland women occupied 47 per cent of the professional, technical and related jobs (very slightly above the EU average of 45 per cent: Bulletin on Women and Employment, October, 1994). In the Irish Labour Force Survey, 1996 (CSO. 1997:30) on the other hand, women constituted 65 per cent of those in the professional services sector.

It is suggested that predominantly female areas of activity are likely to have greater difficulty accessing resources than areas of predominantly male employment, even at the professional level. Davies (1991) saw the lack of priority attached to resourcing a particular area as ultimately reflecting a gendered division of labour within the professions. It is reflected in the pay and working conditions in predominantly female professions such as primary teaching and nursing. Systematic data are limited. Indeed even in the early 1990s research undertaken on behalf of the nursing unions was more concerned with highlighting stress (Wynne *et al*, 1993) than with exploring such structural issues, although a Nursing Commission is currently considering them.

Davies (1991) argued that when predominantly female professions had difficulties accessing resources, a coping style of management emerged. She suggested that this was a response to neglect by the 'powerful' and merely perpetuated the problem. This style of management was characterised by:

> a fire fighting approach to management that is accompanied by a strong personal commitment to the task, a weak sense of status and position, and a willingness, sometimes quite literally on the part of the manager, to 'roll up the sleeves' and get on with whatever needs to be done (Davies, 1991: 238).

Davies recognised that typically with this sort of manager there was overload, stress and burnout among subordinates and a kind of isolation from senior management bred by exhaustion; the coping manager was typically too exhausted to look for additional resources from further up the hierarchy. This style was frequently described by women in the health board study (O'Connor, 1996a). It was seen by them as being generated by the failure of administration to understand the needs of their services, a problem which was compounded by their remoteness from the structures allocating resources and by a kind of defensive isolation ('don't hassle them in Admin') which made it very difficult for the needs of their services to be 'visible'.

As the women at middle and senior level in these health boards saw it, those in positions of responsibility who asked for additional resources were put under considerable pressure: 'If you asked, you were the worst in the world'. Some highlighted the difficulties of women 'taking a stand', particularly if they were working in isolated settings. The word 'intimidation' was spontaneously referred to in a small number of cases to capture the very real pressure they were put under as individuals to 'encourage' them to fall into line. This typically occurred in the face of requests by individuals for additional resources. Typically, in these situations, a woman's request to a (male) administrator was construed by him as an inability to take responsibility for running the service under the existing parameters. As the women involved perceived it, they were threatened by being told: 'If you can't take the responsibility, I'll get someone who will.' Perhaps the most important aspect of such interaction was that it was perceived as a mechanism to ensure female compliance and to perpetuate a situation where 'we (women) are not willing to stir it'. Such remarks were made spontaneously by respondents. It is worth stressing that these experiences of intimidation were not mentioned frequently, but that they did create a climate of fear, and increased a reluctance to ask for additional resources.

Summary

In this chapter, attention has been focused on a group of women who have attracted comparatively little attention, viz. women in 'top jobs', i.e. in managerial and professional occupations. Despite women's higher educational levels; a formal commitment to equal opportunity by nation states and the EU; and a concern with profitability in a capitalist economy, women remain under-represented in positions of authority in Europe.

Traditionally there has been a good deal of ambivalence about a focus on women's access to such positions within the paid employment arena, not least because it was seen as copper-fastening the existing privileges of middle-class women and creating and reflecting a situation where 'tokenism' was likely to occur. There is no doubt that these dangers are very real. However, there is no stronger indication of the continued perception of women as 'outlaws', 'suspect', 'not like us' than their exclusion from the higher echelons: breaking the link between subordination and femaleness is an important element in undermining a structure which is rooted in such subordination.

In Ireland women constitute 65 per cent of those in the professional services sector but only 24 per cent of those in administrative, executive and managerial occupations (Labour Force Survey, 1996 [CSO, 1997]). The proportion of women in such positions of 'expertise' and 'authority' (Savage, 1992) has increased dramatically over the past twenty-five years. However, women still make up only a tiny proportion of those at senior management level even in areas such as the civil service, where there has been continuous monitoring of these patterns for ten years. This pattern is not peculiar to the civil service, nor indeed is it peculiar to Ireland.

In one sense the persistence of these trends is extraordinary. At another level it illustrates the importance of understanding how men's access to such positions is maintained. Finally, women in the professional services sector make up just under one third of all the women in paid employment (Labour Force Survey, 1996 [CSO, 1997:30]). Hence the issue of the value of women's work in predominantly female professional areas and their access to positions of authority is one which is relevant to a sizeable proportion of the female labour force in Ireland.

9

Ireland: A Country for Women?

Introduction

WRITERS and dramatists have consistently depicted Irish women as strong, coping and courageous, while Irish men have been presented as weak, sometimes over-dependent on maternal approval, and often as rather pathetic figures (Mahoney, 1993; J.B. Keane etc). Indeed, this very weakness is often used to justify women's support of what is privately seen as the illusion of male authority. Women see themselves as the strong ones, and 'play along' in the interests of the family and of social harmony, almost like a mother 'playing along' with a child's deluded notions of power. This view is difficult to sustain in the light of the increasing importance of the machinery of the state and the subordinate position of women both within it and in the wider public arena.

Connell argued that although we typically think of gender as a property of individuals (i.e. male/female) it is necessary to go beyond this, and think of it as a property of institutions. Connell suggested that the gendered reality of institutional structures reflected 'the commitments implicit in conventional and hegemonic masculinity and the strategies pursued in an attempt to realise them' (1995a: 215). Only a minority of men, he argued, actively subordinate women (i.e. hegemonic masculinity). However, the majority benefit from 'the patriarchal dividend' (in terms of 'honour, prestige, and the right to command. They also gain a material dividend.' Connell 1995b: 82). They are most comfortable if it appears that 'it is given to them (i.e. heterosexual men) by an external force, by nature or convention, or even by women themselves, rather than by an active social subordination of women going on here and now' (Connell, 1995a:215). In Ireland, the social subordination of women was seen, until very recently, as 'natural', 'inevitable', 'what women want'. It was reflected in women's allocation to the family arena, where their position was given rhetorical validation. Married women's ability to effectively use this arena as a social and emotional power base obscured the fact that their position was ultimately shaped by a system in which they were seen as subordinate.

It was suggested in Chapter 1 that the social and cultural changes in Irish society reflected what Connell (1995a) called 'crisis tendencies'. At a structural level the most obvious of these involves the changing relationship between church and state. There are however other tensions such as those generated by an increasingly service-oriented economic system where women's employment has risen substantially and men's has barely held its own. There are tensions too arising from the state's need for inclusiveness as a basis for its own legitimacy, in the context of the patriarchal nature of Irish public life, where the 'normal' situation is for men to represent women's interests.

Furthermore within each of the major institutional structures (the institutional church, the state, the economic system, the social and cultural construction of heterosexuality) the taken-for-granted nature of male authority is being steadily eroded. In Ireland, the process has been accelerated by a series of revelations concerning the abuse of male power within these structures (see O'Connor, 1995c). In this context, the appropriateness of defining the common good in terms of male interest has become visibly problematic. Nevertheless, concepts of womanhood continue to revolve around caring, reproduction, familism, love, sexual attractiveness, and gendered employment. These concepts sit uneasily with the dilution of trust and the heightened need for an awareness of gendered self-interest which are by-products of the diminished acceptance of male authority.

Many of these crisis tendencies are international phenomena. The impact of them however is particularly acute in Ireland, given the size of the society (3.6 million). Furthermore it is a society where women have been encouraged to exclude themselves from the public arena for 'the sake of the family' although their educational levels have traditionally been higher than those of their male counterparts (Rubery *et al*, 1996). It is increasingly a materialistic society where family size is falling and where the value attached to women's work within the home is becoming more problematic. In all sorts of ways, and in many arenas, women's voices and their concerns are beginning to be heard. Yet, the perceived legitimacy of those voices, especially insofar as they articulate women's needs and perspectives, is still problematic: 'the alternative vision offered by female knowledge and insight is suspect and a source of fear' (O'Carroll, 1991:57-58).

In this book, women have first been located in the context of Irish society and its concepts of womanhood; the problematic nature of the distinctions made between paid work and family have been discussed; and the issue of the family as the source of women's strength and vulnerability has been explored. The tensions and ambiguities in the position of young women have been summarised. The book has concluded by looking at married women's increasing presence in the paid employment arena, and their increasing occupancy of positions in the professional services and to a very much lesser extent in management. In this chapter we shall briefly locate some of the changes which have occurred and will speculate about the issues which are likely to arise in the future.

Changing places: the limits and extent of such change

In looking at the position and experiences of women in Ireland in the past twenty-five years, the many nuances implicit in the phrase 'changing places' seem very appropriate. Some 'places' (e.g. families) have changed; married women have increasingly participated in others (e.g. in paid employment); and the world of education and training seems to be available to young women regardless of gender. Yet in many ways the institutional realities of the church, the state and the economic system have changed very little.

The changes that have been most obvious have been the dramatic fall in the number of children and the dramatic rise in the participation of married women in paid employment at a time when male employment has been more or less static. Family size has halved over the past twenty-five years, and the participation of married women in paid employment has increased from 38,300 in 1971 to 241,000 in 1996, with 63 per cent of married women aged 25-34 years now in the labour force (Labour Force Survey, 1996 [CSO, 1997]). Furthermore, women in Ireland are predominantly involved in full-time rather than part-time paid employment. In a society with one of the lowest levels of state support in the EU, 43 per cent of mothers with one or two dependent children are in paid employment (CSO, 1997). Indeed in 1996, the labour force participation rate of Irish women (at 41 per cent) was coming close to the EU average (45.3 per cent).

There have been other changes. The number of births to lone mothers has increased dramatically with one in three first time births and one in four of all births now being to lone mothers. This raises issues about the definition of the family. The definition of work has been more subtly problematised, challenges in this area stemming from the high levels of male unemployment and from the increasing recognition of the value and importance of women's unpaid work in the home and community.

Irish women now constitute approximately two thirds of those in the professional services area and this is projected to increase. Many of these women are in predominantly female professional areas, such as nursing or primary teaching, and this raises issues as regards the valuation of women's work, since these professions are typically less well paid than predominantly male ones. From what little we know, it appears that even young unmarried women need to be more educated than their male counterparts to 'compensate' for their gender. It also appears that a 'gender bonus' for maleness is reflected in the greater possibilities of promotion enjoyed by men both in predominantly female and in predominantly male occupations. In contrast to the position twenty-five years ago, Irish women now occupy roughly a quarter of administrative managerial and executive positions.

However, a wide range of organisational processes and practices (see Chapter 8) ensure that men still overwhelmingly occupy senior management positions. These characteristics are of course not peculiar to Ireland.

The sheer extent of women's contribution to the family and community has affected their emotional power in both areas, in the face of men's ongoing limited participation in housework and disproportionate access to personal spending money (Second Commission on the Status of Women, 1993; Rottman, 1994a, 1994b).

The evidence is sketchy and incomplete, but it is difficult to avoid the conclusion that women, particularly in working-class areas, have become more visible within their communities. Yet poverty is a reality in the lives of a sizeable proportion of such women and children. Within more middle-class areas, the increasing participation of women in paid employment has potentially reduced the pool of neighbourhood women for informal sociability. Nevertheless women's access to personal spending money, within a context where they are increasingly seen as 'entitled' to some time and money for themselves, has made it possible for them to meet for drinks, in keep fit clubs etc., arenas which are arguably conducive to 'a culture of affiliation' (based on their strength and resources), rather than one simply based on 'shared victimisation' (Woolf, 1993: 315-316).

However, although women are increasingly present within public arenas, there are clear limits to the extent to which such arenas have changed. The existence of opportunities as regards paid employment has offered women choices, but for many women these choices have been highly constrained. The kinds of jobs that are available to them, with the exception of those in professional services and management areas, are to a considerable extent poorly paid and characterised by low possibilities as regards promotion. Thus, the 'solution' at an individual woman's level has reflected and reinforced the overall problem, viz. a highly gendered system of paid employment where wages, benefits and other 'privileges' are disproportionately obtained by those who 'fit' best within the system – men, particularly middle class men.

The changes which have come about in the lives of young women appear obvious in some ways, although because of a paucity of data they are more difficult to quantify. On the one hand, young women occupy a world which is increasingly sexually permissive. On the other hand, double standards and the fear of being seen as a 'slag' 'a tight bitch' or a 'lezzie' appear to be a reality. Subject choice, career choice and recreational activities are 'officially' gender neutral, although what evidence we have suggests that the picture is a good deal more complex. There is some suggestion that the ethos of girls' schools is rather different from that of boys'; and that in mixed schools sexual harassment is a reality. What evidence we have also suggests a greater valuation of 'male' subjects. Thus, despite the fact that girls are out-performing boys at Leaving Certificate level, they still occupy a world where the implicit message is that women are less valuable than men.

Young middle-class women appear to be offered the possibility of full participation in this world. However, clubs and organisations are geared to the needs of middle-class boys, with positions of authority overwhelmingly being held by such boys. We do not know to what extent young women have an awareness of their interests as women. It is ironical, and worrying, that young women still have low levels of self-esteem (Hannan *et al*, 1996). It seems possible to suggest that they assess themselves, and their skills and abilities, on male terms in a male world and that by definition, as young women, they are less than adequate. The needs of girls, and particularly working-class girls, have a low priority in this world. It is not difficult to see that for some of them, a withdrawal from it into lone parenthood may be an emotionally, if not financially, attractive option.

The lives of Irish women have changed substantially but the themes of caring, familism, reproduction, sexual attractiveness and love continue to be important, although they are being differentially weighted by various women with all the possibilities for change that such variation involves. New themes, such as those related to the family (the family feminist), the degendered worker, and the acceptance of 'difference' are emerging. Within Irish society there is at least a rhetorical recognition of the desirability of women playing a part in society and making choices about their own lives. Wider cultural developments have eroded the boundaries of loyalty and secrecy surrounding marriage and family life. Through the development of talk shows; through the initiation of a wide variety of personal development, health, leadership and community development programmes; through legislative activity to protect the rights of the woman in the home as well as through the perceived reality of the women's movement, the needs and experiences of women have come into the public arena. Their sheer presence has implicitly undermined the ability of individual men and the ability of church and state to put forward accounts which are at odds with their reality. In this situation questions might be raised about the appropriate extent and nature of male control. However, since the reality of that control still tends to be denied, or is assumed to be 'natural', or what women want, it is difficult to make this issue explicit. Grint (1991:223) has suggested that the picture is one 'of increasingly embattled senior men confronted by young women undeterred by history or tradition'.

This indeed may be the way such men perceive the situation. To many women the reality is a good deal more complex.

Issues for the future

The most fundamental issue for the future is the relative value of men and women. The differential valuing of women and men underlies our ideas about the nature and value of their work in the home and in the area of paid employment. It underpins our ideas about their appropriate relationship with each other and their place in the wider society. In this section an attempt will be made to speculate about the choices which confront men and women, individually and collectively, and their likely outcome over the next twenty-five years.

The choice for men both in the public and private arena is clear. At heart it is one of choosing whether they want to enforce the subordination of women, through physical or sexual violence; through the denigration of the value of their work inside and outside the home; through the devaluing of their skills; through the de-legitimation of their emotional power and through their exclusion from centres of power that men define as key. Insofar as men do not wish to do this then it is clearly necessary to eliminate privileges based on gender (i.e. 'the patriarchal dividend': Connell, 1995b: 82). This will require a rethinking of the whole nature of manhood, sexuality, work and power and the creation of structures which embody these ideas in the context of a renegotiation of their relationship with women, and a restructuring of society.

It is ironical that this appears to be such a radical proposal. John Stuart Mill in the middle of the nineteenth century recognised that the privileging of men was implicit in, for example, the very structure of marriage, and attempted to waive the unearned privileges which he saw accruing to himself in this situation. The apparent novelty of this idea as we approach the second millennium highlights the extent to which our consciousness of male privilege has become dulled, despite the second wave of the women's movement, and despite the heightened awareness of the relationship between power and knowledge in a post-modern world.

The choice for women at the most fundamental level revolves around whether we are willing to recognise and challenge the gendered nature of power, i.e. to problematise the patriarchal dividend both in public and private areas. It is hard not to see this as involving a tedious series of skirmishes, occasional victories and wearysome reversals. The legitimacy of a woman's agenda, with its prioritising of women's needs, particulary those relating to their vulnerability to poverty and to domestic violence and their under-representation in positions of authority in the wider society, will be key. Underlying these are issues related to the value of 'women's work' inside and outside the home; the nature of a genuinely woman-centred sexuality and the possibilities for male/female relationships within a world where these relationships with men are not inevitably hierarchical.

The reality of Irish society in the past twenty-five years has been transformed by individual incremental change, as reflected in family size, women's education, women's participation in paid employment, etc. Of course these changes have been facilitated by technology, and by a post-modern deconstruction of taken-for-granted ideologies. Ironically, perhaps, the ability of women to change the parameters of their own private lives has generated in some an optimism which fails to recognise the implicit male bias in these systems and under-estimates the strength and flexibility of the processes and practices involved in the maintenance of patriarchy. This optimism is legitimated by ideas about meritocracy and equality which are fostered within what purport to be gender neutral structures. The implication is that there is no need for women to face the gendered reality of power; that their interests are 'no different to anyone else's' (i.e. men's); and that attempts to suggest this are divisive and unhelpful. Within the private arena the possibility of gendered opposing interests can be obscured by love. Yet, 'a gender order where men dominate women cannot avoid constituting men as an interest group concerned with defense and women as an interest group concerned with change' (Connell, 1995b: 82). Women will need to confront this. To fail to do so constitutes one of the greatest threats to improvements in the position of women in the future.

It is clear that there are considerable difficulties arising from the fact that women's work in the home and in the wider community is unpaid and to a considerable extent undervalued. Indeed within an increasingly materialistic society it is perhaps inevitable that it will be undervalued insofar as it is unpaid. Yet it is equally clear that it is socially valuable. Mahon (1994) suggested that state policies in the area of taxation, social welfare and child care in Ireland have for the most part effectively underpinned the position of the male head of the household. It seems probable that this will change slowly, with Ireland moving from being a strong to a weak breadwinner state (O'Connor and Shortall, 1998). The idea of a social wage for every man, woman and child is attractive. However, since it would erode the financial control which has been seen as an important element in Irish men's definition of themselves, it is likely to be resisted.

Increasingly, both men and women will be involved in paid employment. The employment of women, not least because they are a low paid, relatively unconscientised labour force is likely to increase, particularly given the prioritising of the service sector, and the fact that women are predominantly located in this sector. It is probable that a minimum wage will be introduced in Ireland. Nevertheless, it seems likely that women will continue to be over-represented among the low paid, as they are throughout Europe.

There has been little evidence of the willingness of the Irish state to reconcile work and family life, although pressure from Europe, as in the past, may encourage some movement in this direction. For the most part it is women who cope with the difficulties consequent on a failure to do this. Since almost four fifths of the Irish women who are in paid employment are in full-time work, they are already coping with this situation. It seems likely that they will continue to do so, more or less unaided by the state.

What evidence we have suggests that the existence of substantial areas of predominantly female employment, and the equation between 'natural' femininity and skills, has been associated with the devaluing of such skills, and with lower pay levels in those areas where women are concentrated. This appears to apply both to the hourly wages of women industrial workers and to the salaries paid to nurses and primary teachers (who are predominantly women) as opposed to computer programmers and university lecturers (who are predominantly men). There is some evidence that women themselves, their unions and the EU are beginning to challenge gender-biased job evaluation schemes although this can be expected to be strongly resisted. Indeed it is salutary to note that the only case taken to date in this area, a case in the UK involving the payment of lower wages to speech therapists (a predominantly female occupation) than to psychologists (a predominantly male occupation), has already gone on for fourteen years (See Chapter 2; also Lester, 1997). Thus progress in this area, although critical, seems likely to be slow.

Women's educational achievements are being reflected in their increasing dominance in the professional services. It seems inevitable that, when this is combined with the increasing participation of married women in paid employment, these trends will continue and will become stronger. One can expect that women will increasingly move into the 'male' professional bastions such as law and medicine and will increasingly occupy positions of authority within the state structures. Over the next twenty-five years, it seems probable that individual and collective legal skirmishing and political lobbying will be part of such women's lives within these structures.

Up to very recently it has been almost impossible to envisage a concept of woman which embraced authority in the public arena. This has begun to change. A handful of women have recently exemplified this possibility, including Mary Robinson, as former President of Ireland, and Mary McAleese as the current President. There have been others in the world of politics. However, the ambivalence towards them was soberingly demonstrated by the electoral annihilation of most of those who were ministers in the last government. Clearly there are issues here which need to be confronted by men and women alike.

The extent and nature of the solidarity between women and their ability to create and maintain structures which recognise variation in their experiences of discrimination, their different choices and lifestyles and their different levels of gender awareness is likely to be critical as regards the perpetuation of male control, a control which is increasingly likely to be mediated through women who support the system. In that context the short-term rewards available to those who are willing to be 'hard on women' as the price of their apparent acceptance by male-dominated structures are likely to be considerable. Ironically this is barely beginning to be an issue in Irish society, partly because of women's strength and partly because it has simply not occurred to men to use them in this way. Attempting to deal with the increasing use of this strategy is likely to be one of the most painful issues to be faced in the future.

It is clear that some women may choose not to pursue such options, an outcome which is heartily desired by conventional masculinity. However, in the face of decreasing family size, and an increasingly materialistic culture, even if women do not participate in paid employment or seek promotion when their children are young, they may well have a contribution to make to the public arena at a later stage. It is possible that the processes (outlined in Chapter 8) which have been very effective in maintaining male control over institutional structures will continue to operate, with age limits, restrictions on re-entry, etc. continuing to be used to effectively limit such women's options. The need for vigilance in resisting the imposition of such barriers is likely to be crucial.

The EU's concern with the nature of democracy and citizenship and the Irish Government's own commitments in the gender area have created pressure for change. Quotas have been introduced to a wide range of state bodies. In many cases these have been vigorously resisted. Indeed, it is fair to say that some women have been uncomfortable with the sort of positive discrimination implicit in such arrangements, while others have highlighted the fact that they merely counterbalance the implicit positive discrimination in favour of men which has become the norm. The continuance of such measures is seen as crucially important: it is the 'structural stuff that gives women confidence' (O'Connor, 1996a).

Despite much rhetoric there is a continued implicit prioritising of men and their interests by male-dominated institutional structures. There remains a residual feeling within the wider society and in state agencies, that men and their needs are in some way more important than women and their needs. It is implicit in the prioritising of long-term unemployment, which predominantly involves men, above the re-integration of women who have left, or indeed been excluded from, the labour force because of marriage and family responsibilities. This approach, which in fact raises issues of indirect discrimination, is typically justified by referring to the need to deal with the unemployment figures and the live register. It fails to see the potential contribution of such women to the economic well-being of the country. It also ignores the issue of the appropriateness of excluding them in view of the EU's concern with social integration and the requirement to gender-audit EU funds. The failure to produce a national report outlining the extent to which EU structural funds are actually targeted at women is a very effective method of obscuring this issue (CWC and NICVA, 1996). There has been no attempt to introduce contract compliance as a way of bringing about equality at the level of outcome, despite the fact that it has been shown to be a very effective way of challenging discrimination in the North of Ireland, and one which is compatible with EU law (Lester, 1997). It is difficult to see such patterns changing unless and until women-oriented women constitute a critical mass (at least 30 per cent) of senior management within the structures of the state. It remains to be seen if this will be possible within the next twenty-five years.

In a society where women see themselves in terms of their relationship with others and are accustomed to 'humouring' men in the interests of family solidarity, the attractiveness of autonomy is limited. Nevertheless, to a degree to which one would not suspect from the media, positive attitudes exist towards 'developing women's confidence in themselves', and to ensuring 'that the things which women value receive full consideration in society', and developing society 'in such a way that women play a part'. It is interesting that none of these definitions make any explicit reference to men. They do, however, implicitly advert to the invisibility/exclusion of women and the things they value from the public arena. It is clear that a fundamental restructuring is what is being envisaged by women within a changing Ireland (MRBI, 1994).

Many men, at a personal level, have come to terms with the redefinition of manhood which is implicit in these ideas. However, such ideas have not yet been assimilated into the social and cultural construction of heterosexuality nor have they been dealt with by the main institutional structures such as the institutional church, the state or even the economic system. Indeed they have tended to be ignored, occasionally surfacing in crises concerning male authority or in vituperative reactions to specific issues. Among young men and women, within what purports to be a gender neutral world, active (hetero) sexuality seems to be an increasingly important element, although issues related to the gendered reality of power, reflected in sexual double standards and in ambivalence towards the use of force in sexual relationships, seem to be obscured.

The widespread adoption of a feminised concept of love has implicitly devalued the typically male contributions to family life, such as financial support, practical help, etc. On the other hand, typically female contributions and areas of expertise, such as talking about feelings and relationships, are implicitly highly valued. In this context, women are legitimately perceived as the key resource providers, and the people with the emotional expertise to maintain the cohesion of the family unit. Elements such as caring, when separated from the 'appropriate heterosexual context', can be seen as further eroding male power within the family and bode ill for the future ability of the state to legitimise attempts to compel lone mothers to undertake paid employment (as has been done in other societies, e.g. the US). Such has been Irish women's desire for financial independence that to date this has not even become an issue here.

Women in Ireland are accustomed to making choices and creating meaning and identity within structures which, to a greater or lesser extent, are not of their own choosing. They have shown a formidable ability, even within the social and cultural constraints operating in Ireland from the 1920s to the 1960s, to ensure that their daughters received an education. Indeed, as previously mentioned, Ireland is the only OECD country where women aged 55-64 years have been more educated than their male counterparts. Because of the conservative nature of the educational content and process, this did not immediately subvert the system. However, the support of mothers for their daughters' endorsement of lone parenthood (McCashin, 1996) has had a much more immediate effect. It is by no means clear where mothers' concern for their daughters might end, or what lifestyles it might lead them to condone. The implications of these changes for their sons is an issue which will need to be faced by many women. However, to the extent to which they see the changing social and cultural landscape increasing their children's possibilities as regards personal happiness, the more likely they are to feel comfortable with them.

It is perhaps not surprising that in this situation many men and women will yearn for the certainties of what is nostalgically seen as a simpler world. Some men will turn to violence to extract that submission from women which 'should' be given to them as men. Others will react with despair to a situation where they feel diminished because gendered privileges are not available to them or where they see themselves as having no value because they are not breadwinners. Some will recognise that in this changed social and cultural context there are possibilities for a different kind of relationship with women, and indeed a different lifestyle. Such a route is one which Connell, himself a heterosexual man, sees as having benefits, not least of which are related to the fact that most men have loved at least one woman, whether mother, daughter, wife or lover.

It is unclear which route will be taken by Irish men. It has been noted that the class structure in Ireland has been remarkably resilient, and it is possible that patriarchy will be equally so. Resistance to date has involved effectively ignoring the changes which are occurring. Perhaps the most striking manifestation of this has been the widespread misperception of the gender of what has become known as the Celtic Tiger, in a situation where male employment has been virtually static and female employment has increased dramatically. It has also involved what can only be described as hostile attempts to undermine women who are successful within 'male' areas (e.g. world class athletes such as Sonia O'Sullivan). There appears to have been an increase in sexual and other violent crimes against women. There have been attempts to co-opt individual women and there has been the beginning of a recognition of the usefulness of right-wing women whose main loyalties are towards men. There has been no evidence of attempts by the dominant institutions to rethink their own definitions of womanhood, or indeed manhood. To an extraordinary degree the changes in women's lives over the past twenty-five years have barely impacted on many institutional structures. Insofar as women wish to be part of them, they do so on male terms. These structures are still controlled by men, and they operate on the assumption that the male is the norm. Yet Irish society remains highly gendered: being a woman is seen as the most important element in most women's identity.

There are some signs of hope, such as the tradition of 'easy', 'decent' men who have peopled our literature, and our lives, and whose relationships with women have been characterised by respect and geniality rather than domination. The crisis tendencies within and between the institutional structures and the visibility of the erosion of male authority within what is a numerically small society suggest that pragmatic concessions will be made. Europe's concern with social solidarity and with the democratic deficit may further legitimise women's visibility and their contribution to the public arena. A small number of men are publicly discussing the redefinition of manhood; others are endorsing a 'woman's agenda' in the public arena, distancing themselves from men who are violent towards women and children, and trying to create structures in the public arena which do not institutionalise indirect discrimination against women.

The position of women in Irish society is in a state of flux. Many of the changes which have occurred are not peculiar to Irish society, although they are particularly visible within it because of the very scale of the society, the emotional power of women within the family, their educational achievements and their disproportionate access to positions in the professional services. However, unless its institutional structures reflect and reinforce a positive valuation of womanhood in all its multifacetedness then, truly, it remains no country for women . . . or indeed for men.

References

A

Abbot, P. and Wallace, C. (1990) *An introduction to sociology: feminist perspectives*. London and New York: Routledge.

Acar, F. (1990) 'Role priorities and career patterns: a cross cultural study of Turkish and Jordanian University Teachers', in S. Stiver Lie and V. O'Leary (eds) *Storming the Tower*. London: Kogan Page.

Acker, J. (1988) 'Class, gender and the relations of distribution', *Signs* 13, 3: 473-497.

Acker, J. (1989) 'The problem with patriarchy', *Sociology* 23, 2: 235-240.

Acker, J. (1990) 'Hierarchies, jobs, bodies: a theory of gendered organisations', *Gender and Society* 4: 139-158.

Acker, J. (1991) 'Thinking about wages: the gendered gap in Swedish banks', *Gender and Society* 5, 3: 390-407.

Adams, B.N. (1968) *Kinship in an urban setting*. Chicago, Ill: Markham.

Alcoff, L. (1988) 'Cultural feminism versus post-structuralism: the identity crisis in feminist theory', *Signs* 13, 3: 405-436.

Andrews, B. and Brown, G.W. (1988) 'Marital violence in the community: a biographical approach', *British Journal of Psychology* 153: 305-312.

Aontas (1986) *Priority areas in adult education*. Dublin: Aontas.

Aontas (1993) *Advice, guidance and training for local women's groups*. Dublin: Aontas, New Opportunities for Women Project.

Arensberg, C. and Kimball, S. (1940) *Family and community in Ireland*. Cambridge, Mass: Harvard University Press.

Ashbridge Management School (1980) *Employee potential: issues in the development of women*. London: Institute of Personnel Management.

ASTI (1991) *The promotional expectations and achievements of teachers*. Dublin: Association of Secondary Teachers of Ireland.

B

Ballaster, R., Beetham, M., Frazer, E. and Hebron, S. (1991) *Women's worlds*. London: Macmillan.

Barker, P. and Monks, K. (1994) *Career progression of chartered accountants*. Dublin: Dublin City University Business School.

Barker, D., Halman, L. and Vloet, A. (1992) *The European Values Study (1981-1990) Summary Report*. London: Gordon Cook.

Barrett, M. (1980) *Women's oppression today*. London: Verso.

Barrett, M. and McIntosh, M. (1991/1982) *The anti-social family*. Second edition. London: Verso.

Barrett, M. (1992) *The politics of truth*. Cambridge: Polity Press.

Barry, U. (1986) 'Exploring feminism' in *Exploring feminism, Women's Studies Bulletin Special Issue*. Proceedings of the Annual Conference of the Women's Studies Association of Ireland, Limerick: September 1-6.

Barry, U. (1992) 'Movement, change and reaction: the struggle over reproductive rights in Ireland', in A. Smyth (ed) *The abortion papers, Ireland*. Dublin: Attic Press.

Barry, U. (1996) *Trends and prospects for women's employment in the 1990s in the Irish economy*. Brussels: European Network of Experts on the situation of women in the Labour Market.

Barry, U. and Jackson, P. (1988) 'Women on the edge of time: part time work in Ireland, North and South', in M. Buckley and M. Anderson (eds) *Women, equality and Europe*. London: Macmillan.

Beale, J. (1986) *Women in Ireland*. London: Macmillan.

Beechey, V. (1977) 'Some notes on female wage labour in capitalist production', *Capital and Class*, Autumn: 45-66.

Beechey, V. (1989) 'Women's employment in Britain and France: some problems of comparison', *Work, Employment and Society* 3, 3, 369-378.

Beck, U. and Beck-Gernsheim, E. (1995/1990) *The normal chaos of love*. Cambridge: Polity Press.

Bell, D. (1991) 'Cultural studies in Ireland and the post-modernist debate', *The Irish Journal of Sociology* 1:83-95.

Bell, C. and Newby, H. (1991), 'Husbands and wives: the deferential dialectic', in D. Leonard and S. Allen (eds) *Sexual divisions revisited*. London: Macmillan.

Benston, M. (1969) 'The political economy of women's liberation', *Monthly Review* 21(4) September: 13-27.

Benton, T. (1981) 'Objective interests and the sociology of power', *Sociology* 15:161-184.

Bergusson, B. and Dickens, L. (1996) *Equal opportunities and collective bargaining in Europe*. Dublin: European Foundation for Living and Working Conditions.

Blackwell, J. (1987) 'Gender and statistics', in C. Curtin, P. Jackson, B. O'Connor (eds) *Gender in Irish society*. Galway: University Press.

Blackwell, J. (1989) *Women in the labour force*. Dublin: Employment Equality Agency.

Bottero, W. (1992) 'The changing face of the professions? Gender and the explanations of women's entry into pharmacy', *Work, Employment and Society* 6, 3: 329-346.

Bourdieu, P. (1977) *Towards a theory of practice*. Oxford: Oxford University Press.

Bourdieu, P. (1985) 'The social space and the genesis of groups', *Theory and Society* 14 (6). 723-749.

Bourdieu, P. (1986) 'The forms of capital', in J. Richardson (ed) *Handbook of theory and research for the sociology of education*. New York: Greenwood.

Bourdieu, P. (1989) 'Social space and symbolic power', *Sociological Theory* 7(1):14-63.

Boulton, M. (1983) *On being a mother*. London: Tavistock.

Brannen, J. and Collard, J. (1982) *Marriages in trouble: the process of seeking help*. London: Tavistock.

Brannen, J. (1995) 'Young people and their contribution to household work', *Sociology* 29, 2:317-338.

Brannen, J. and Wilson, G. (eds) (1987) *Give and take in families*. London: Allen and Unwin.

Breathnach, P. (1992) 'Employment in Irish tourism: a gender analysis', *Labour Market Review* 3, 2: 15-24.

Breathnach, P. (1993) 'Women's employment and peripheralisation: the case of Ireland's branch plant economy', *Geoforum* 24,1:19-29.

Breathnach, P., Henry, M., Drea, A. S., and O'Flaherty, M. (1994) 'Gender in Irish tourism employment' in V. Kinnary and D. Hall (eds) *Tourism: a gender analysis*. Chicester: Wiley and Sons.

Breen, R. (1984a) 'Status attainment or job attainment? The effects of sex and class on youth unemployment', *British Journal of Sociology* 35, 3: 363-386.

Breen, R. (1984b) *Education and the labour market: work and unemployment amongst recent cohorts of Irish school leavers*. General Research Series No. 119. Dublin: ESRI.

Breen, R. (1985) 'The sociology of youth unemployment', *Administration* 33, 2: 167-186.

Breen, R. (1991) *Education, employment and training in the youth labour market*. General Research Series No. 152. Dublin: ESRI.

Breen, R., Hannan, D.F., Rottman D.B. and Whelan, C.T. (1990) *Understanding contemporary Ireland*. Dublin: Gill and Macmillan.

Britten, A. (1977) *The privatized world*. London: Routledge and Kegan Paul.

Britten, N. and Heath, A. (1983) 'Women, men and social class', in E. Gamarnikow, D.H.J. Morgan, J. Purvis and D.E. Taylorson (eds) *Gender, class and work*. London: Heinemann.

Brody, H. (1973) *Inishkillane*. London: Penguin.

Browne, D. (1995) 'Legal changes in the law concerning marital breakdown in Ireland', in M. O'Brien (ed) *Divorce? Facing the issues of marital breakdown*. Dublin: Attic Press.

Brown, G.W., Davidson, S., Harrus, T., Maclean, U. and Prudo, R. (1977) 'Psychiatric disorder in London and North UIST', *Social Science and Medicine* 11, 367-377.

Brown, G.W. and Harris, T. (1978) *Social origins of depression: a study of psychiatric disorder in women*. London: Tavistock.

Brown, G.W. (1987) 'Social factors and the development and course of depressive disorders in women', *British Journal of Social Work* 17:615-634.

Brown, G.W., Andrews, B., Harris, T., Adler, Z. and Bridge, L. (1986) 'Social support, self esteem and depression', *Psychological Medicine* 16:813-831.

Bulletin on Women and Employment in the EU (1994) April. No. 4. Brussels: European Commission.

Bulletin on Women and Employment in the EU (1994) October, No. 5. Brussels: European Commission.

Bulletin on Women and Employment in the EU (1995) April, No. 6. Brussels: European Commission.

Bulletin on Women and Employment in the EU (1995) October, No 7. Brussels: European Commission.

Bulletin on Women and Employment in the EU (1996) April, No. 8. Brussels: European Commission.

Bulletin on Women and Employment in the EU (1996) October, No. 9. Brussels: European Commission.

Bulmer, M. (1987) *The social basis of community care.* London: Allen and Unwin.

Burgoyne, J. *et al* (1987) *Divorce matters.* Penguin: Harmonsworth.

Burke, H. (1984) 'Continuity and change: the life cycle of Irish women in the 1980s', in *The changing family.* Dublin: UCD, Family Studies Unit.

Byrne, A. (1988a) *A review of the statistics on low pay, social welfare and the health status of Irish women.* Dublin: Combat Poverty.

Byrne, A. (1988b) *Women and poverty report.* Dublin: Council for the Status of Women.

Byrne, A. (1989) 'National tribunal on women's poverty'. Draft Report submitted to Combat Poverty Agency, Dublin.

Byrne, A. (1992) 'Statistics – what do they tell us about women?', *UCG Women's Studies Review* 1:1-13.

Byrne, A. (1992) 'Academic women's studies in the Republic of Ireland', *Women's Studies Quarterly*, 15-27.

Byrne, A. (1993) 'Revealing figures? Official statistics and rural Irish women', in A. Smyth (ed) *Irish women's studies reader,* Dublin: Attic Press.

Byrne, A., Byrne, P. and Lyons, A. (1996) 'Inventing and teaching women's studies: considering feminist pedagogy', *Irish Journal of Feminist Studies* 1, 1: 78-99.

Byrne, S. and Kamikaze, I. (1994) 'Lies, myths and stereotypes: a satirical look at lesbians in the media', Unpublished paper presented at Conference on *Who's news? Whose views?: Women and the media in Ireland.* March, Dublin: Women's Education Research and Resource Centre.

C

Caldwell, M.A. and Peplau, L.A. (1982) 'Sex differences in same sex friendships', *Sex Roles* 8: 721-732.

Callan, T. and Farrell, B. (1991) *Women's participation in the Irish labour market.* Dublin: ERSI.

Callan, T., Nolan, B. and Whelan, C.T. (1992) 'Resources, deprivation and the measurement of poverty', *Journal of Social Policy* 22 (2), 141-172.

Callan, T. (1994) 'Poverty and gender inequality', in B. Nolan and T. Callan (eds) *Poverty and policy in Ireland.* Dublin: Gill and Macmillan.

Callan, T., Nolan, B. and Whelan, C. (1994) 'Income, deprivation and exclusion', in B. Nolan and T. Callan (eds) *Poverty and policy in Ireland.* Dublin: Gill and Macmillan.

Callan, T., Nolan, B., Whelan, C.T. and Williams, J. (1996) *Poverty in the 1990s: evidence from the 1994 living in Ireland survey.* Dublin: Oaktree Press.

Callan, T. and Wren, A. (1994) *Male-female wage differentials: analysis and policy issues.* Dublin: NESC.

Canadian Government (1990) *Beneath the veneer: the report of the task force on barriers to women in the public service.* Ottawa: Canadian Government Publishing Centre.

Cancian, F.M. (1986) 'The feminisation of love', *Signs: Journal of Women in Culture and Society* 4:692-709.

Carey, M. (1994) 'Gender and power: boys will be boys and so will girls', *Irish Journal of Sociology* 4: 105-125.

Casey, M. (1987) *Domestic violence against women – the women's perspective.* Dublin: UCD.

Cathcart, H. (1989) 'Adult education values and Irish society' in D. O'Sullivan (ed) *Social commitment and adult education.* Cork: Cork University Press.

Central Statistics Office (1993a) *Labour Force Survey 1991.* Dublin: Government Publications.

Central Statistics Office (1993b) *Census: Summary Population Report.* Dublin: Government Publications.

Central Statistics Office (1994) *Census 1991: Household Composition and Family Units.* Dublin: Government Publications.

Central Statistics Office (1995a) *Labour Force Survey 1993.* Dublin: Government Publications.

Central Statistics Office (1995b) *Vital Statistics 1994.* Dublin: Government Publications.

Central Statistics Office (1997a) *Labour Force Survey 1996.* Dublin: Government Publications.

Central Statistics Office (1997b) *Women in the workforce.* Dublin: CSO.

Central Statistics Office (1997b) *Household Budget Survey 1994-95: Preliminary Results.* Dublin: Government Publications.

Cheal, D. (1991) *Family and the state of theory.* London: Harvester.

Chodorow, N. (1978) *The reproduction of mothering.* London: University of California Press.

Claffey, U. (1993) *The women who won.* Dublin: Attic Press.

Clancy, P. (1988) *Who goes to college?* Dublin: Higher Education Authority.

Clancy, P. (1989) 'Gender differences in student participation at third level' in C. Hussey (ed) *Equal opportunities for women in higher education.* Dublin: UCD.

Clancy, P. (1990) 'Socio-economic group, gender and regional inequalities in student participation in higher education', in C. Fennell and M. Mulcahy (eds), *Equality of opportunity in Irish third level institutions.* Proceedings of a Forum held September, 1990. Cork: UCC.

Clancy, P. (1991) 'Irish nuptuality and fertility patterns in transition', in G. Kiely and V. Richardson (eds) *Family policy: European perspectives.* Dublin: Family Studies Centre.

Clancy, P. (1995a) 'Education in the Republic of Ireland: the project of modernity', in P. Clancy *et al* (eds) *Irish society: sociological perspectives.* Dublin: IPA.

Clancy, P. (1995b) *Access to college: patterns of continuity and change.* Dublin: Government Publications.

Clancy, P. (1994) *Report on the cultural sector.* Dublin: Business School.

Cleary, A. (1986) 'A study of depression among women – implications for preventive mental health'. Unpublished ms.

Clancy, A. (1997) 'Madness and mental health in Irish women', in A. Byrne and M. Leonard (eds) *Women in Irish society: a sociological reader.* Belfast: Beyond the Pale.

Clark, L. (1995) 'The role of the law in equal opportunities', in *Making gender work: managing equal opportunities.*

Clarke, C. and Healy, S. (1997) *Pathways to a basic income.* Dublin: Cori.

Cockburn, C. (1991) *In the way of women: men's resistance to sex equality in organization.* London: Macmillan.

Cohen, G. (1978) 'Women's solidarity and the preservation of privelige', in P. Caplan and J. Bujra (eds) *Women united, women divided.* London: Tavistock.

Collins, N. (1987) *Local government managers at work.* Dublin: IPA.

Combat Poverty Agency (1989) *Pictures of poverty.* Dublin.

Comer, L. (1982) 'Monogamy, marriage and economic dependence', in E. Whitelegg *et al* (eds) *The changing experience of women.* Oxford: Martin Robertson.

Commission of the European Communities (1986) *Equal opportunities for women: medium term community programme 1986-1990.* Supplement 3/86 Luxembourg: Office for Official Publications of the European Communities.

Commission of the European Communities (1990) *Men and women of Europe in 1987,* Supplement No. 26, Women of Europe. Brussels.

Commission on Adult Education (1983) *Lifelong learning: report of the Commission on Adult Education.* Dublin: Stationery Office.

Community Workers Cooperative and the Northern Ireland Council for Voluntary Action (1996) *Equality and the structural funds.* Dublin: Combat Poverty.

Condren, M. (1989) *The serpent and the goddess: women, religion and power in Celtic Ireland.* San Francisco: Harper and Row.

Conlon, C. (1994a) 'Women: an anomaly in Irish society? Abortion in the Republic of Ireland'. Paper presented at Sociological Association of Ireland Annual Conference, Clonmel.

Conlon, C. (1994b) 'A profile of 231 women who sought pregnancy counselling, 193 of whom chose abortion', in *Irish Family Planning Association Report.* Dublin: IFPA.

Connell, R.W. (1994) 'The state, gender and sexual politics: theory and appraisal', in H.L. Radthe and H.J. Stam (eds) *Power and gender: social relations in theory and practice*. London: Sage.

Connell, R.W. (1995a/1987) *Gender and power*. Oxford: Blackwell.

Connell, R.W. (1995b) *Masculinities*. Cambridge: Polity Press.

Connolly, L. (1996) 'The women's movement in Ireland 1970-1995: a social movements analysis', *Irish Journal of Feminist Studies* 1, 1: 43-77.

Connolly, L. (1997) 'From revolution to devolution: a social movements analysis of the contemporary women's movement in Ireland', Unpub Ph.D. thesis submitted to Maynooth University.

Conroy Jackson, P. (1986) 'Women's movement and abortion: the criminalisation of Irish women', in D. Dahlerup (ed) *The new women's movement: feminism and political power in Europe and the USA*. London: Sage.

Conroy Jackson, P. (1990) *The impact of the completion of the internal market on women in the EC*. Commission of the European Communities: V/506/90-EN.

Conroy Jackson, P. (1991) 'The investment of women in the labour market'. Discussion Paper for Combat Poverty: Referred to in the *Report of the Second Commission on the Status of Women, 1993*. Dublin: Government Publications.

Conroy Jackson, P. (1992) 'Outside the jurisdiction: Irish women seeking abortion', in A. Smyth (ed) *The abortion papers Ireland*. Dublin: Attic Press.

Co-ordinating Group of Secretaries (1996) *Delivering better government: strategic management initiative second report to government*. Dublin: Government Publications.

Coolahan, J. (1994) *Report on the national education convention*. Dublin: Government Publications.

Cook, J. (1997) *The Marley Grange multi-denominational school challenge 1973-78*. Dublin: Rathfarnham.

Corcoran, T., Hughes, G., and Sexton, J.J. (1993) *Occupational employment forecasts: 1996*. Dublin FÁS/ESRI.

Corcoran-Nantes, Y. and Roberts, K. (1995) '"We've got one of those": the peripheral status of women in male-dominated industries', *Gender, Work and Organisation* 2, 1: 21-33.

CORI (1997) *Religious congregations in Irish education: A role for the future*. Dublin: Conference of Religious of Ireland, Education Commission.

Coulter, C. (1990) *Ireland: between the first and the third worlds*. Dublin: Attic Press.

Coulter, C. (1993) *The hidden tradition: feminism, women and nationalism in Ireland*. Cork: Cork University Press.

Cousins, M. (1996) *Pathways to employment for women returning to paid work*. Dublin: EEA.

Coverman, S. (1989) 'Women's work is never done: the division of domestic labour', in J. Freeman (ed) *Women: a feminist perspective*, 4th ed. Mountain View, CA: Mayfield.

Cowan, R.S. (1985) 'The industrial revolution in the home', in D. MacKenzie and J. Wajkman (eds) *The social shaping of technology*. Milton Keynes: Open University.

Crickley, A. (1989) 'Women and community work – a perspective on the late 80s' in *Co-options: Journal of the Community Workers Co-Op*. Dublin: 31-33.

Crompton, R. and Jones, G. (1984) *A white collar proletariat? Deskilling and gender in clerical work*. Bastingstoke: Macmillan.

Crompton, R. and Mann, M. (eds) (1986) *Gender stratification*. Cambridge: Polity Press, in association with B. Blackwell.

Crompton, R. (1995) *Paying the price: comparative studies of women's employment,* Working paper 4. London: Demos.

Crone, J. (1989) 'Lesbianism in Ireland' in *Co-options: Journal of the Community Workers Co-Op*. Dublin: 22-25.

Crone, J. (1986) 'Elements of a radical feminist spirituality' in *Exploring feminism, Women's Studies Bulletin Special Issue*. Proceedings of the Annual Conference of the Women's Studies Association of Ireland. September: 31-36.

Cronin, C. (1992) 'Women into engineering: issues, challenges and strategies'. Unpublished MA thesis submitted to the University of Limerick.

Cunningham, C. (1994) 'Women in trade unions: policies, practices and patriarchy'. Unpublished Masters Thesis submitted to the University of Limerick.

Curry, J. (1993) *Irish social services: second edition*. Dublin: Institute of Public Administration.

Curtin, C., Kelly, M., O'Dowd, L. (eds) (1984) *Culture and ideology in Ireland*. Galway: Galway University Press.

Curtin, C., Jackson, P. and O'Connor, B. (eds) (1987) *Gender in Irish society*. Galway: University Press.

Curtin, C. and Varley, A. (1984) 'Children and childhood in rural Ireland: a consideration of the ethnographic literature', in C. Curtin, M. Kelly and L. O'Dowd (eds) *Culture and ideology in Ireland*. Galway: Galway University Press.

Curtin, C. (1986) 'Marriage and family', in P. Clancy, S. Drudy, K. Lynch and L. O'Dowd (eds) *Ireland: a sociological profile*. Dublin: IPA.

Curtin, D. (1989) *Irish employment equality law*. Dublin: Round Hall Press

D

Dahlerup, D. (ed) (1986) 'Introduction' *The new women's movement: feminism and political power in Europe and the USA*. London and New York: Sage.

Dalla Costa, M. and James, S. (1972) *The power of women and the subversion of the community*. Bristol: Falling Wall Press.

Dalley, G. (1988) *Ideologies of caring: rethinking community and collectivism*. London: Macmillan.

Daly, M. (1978) *Gyn/Ecology*. Boston: Beacon Press.

Daly, M. (1984) *Pure lust*. London: The Women's Press.

Daly, M. (1986/73) *Beyond God the father*. London: The Woman's Press.

Daly, M. (1985) *The hidden workers*. Dublin: Employment Equality Agency.

Daly, M. (1989) *Women and poverty*. Dublin: Attic Press.

Daly, M. and Walsh, J. (1991) *Moneylending and low income families*. Dublin: Combat Poverty.

Davidson, M. and Cooper, C. (1992) *Shattering the glass ceiling*. London: PCP.

Davidson, M. and Cooper, C. (1993) *European women in business and management*. London: Chapman.

Davis, K., Leijenaar, M. and Aldersma, J. (1991) (eds) *The gender of power*. London: Sage.

Davies, C. (1991) 'Gender, history, and management style in nursing: towards a theoretical synthesis', in M. Savage and A. Witz (eds) *Gender and bureaucracy*. Oxford: Blackwell/Sociological Review.

Davies, C. (1995) 'The sociology of the professions and the profession of gender', *Sociology* 30, 4:661-678.

De Beauvoir, S. (1972/49) *The second sex*. Middlesex: Penguin.

Delamere, R. (1985) 'Sexuality', in L. Steiner Scott (ed) *Personally speaking: women's thoughts on women's issues*. Dublin: Attic Press.

Delphy, C. and Leonard, D. (1992) *Familiar exploitation: a new analysis of marriage in contemporary western societies*. Cambridge: Polity Press.

Department of Agriculture (1994) *Information note*: Leader 2. Dublin.

Department of Enterprise and Employment (1994). *Evaluation report: impact indicators*. Dublin: ESF Programme Education Unit.

Department of Equality and Law Reform (1994a) *National report of Ireland*. Dublin: Government Publications.

Department of Equality and Law Reform (1994b) *Report on a survey of equal opportunities in the public sector*. Dublin: Department of Equality and Law Reform.

Department of Equality and Law Reform (1997) *Statement of strategy 1997-2000*. Dublin: Department of Equality and Law Reform.

Department of Equality and Law Reform (1998) Press Release: Equal Opportunity Child Care Programme. Dublin: Press Office.

Department of Education (1994) Personal communication.

Department of Finance (1997a) *Equality of opportunity in the civil service 1994 and 1995. Eighth annual report on the implementation of the equal opportunity policy and guidelines for the civil service*. Dublin.

Department of Finance (1997b) *Tabular statement to accompany equality of opportunity in the civil service 1994 and 1995. Eighth annual report on the implementation of the equal opportunity policy and guidelines for the civil service*. Dublin.

Department of Foreign Affairs (1996) *Ireland and the European Union*. Dublin: Department of Foreign Affairs.

Department of Health (1993) *Shaping a healthier future*. Dublin: Government Publications.

Department of Health (1995) *Developing a policy for women's health*. Dublin: Government Publications.

Derrida, J. (1978) *Writing and difference*, Trans. by A. Bass. Chicago: University of Chicago Press.

Dean, G. (1984) *Termination of pregnancy*. Dublin: Medico-Social Research Board.

Dineen, D. (1992) 'Atypical work patterns in Ireland: short term adjustments or fundamental changes?', *Administration* 40, 3:248-274.

Dixon, A. and Baker, A. (1996) *A management development strategy for the health and personal social services in Ireland*. Dublin: Department of Health.

Dobash, R.E. and Dobash, R.P. (1992) *Women, violence and social change*. London: Routledge and Kegan Paul.

Dohrenwend, B.B., Shrout, P., Egri, G. and Mendelsounm, F. (1980) 'Measures of non-specific psychological distress and other dimensions of psychopathology in the general population', *Archives of General Psychiatry* 37:1229-1236.

Doherty, D. (1997) Office of Health Management. Personal communication.

Dorgan, M. (1989) 'Women in Irish society – the need for radical social change', *Co-options: Journal of the Community Workers Co-Op*. Dublin: 20-21.

Dorgan, J., Drew, E. and Murphy, C. (1994) 'Consultants' report to the Joint Oireachtas Committee on Women's Rights', in *Women and rural development*. Dublin: Government Publications.

Drew, E. (1992) 'The part time option? Women and part time work in the European Community', *Women's Studies International Forum* 15, 5/6: 607-614.

Drudy, S. (1993) 'Equality of all: sociological perspectives', in *Women in the church in Ireland*: Proceedings of a study day, 23rd October in Clonliffe College, Dublin. Irish Commission for Justice and Peace: A Commission of the Catholic Bishops Conference.

Drudy, S. and Lynch, K. (1993) *Schools and society in Ireland*. Dublin: Gill and Macmillan.

Durkan, J. Assisted by A. O'Donohue, M. Donnelly and J. Durkan (1995) *Women in the labour force*. Dublin: Employment Equality Agency.

Dublin Lesbian and Gay Men's Collectives (1986) *Out for ourselves*. Dublin: Women's Community Press.

Duffy, C. (1994) 'Female poverty, powerlessness and social exclusion in Ireland', *Administration* 42, 1: 47-66.

Duggan, C. (1987) 'Farming women or farmers' wives? Women in the farming press', in C. Curtin, P. Jackson and B. O'Connor (eds) *Gender in Irish society*. Galway: University Press.

Dworkin, A. (1983) *Right-wing women*. London: The Women's Press.

E

Economist Intelligence Unit (1997) *Ireland Country Report – 3rd Quarter*. London.

EC (1988) *Positive action: equal opportunities for women in employment: a guide*. Brussels.

EC (1994) *European white paper on social policy: a way forward for the union*. Brussels.

Edholm, F. (1982) 'The unnatural family', in E. Whitelegg *et al* (eds) *The changing experience of women*. Oxford: Martin Robertson in association with Open University.

Egan, O. (1994) 'Overview of equal opportunities in third level education in Ireland', in *Equality of opportunity in third level education in Ireland*. Cork: National Unit on Equal Opportunities at Third Level.

Egan, O. (1997) 'Homophobia: not just a lesbian thing', in C. C. Aniagolu (ed) *In From the Shadows*, Vol 3. Limerick: University of Limerick Press.

Egan, R. (1986) 'Feminism and politics in Ireland', *Exploring feminism, Women's Studies Bulletin*: Proceedings of the Annual Conference of the Women's Studies Association of Ireland, Sept. 1986.

Ehrenreich, B., Heiss, E. and Jacobs, G. (1986) *Remaking love: the feminisation of sex*. New York: Anchor Press/Doubleday.

Elliot, F. (1986) *The family: change or continuity*. London: Macmillan.

Employment Equality Agency (–) *Equality at work: positive approaches*. Dublin.

Employment Equality Agency (1983) *Code of practice on equality of opportunity in employment*. Dublin.

Equal Opportunities Commission (1993) *Women and men in Britain, 1993*. Manchester: 1993 Equal Opportunities Commission.

Equal Opportunities Commission (1997) *Management and the professions: briefings on women and men in Britain*. Manchester: EOC.

Erikson, R. and Goldthorpe, J.H. (1988) 'Debate: women at cross-classroads: a critical note', *Sociology* 22, 4:545-553.

Eurobarometre (1997) *Women and men in Europe and equal opportunities*: summary report. Brussels: European Commission.

European Commission (1993) *Rapid Research Reports*. Brussels: ECSC-EEC-EAEC.

European Commission (1996) *Eurobarometer 45*. Brussels.

European Commission (1995) *Employment in Europe, 1995*. Brussels: Directorate-general for employment, Industrial Relations and Social Affairs.

European Commission (1997) *Social Europe: progress report on the implementation of the medium term social action programme 1995-97*. Luxembourg: Office for Official Publications of the European Community.

European Social Policy White Paper (1994) EC: Brussels.

European Observatory on National Family Policies (1990) *Families and policies: evaluation and trends in 1988/89*. Brussels.

Eurostat (1985) 'Employment and unemployment', Bulletin No. 2, EC Commission of the European Communities.

Eurostat (1987) *Women in Europe, their economic and social position:* Luxembourg: EC.

Eurostat (1991) *Basic statistics of the Community*. Luxembourg: Office for Official Publications of the European Community.

Eurostat (1993) *Unemployed women in the EC*. Luxembourg: Office for Official Publications of the European Community.

Eurostat (1994) *Labour Force Survey 1992*. Luxembourg: Office for Official Publications of the European Community.

Eurostat (1995a) *Demographic statistics*. Luxembourg: Office for Official Publications of the European Community.

Eurostat (1995b) *Women and men in the European Union*. Luxembourg: Office for Official Publications of the European Community.

Eurostat (1995c) *Statistics in focus: population and social conditions, households and families in the European Economic area*. Luxembourg: Office for Official Publications of the European Community.

Eurostat (1996) *Statistics in focus: population and social conditions, Labour Force Survey*. Luxembourg: Office for Official Publications of the European Community.

Eurostat (1997) European Commission Childcare Network (1990) *Mothers, fathers and employment*. Brussels: Commission of the European Communities.

Evanson, E. (1982) *Hidden violence: a study of battered women in Northern Ireland*. Belfast: Farset Press.

Evetts, J. (1993). 'Women in engineering, educational concomitants of a non traditional career choice', *Gender and Education 5*, 2: 167-178.

F

Faderman, L. (1981) *Surpassing the love of men*. London: Junction Books.

Fahey, T. (1990) 'Measuring the female labour supply: conceptual and procedural problems in Irish official statistics', *Economic and Social Review 21*, 2:163-191.

Fahey, T. (1992) 'Housework, the household economy and economic development in Ireland since the 1920s', *Irish Journal of Sociology 2*:42-69.

Fahey, T. (1993) 'Full citizenship for the next generation', in B. Reynolds and S. Healy (eds) *New frontiers for full citizenship*. Dublin: CMRS.

Fahey, T. (1995) 'Family and household in Ireland', in P. Clancy, S. Drudy, K. Lynch and L. O' Dowd (eds) *Irish society: sociological perspectives*. Dublin: Institute of Public Administration.

Fahey, T. and Lyons, M. (1995) *Marital breakdown and family law in Ireland*. Dublin: Oak Tree Press.

Faith, K. (1994) 'Resistance: lessons from Foucault and feminism', in H.L. Radtke and J. Stam (eds) *Power/gender: social relations in theory and practice*. London: Sage.

FÁS (1993) *Positive action programme for women: report on 1992 programme, outline of 1993 programme*. Dublin: FÁS, Training and Employment Authority.

FÁS (1994) *Women in focus 1994-95*. Dublin: FÁS.

Fennell, N. (1987) *Irish women: agenda for practical action*. Dublin: Department of Taoiseach.

Ferguson, A. (1989) *Blood at the root: motherhood, sexuality and male dominance*. London: Pandora.

Finch, J. (1989) *Family obligations and social change*. Oxford: Polity and Blackwell.

Finch, J. (1996) 'Women, the family and families', in T. Coslett, A. Easton, and P. Summerfield (eds) *Women, power and resistance*. Buckingham: OUP.

Finch, J. and Mason, J. (1990) 'Filial obligations and kin support for elderly people', *Ageing and Society* 10, 151-175.

Fine-Davis, M. (1983) *Women and work in Ireland: a social psychological perspective*. Dublin: Council for the Status of Women.

Fine-Davis, M. (1988a) *Changing attitudes to the role of women in Ireland: attitudes towards moral issues in relation to voting behaviour in recent referenda*. Third Report of the Second Joint Oireachtas Committee on Womens' Rights. Dublin: Government publications.

Fine-Davis, M. (1988b) *Changing gender role attitudes in Ireland 1975-1986*. Report of the Second Joint Oireachtas Committee on Women's Rights. Dublin: Government Publications.

Fine-Davis, M. (1992) *Attitudes and structural barriers to women's full participation in employment: two case studies of women operatives and managers in public and private sector organizations*. Dublin: CSW.

Firth, J., Hubert, J. and Forge, A. (1969) *Families and their relatives*. London: Routledge and Kegan Paul.

First Monitoring Committee (1994) *First progress report of the monitoring committee on the implementation of the recommendations of the Second Commission on the Status of Women (1994)*. Dublin, Department of Equality and Law Reform: Stationery Office.

First Report of the Third Joint Oireachtas Committee on Women's Rights (1991) *Motherhood, work and equal opportunity*. Dublin: Government Publications.

Fitzgerald, J. (1996) 'At the academy's front door? Irish women's studies periodicals', *Irish Journal of Feminist Studies* 1:107-114.

Fitzgerald, J. and Hughes, G. (1994) 'Labour market outlook and the structure of employment in Ireland', *Labour Market Review* 5, 1: 21-46.

Fitzgerald, M. and Jeffers, A. (1994) 'Pyschosocial factors associated with psychological problems in Irish children and their mothers', *Economic and Social Review* 25, 4: 285-301.

Fitzgerald, E. (1994) 'Women influencing future policy: let's shift the balance'. Paper presented at the Conference on Celebrating Women's Work, Grand Hotel, Malahide, Dublin, May 20-22 1994.

Flanaghan, N. and Richardson, V. (1993) *Unmarried mothers: a social profile*. Dublin: UCD.

Flynn, S. and O'Connell, J. (1990) 'The catholic church and community work', in *Community work in Ireland: trends in the 80s, options for the 90s*. Dublin: Combat Poverty.

Forgacs, D. (ed) (1988) *A Gramsci reader*. London: Lawrence and Wishart.

Fogarty, M., Ryan, L. and Lee, J. (1984) *Irish values and attitudes*. Dublin: Dominican Publications.

Foster, R. (1984) *Health in rural Ireland: a study of selected aspects: Dublin and Leitrim*. Health Education Bureau and the North Western Health Board.

Fourth Report of the Fourth Joint Oireachtas Committee on Women's Rights (1996) *The impact of European equality legislation on women's affairs in Ireland*. Dublin: Government Publications.

Fox, R. (1979) 'The visiting husband on Tory Island', *Journal of Comparative Family Studies* 10, 2:163-190.

Foucault, M. (1979) *The history of sexuality, Vol. I: an introduction*. Trans. by R. Hurley. London: Allen Lane.

Foucault, M. (1980) *Power/knowledge; selected interviews and writings 1972-1977*, C. Gordon (ed). New York: Pantheon Books.

Foucault, M. (1984/1991) *The Foucault reader*, R. Rabinow (ed). London: Penguin.

Frazer, H. (1991) 'Child poverty and income support measures', in R. Bowick and M. Burns (eds) *The rights of the child: Irish perspectives on the UN convention*. Dublin: The Council for Social Welfare.

Freire, P. (1972) *Pedagogy of the oppressed*. New York: Penguin.

Friedan, B. (1965/63) *The feminine mystique*. Middlesex: Penguin.

G

Gaffney, M. (1991a) 'How men resist equality', *Status Journal*: 4-7. Dublin: Council for the Status of Women.

Gaffney, M. (1991b) *Glass slippers and tough bargains*. Dublin: Attic Press.

Galligan, Y. (1992) 'Women in Irish politics', in J. Coakley and M. Gallagher (eds) *Politics in the Republic of Ireland*. Galway: PSAI Press.

Garavan, R. (1994) 'The managerial careers of women and men in the Bank of Ireland', Unpublished MA thesis submitted to the University of Limerick.

Gardiner, F. (1993) 'Political interest and participation of Irish women 1922-1992: the unfinished revolution', in A. Smyth (ed) *Irish women's studies reader*. Dublin: Attic Press.

Gardiner, F. (1996) 'Gender gaps and dual cultures: are these the missing links in Irish Politics?', *Irish Journal of Feminist Studies* 2:36-57.

Gay and Lesbian Equality Network and Nexus (1995) *Poverty: lesbians and gay men*. Dublin: Combat Poverty.

Geary, R.C. and Ó Muirceartaigh, F.S. (1974) *Equalization of opportunity in Ireland: statistical aspects*. Dublin: ESRI.

Giddens, A. (1992) *The transformation of intimacy: sexuality, love and eroticism in modern societies*. Cambridge: Polity Press.

Gilligan, C. (1982) *In a different voice*. Cambridge, Mass: Harvard University Press.

Gilligan, R. (1991) *Irish child care services*. Dublin: Institute of Public Administration.

Gilligan, A.L. and Zappone, K. (1994) 'The cutting edge: women's community education'. Unpublished ms.

Girvin, B. (1996) 'The Irish divorce referendum, November 1995', *Irish Political Studies*, Vol. 2: 174-181.

Gleeson, J. (1992) *Gender equality in education in the Republic of Ireland (1984-1991)*, Second Report of the Third Oireachtas Committee on Women's Rights. Dublin: Government Publications.

Glendennings, C. and Millar, J. (eds) (1988) *Women and poverty in Britain*. Brighton: Wheatsheaf.

Goldthorpe, J.H. (1983) 'Women and class analysis: in defence of the conventional view', *Sociology* 17: 465-488.

Goldthorpe, J. and Whelan, C. (eds) (1992) *The development of industrial society in Ireland*. New York: Oxford University Press.

Goss, S. and Browne, H. (1991) *Equal opportunities for women in the NHS*, NHS Management Executive Office for Public Management. London: Department of Health.

Gove, W. (1972) 'The relationship between sex roles, marital status and mental illness', *Social Forces* 51:34-44.

Gove, W.R. (1978) 'Sex differences in mental illness among adult men and women', *Social Science and Medicine* 12B: 187-198.

Government Publications (1993) *Summary population report: census 1991*. Dublin.

Graham, H. (1983) 'Caring: a labour of love', in J. Finch and D. Groves (eds) *A labour of love: women, work and caring*. London: Routledge and Kegan Paul.

Greaney, V. and Kelleghan, T. (1984) *Equality of opportunity in Irish schools: a longitudinal study of 500 students*. Dublin: Educational Co.

Greene, E., Hebron, S. and Woodward, D. (1990) *Women's leisure, what leisure?* London: Macmillan.

Griffin, C. (1985) *Typical girls*. London: Routledge and Kegan Paul.

Grint, K. (1991) *The sociology of work*. Cambridge: Polity.

Gullestad, M. (1984) *Kitchen table society*. Oslo: Universities Forlaget.

H

Hakim, C. (1991) 'Grateful slaves and self-made women: fact and fantasy in women's work orientations', *European Sociological Review* 7, 2: 97-120.

Hakim, C. (1995) 'Five feminist myths about women's employment', *The British Journal of Sociology* 46, 3:429-457.

Hakim, C. (1996) 'The sexual division of labour and women's heterogeneity', *The British Journal of Sociology* 47, 1:178-188.

Halford, S. (1992) 'Feminist change in a patriarchal organization: the experience of women's initiatives in local government and implications for feminist perspectives on state institutions', in *Gender and bureaucracy* op. cit.

Hanafin, Joan (1992) 'Co-education and educational attainment'. Unpublished Ph.D. thesis submitted to the University of Limerick.

Handy, C.B. (1985) *Understanding organisations*. Second edition. Middlesex: Penguin.

Hannan, D. and Katsiaouni, L. (1977) *Traditional families? From culturally prescribed to negotiated roles in farm families*. Dublin: ESRI Paper No. 87.

Hannan, D.F. (1979) *Displacement and development: class, kinship and social change in Irish rural communities*. Dublin: ESRI.

Hannan, D., Breen, R., Murray, B., Watson, D., and Hardiman, N. (1983) *Schooling and sex roles: sex differences in subject provision and student choice in Irish post-primary schools*. Dublin: ESRI.

Hannan, D.F. and Shortall, S. (1991) *The quality of their education*. Dublin: ESRI.

Hannan, D. and Boyle, M. (1987) *Schooling decision: the origins and consequences of selection and streaming in Irish post-primary schools*. Dublin: ESRI.

Hannan, D.F. and Ó Riain, S. (1993) *Pathways to adulthood in Ireland*. Dublin: ESRI.

Hannan, D., Smyth, E., McCullagh, J., O'Leary, R. and McMahon, D. (1996) *Co-education and gender equality*. Dublin: Oak Tree Press.

Hansard Society (1990) *Report of the Hansard Society Commission on women at the top*. London: HMSO.

Hardiman, N. (1992) 'The state and economic interests: Ireland in a comparative perspective', in J.H. Goldthorpe and C. T. Whelan (eds) *The development of industrial society in Ireland*. Proceedings of the British Academy, Oxford: OUP.

Hardiman, N. and Whelan, C.T. (1994) 'Values and political partisanship', in C. Whelan (ed) *Values and social change in Ireland*. Dublin: Gill and Macmillan.

Harris, L. (1984) 'Class, community and sexual divisions in North Mayo', in C. Curtin, M. Kelly and L. O'Dowd (eds) *Culture and ideology in Ireland*. Galway: University Press.

Hartmann, H. (1976) 'Capitalism, patriarchy and job segregation by sex', *Signs* 1 (3): 737-776.

Hartmann, H. (1981) 'The unhappy marriage of marxism and feminism: towards a more progressive union, in L. Sargent (ed) *Women and revolution*. London: Pluto Press.

Hartmann, N. (1994) 'The unhappy marriage of marxism and feminism', in J. Kourany, J.P. Sterba and R. Tong (eds) *Feminist philosophies: problems, theories and applications*. London: Harvester/Wheatsheaf.

Hayden, J. (1990). 'Equality of opportunity in Irish third level institutions', in C. Fennell and M. Mulcahy (eds) *Equality of opportunity in Irish third level institutions*. Cork: Proceedings of Forum in UCC.

Hayes, L. (1990) *Working for change: a study of three women's community projects*. Dublin: Combat Poverty Agency.

Health Research Board (1991) *Report on activities of Irish psychiatric hospitals*. Dublin: HRB.

Hearn, J. (1982) 'Notes on patriarchy, professionalization and the semi-professions', *Sociology* 16 (2): 18 4-202.

Hearn, D. (1995) 'Global restructuring and the Irish political economy', in P. Clancy, S. Drudy, K. Lynch and L. O'Dowd (eds) *Irish society: sociological perspectives*. Dublin: Institute of Public Administration.

Hedstrom, P. (1991) 'Comments', in P. Bourdieund and J. S. Coleman (eds) *Social theory for a changing society*. New York: Russell Sage.

Heffernan, L.M. (1993) 'About the ICJP's women in the church working group', in *Women in the church in Ireland*. Proceedings of a study day held on 23 October, in Clonliffe College, Dublin. The Irish Commission for Justice and Peace, a Commission of the Catholic Bishops Conference.

Henderson, S., Byrne, D.G. and Duncan-Jones, P. (1981) *Neuroses and the social environment*. London: Academic Press.

Henley Centre (1991) 'Irish women, issues and concerns for change: a survey conducted by Council for the Status of Women/Women's Way'. Dublin: CSW.

Henley Centre Report (1991) *An equal future: policy and women in the 1990s*. Dublin: Council for the Status of Women.

Hickey, B.L. and Martin, M.O. (1994) *The 1992 leaving cert examination*. Dublin: NCCA.

Hicks, L. (1990) 'Excluded women: how can this happen in the hotel world?', *Services Industry Journal* 10, 2, 348-363.

Hite, S. (1976) *The Hite report*. New York: Macmillan.

Hite, S. (1987) *Women and love: a cultural revolution in progress*. Harmondsworth: Penguin.

Hochschild, A. (1983) *The managed heart*. Berkeley: University of California Press.

Holland, J., Ramazonoglu, C., Sharpe, S. and Thomson, R. (1992) 'Pleasure, pressure and power: some contradictions of gendered sexuality', *The Sociological Review* 1992, 40, 4 (Nov.) 645-673.

Honan, M. (1997) 'Recent developments on indirect discrimination', *Equality News* 9:16.

Hood, E.F. (1984) 'Black women, white women: separate paths to liberation', in A.M. Jaggar and P. Rothenberg (eds) *Feminist frameworks*. Second edition. New York: McGraw Hill.

Hornsby-Smith, M. (1992) 'Social and religious transformation in Ireland: a case of secularisation', in J.H. Goldthorpe and C.T. Whelan (eds) *The development of industrial society in Ireland*. Oxford: Oxford University Press.

Hornsby-Smith, M.P. and Whelan, C.T. (1994) 'Religious and moral values', in C. Whelan (ed) *Values and social change in Ireland*. Dublin: Gill and Macmillan.

Hoskyns, C. (1992) 'The European Community's policy on women in the context of 1992', *Women's Studies International Forum* 15, 1: 21-28.

Humphreys, A. (1966) *The new Dubliners*. London: Routledge and Kegan Paul.

Hussey, G. (1993) *Ireland today: anatomy of a changing state*. Dublin: Townhouse, Viking.

Hyde, A. (1996a) Unmarried women's experiences of pregnancy and the early weeks of motherhood in an Irish context: a qualitative analysis. Unpublished Ph.D. thesis submitted to TCD.

Hyde, A. (1996b) 'Contraceptive practices', *The Irish Journal of Sociology* 6: 179-211.

I

IFPA (1994a) *Your guide to contraception*. Dublin: IFPA.

IFPA (1994b) *Annual report*. Dublin: IFPA.

IMS (1993) *Childhood experiences and attitudes: an IMS survey*. Dublin: Irish Marketing Surveys.

IMS (1996) *Teenagers poll*. Dublin: Irish Marketing Surveys.

Inglis, T. (1987) *Moral monopoly: the catholic church in modern Irish society*. New York and Dublin: St Martin's Press, Gill and Macmillan.

Inglis, T. (1994) 'Revealing issues on Irish sex', Paper presented at SAI Annual Conference, Derry: 13-15 May.

Inglis, T. and Bassett, M. (1988) *Live and learn - day time adult education in Coolock*. Dublin: Aontas.

Ingram, A. (1992) 'Home and away: the unequal vista for Irish women' in A. Smyth (ed) *The abortion papers Ireland*. Dublin: Attic Press.

INTO (1991) *A decade of progress: an INTO handbook on gender equality in primary education*. Dublin: INTO.

Ireland (1993) *Matrimonial Home Bill*. Dublin: Government Publications.

Ireland (1993) *Statistical bulletin* (1993). Dublin: Government Publications.

Ireland (1994) *Family Law Bill*. Dublin: Government Publications.

Ireland (1995) *Vital statistics fourth quarter and yearly summary 1994*. Dublin: Government Publications.

Ireland (1995) *Domestic Violence Bill*. Dublin: Government Publications.

Ireland (1995) *Social Welfare (No.2) Bill*. Dublin: Government Publications.

Ireland (1997) *National anti-poverty strategy*. Dublin: Government Publications.

Ireland (1997) *Employment Equality Bill*. Dublin: Government Publications.

Irigaray, L. (1985/1977) *This sex which is not one*. Translated by C. Porter and C. Burke. New York: Ithaca, Cornell University Press.

Irigaray, L. (1993) *Je, tu, nous, towards a culture of difference*. Trans by A. Martin. London: Routledge.

Irish Congress of Trade Unions (1990) 'Implementation of equality report'. Progress report to Women's Conference. Dublin: ICTU.

Irish Congress of Trade Unions (1993) *Irish Congress of Trade Unions: mainstreaming equality*. Dublin: ICTU.

J

Jackson, P. (1986) 'Worlds apart – social dimensions of sex roles', in P. Clancy, S. Drudy, K. Lynch and L. O'Dowd (eds) *Ireland: a sociological profile*. Dublin: Institute of Public Administration.

Jackson, P. (1986) 'Exploring feminism: notes on feminism and the family', *Women's Studies Bulletin*: Special Issue. Proceedings of the Annual Conference of the Women's Studies Association of Ireland: 12-21.

Jackson, P. (1987) 'Outside the jurisdiction – Irishwomen seeking abortion', in C. Curtin, P. Jackson and B. O'Connor (eds) *Gender in Irish society*. Galway: Galway University Press.

Jackson, S. (1993) 'Women and the family', in D. Richardson and V. Robinson (eds) *Introducing women's studies*. London: Macmillan.

Jackson, S. (1996) 'Heterosexuality and feminist theory', in D. Richardson (ed) *Theorizing heterosexuality – telling it straight*. Buckingham: Open University Press.

Jaggar, A. (1988/83) *Feminist politics and human nature*. New Jersey: Roman and Allanheld.

James, N. (1989) 'Emotional labour: skill and work in the social regulation of feelings', *Sociological Review* 37, 1:15-42.

Jorgensen, P.S. (1991) 'The family with dependent children in Denmark', in G. Kiely and V. Richardson (eds) *Family, policy; European perspectives*. Dublin: Family Studies Centre.

Jortay, F., Maulders, D. and Plasman, R. (1990) *Evaluation of the impact of the single market competition on women's employment in the banking sector: a synthesis report*. Brussels: EC.

K

Kanter, R. (1993/77) *Men and women of the corporation*. Second edition. New York: Basic Books.

Kanter, R.M. (1991) 'The future of bureaucracy and hierarchy in organizational theory: a report from the field', in P. Bourdieu and J.S. Coleman (eds) *Social theory for a changing society*. New York: Russell Sage Foundation.

Kaplan, G. (1992) *Contemporary western European feminism*. London: Allen and Unwin.

Keane, M. and Quinn, J. (1990) *Rural development and rural tourism.* Galway: Social Sciences Research Centre. Report No. 5.

Kearney, B., Boyle, G.E. and Walsh, J. (1994) *EU Leader 1 Initiative in Ireland: evaluation and recommendations.* Dublin: Department of Agriculture.

Kellaghan, T., Fontes, P. *et al* (1985) *Gender inequalities in primary school teaching.* Dublin: The Educational Company.

Kelleher, P. and Whelan, M. (1992) *Dublin communities in action.* Dublin: Combat Poverty.

Kelleher and Associates with O'Connor, M. (1995) *Making the links.* Dublin: Women's Aid.

Kelly, M. (1991) 'Review symposium', *Economic and Social Review* 22, 3:239-252.

Kelly, M., O'Dowd, L. and Wickham, J. (1982) *Power, conflict and inequality.* Dublin: Turoe Press.

Kelly, M. and Rolston, B. (1995) 'Broadcasting in Ireland: issues of national identity and censorship', in P. Clancy *et al* (ed) *Irish society: sociological perspectives.* Dublin: IPA.

Kennedy, F. (1986) 'The family in transition', in K.A. Kennedy (ed) *Ireland in transition.* Cork: Mercier Press.

Kennedy, F. (1989) *Family, economy and government in Ireland.* ESRI Paper No. 143.

Kennedy, F. (1993) 'Developments in the Irish family in the European context'. Paper given to the Annual General Meeting of the Commission on the Laity, Dublin.

Kennedy, K. A. (1992) 'The context of economic development', in J. Goldthorpe and C.T. Whelan (eds) *The development of industrial society in Ireland.* Published for the British Academy by Oxford University Press.

Kennedy, K. (1993) *Unemployment: crisis in Ireland.* Cork: Cork University Press.

Kennedy, K. (1993) *Facing the unemployment crisis in Ireland.* Cork: Cork University Press.

Kinsey, A.C. *et al* (1953) *Sexual behaviour in the human female.* Philadelphia: W. B. Saunders and Company.

Kiely, G. (1995) 'Fathers in families', in I.C. McCarthy (ed) *Irish Family Studies: selected papers.* Dublin: UCD.

Kitzinger, J. (1995) 'I'm sexually attractive but I'm powerful', *Women's Studies International Forum* 18, 2: 187-196.

Komarovsky, M. (1967) *Blue collar marriage.* New York: Vintage.

Komito, L. (1989) 'Voters, politicians and clientelism: a Dublin survey', *Administration* 37, 2: 171-192.

L

Langford, W. (1996) 'Romantic love and power', in T. Coslett, A. Easton, and P. Summerfield (eds) *Women, power and resistance.* Buckingham: OUP.

Langley, E. (1990) *From Cathleen to anorexia.* Dublin: Attic Press.

Lasch, C. (1977) *Haven in a heartless world.* New York: Basic Books.

Laumann, E. (1991) 'Comments', in P. Bourdieu and J. S. Coleman (eds) *Social theory for a changing society.* New York: Russell Sage.

Lee, J. J. (1978) 'Women and the church since the famine', in M. MacCurtain and D. Ó Corráin, *Women in Irish society.* Dublin: Arlen Press.

Lee, J.J. (1989) *Ireland 1912-1985: politics and society.* Cambridge: Cambridge University Press.

Lees, S. (1993) *Sugar and spice: sexuality and adolescent girls.* London: Penguin.

Lee Treweek, G. (1996) 'Emotion work, order and emotional power in care assistant work', in V. James and J. Gabe (eds) *Health and the sociology of emotions.* Oxford: Blackwell Publishers/Editorial Board.

Leiulfsrud, H. and Woodward, A.E. (1988) 'Women at crossroads: a critical reply to Erikson's and Goldthorpe's note', *Sociology* 22:555-562.

Leonard, D. (1987) *Sex and generation.* London: Tavistock.

Leonard, M. (1992) 'Ourselves alone: household work strategies in a deprived community', *Irish Journal of Sociology* 2:70-84.

Lester, A. (1997) 'Strengthening the legal framework: learning from international experience', Paper presented at EEA 1977-1997, Anniversary Conference Programme, *Look beyond 2000,* Dublin: Royal Hospital Kilmainham.

Levine, J. (1982) *Sisters.* Dublin: Ward River Press.

Levinson, D., Aamador, A.C. and Pari, J.L. (1992) *A question of equity: women and the glass ceiling in the federal government.* A report to the President and Congress of the US by the US Merit Protection Board.

Liddy, S. (1993) 'The impact of feminism on feature writing in Irish women's magazines'. Masters Thesis submitted to the University of Limerick.

Liddy, S. (1995) 'Feature writing in women's magazines: a limited ideological challenge', *Irish Communications Review* 5: 27-35.

Liff, S. and Dale, K. (1994) 'Formal opportunity, informal barriers: black women managers within a local authority', *Work, Employment and Society* 8, 2: 177-198.

Liff, S. and Wajcman, J. (1996) 'Sameness and "difference" revisited: which way forward for equal opportunity initiatives?', *Journal of Management Studies* 33, 1:79-94.

Lindsey, N. (1994) 'Opening address', in O. Egan (ed) *Equality of opportunity in third level education in Ireland.* Cork: National Unit on Equal Opportunities at Third Level.

Lockwood, D. (1964) 'Social integration and system integration', in G. K. Zollschan and W. Hirch (eds) *Explanations in social change.* London: Routledge and Kegan Paul.

Lugones, M. and Spelman E. (1993) 'Have we got a theory for you! Feminist theory, cultural imperialism and the demand for the "woman's voice"', in J. Kourany, J.P. Sterpa and R. Tong (eds) *Feminist philosophies: problems, theories and applications.* London: Harvester/Wheatsheaf.

Lynch, I. (1993) 'Labour law', in A. Connelly (ed) *Gender and the law in Ireland.* Dublin: Oak Tree Press.

Lynch, K. (1989a) 'Solidary labour: its nature and marginalization', *Sociological Review* 37, 1: 1-14.

Lynch, K. (1989b) 'The ethos of girls' schools: an analysis of the differences between male and female schools', *Social Studies* 10, 1-2: 11-31.

Lynch, K. (1991) 'Girls and young women in education in Ireland', in M. Wilson (ed) *Girls and young women in education: a European perspective.* Oxford. Pergamon.

Lynch, K. (1992) 'Ideology and the legitimation of inequality in education', in P. Clancy *et al* (eds) *Ireland and Poland: comparative perspectives.* Dublin: UCD.

Lynch, K. (1994a) 'Women teach and men manage: why men dominate senior posts in Irish education', in *Women for leadership in education.* Dublin: Education Commission of the Conference of Religious in Ireland.

Lynch, K. (1994b) 'An analysis of the differences between educational policies based on principles of equity, equality of opportunity and egalitarianism', in O. Egan (ed) *Equality of opportunity in third level education in Ireland.* Cork: National Unit on Equal Opportunities at Third Level, UCC.

Lynch, K. and McLaughlin, E. (1995) 'Caring labour and love labour', in P. Clancy, S. Drudy, K. Lynch and L. O Dowd (eds) *Irish society: sociological perspectives.* Dublin: Institute of Public Administration.

Lynch, K. and Morgan, V. (1995) 'Gender and education; North and South', in P. Clancy *et al* (eds) *Irish society: sociological perspectives.* Dublin. Institute of Public Administration.

Lyons, M., Ruddle H. and O'Connor, J. (1992) *Seeking a refuge from violence.* Dublin and Limerick: Policy Research Centre, Mid Western Health Board and Adapt House.

M

MacCurtain, M (1993) 'Moving statues and Irish women', in A. Smyth (ed) *Irish women's studies reader.* Dublin: Attic Press.

MacDevitt (1996) 'Barriers to the participation of women in business and business creation', in *Barriers to the participation of women in business and business creation*, Third Report of the Fourth Joint Oireachtas Committee on Women's Rights. Dublin: Government Publications.

Mac Gréil, M. (1991) *Religious practice and attitudes in Maynooth.* Maynooth: Survey Research Unit.

MacKinnon, C. (1987) *'Towards a feminist theory of the state'*, Cambridge, Mass: Harvard University Press.

Maguire, S. (1988) 'Sorry love – violence against women in the house', *Critical Social Policy* 8, 2. (23): 34-43.

Mahon, E. (1987) 'Women's rights and catholicism in Ireland', *New Left Review*, 116 Nov/December: 53-78.

Mahon, E. (1991a) *Motherhood, work and equal opportunity*. First Report of the Third Joint Oireachtas Committee on Women's Rights. Dublin: Stationery Office.

Mahon, E. (1991b) 'The barriers and difficulties women experience in getting to decision making level'. Presented at the *From Participation to Partnership Conference*, hosted by Waterford Women's Federation and the Council for the Status of Women. Nov. 29, Waterford.

Mahon, E. (1991c) 'Equal opportunities in the Irish civil service: an interim review', *Women in Public Service Equal Opportunities International* 10, 2: 2-10.

Mahon, E. (1992) 'Review of T. Callan and B. Farrell: Women's participation in the Irish labour market', *Irish Journal of Sociology* 2: 186-189.

Mahon, E. (1993) 'Feminism and the family'. Paper presented at the Sociological Association of Ireland Conference. Dublin, December.

Mahon, E. (1994) 'Ireland: a private patriarchy?' *Environment and Planning: A*, 26:1277-1296.

Mahon, E. (1995) 'From democracy to femocracy: the women's movement in the Republic of Ireland', in P. Clancy *et al* (eds) *Irish society: sociological perspectives*. Dublin: IPA.

Mahon, E. and Dillon, L. (1996) 'Women in management in local administration', *Second Report of the Fourth Joint Oireachtas Committee on Women's Rights*. Dublin: Government publications.

Mahon, E. and Conlon, C. (1996) 'Legal abortions carried out in England on women normally resident in the Republic of Ireland', in *Report of the Constitutional Review Group*. Dublin: Government Publications.

Mahoney, R. (1993) *Whoredom in Kimmage: Irish women coming of age*. London: Doubleday.

Mann, M. (1986) 'A crisis in stratification theory?' in R.Crompton and M.Mann (eds) *Gender and stratification*. Cambridge: Polity Press.

Marauni, M. (1992) *The position of women in the labour market*. Report No. 36. Brussels: Commission of the European Communities.

Masters, W. and Johnson, V. (1966) *Human sexual response*. Boston: Little Brown and Co.

McCabe, T. (1981) 'Girls and leisure', in A. Tomlinson (ed) *Leisure and social control*. Brighton: Chelsea.

McCarthy, E. and Drew, E. (1994) 'Profile of women in organisations in the Dublin region (1990-1993)', in *The changing face of women and work in the Dublin region*. Dublin: Dublin Technology Partnership.

McCarthy, J. and Ronayne, T. (1984) *The psychological well-being of the young unemployed*. Dublin: YEA.

McCarthy, E. (1986) *Transitions to equal opportunity at work in Ireland: problems and possibilities*. Dublin: EEA.

McCarthy, L. (1996) 'Still not making it to the top: a study of individual and organisational factors affecting lecturers in UL'. Unpublished ms.

McCashin, A. (1993) *Lone parents in the Republic of Ireland: enumeration, description and social implications for social security*. Dublin: ESRI.

McCashin, A. (1996) *Lone mothers in Ireland*. Dublin: Oak Tree Press.

McCullagh, M. (1984) 'Youth employment and the ideology of control in Northern Ireland', in C. Curtin, M. Kelly, L. O'Dowd (eds) *Culture and ideology in Ireland*. Galway: University of Galway Press.

McCullagh, C. (1991) 'The ties that blind: family and ideology in Ireland', *Economic and Social Review* 22, 3:199-211.

McDonough, B. (1994) 'Putting equality into action'. Unpublished ms, Paper presented at University of Limerick.

McGauran, A.M. (1996) 'The effects of EU policy on women's employment: the case of women in Irish and French retailing', *Irish Journal of Feminist Studies* 2: 83-102.

McIntyre, S. (1991) 'Who wants babies?: the social construction of instincts', in D.L. Leonard and A. Speakman (eds) *Sexual divisions revisited*. London: Macmillan.

McKenna, A. (1979) 'Attitudes of Irish mothers to child rearing', *Journal of Comparative Family Studies,* vol x, 2:227-252.

McKenna, A. (1988) *Childcare and equal opportunities*. Dublin: EEA.

McKeown, K. (1991) *St Vincent's Family Resource Centre 1979-1989: an overview*. Dublin: Daughters of Charity.

McKeown, K. and Gilligan, R. (1991) 'Child sexual abuse in the Eastern Health Board region of Ireland in 1988: an analysis of 512 confirmed cases', *The Economic and Social Review* 22, 2:101-134.

McLoughlin, R.J. (1972) 'The industrial development process: an overall view', *Administration* 20: 27-36.

McQuillan, H. (1995) 'Options and opportunities: an exploration of gender differences in subject and career choices', in R. Lentin (ed) *In From the Shadows: the UL women's studies collection*, Vol. 1. Limerick: UL.

McRobbie, A. (1978) 'Working class girls and the culture of femininity', in *Women take issue*. London: Hutchinson.

McRobbie, A. (1991) *Feminism and youth culture*. London: Macmillan

Mc Rae, S. (1986) *Cross-class families*. Oxford: Clarendon Press.

McWilliams, M. (1991) 'Women's paid work and the sexual division of labour', in *Women, employment and social policy in Northern Ireland: a problem postponed?* Belfast: Queens University, and University of Ulster: Policy Research Institute.

McWilliams, M. and McKernan, J. (1993) *Bringing it out in the open: domestic violence in Northern Ireland*. London: HMSO.

Meaney, G. (1991) *Sex and nation: women in Irish culture and politics*. Dublin: Attic Press.

Messinger, J. (1969) *Inis Beg*. New York: Holt Rinehart and Winston.

Miles, A. (1988) *Women and mental illness: the social context of female neurosis*. Sussex: Wheatsheaf.

Millar, J., Leeper, S. and Davies, C. (1992) *Lone parents: poverty and public policy in Ireland*. Dublin: Combat Poverty.

Minturn, L. and Lambert, W.L. (1964) *Mothers of six cultures: antecedents of child rearing*. New York: Wiley.

Morgan, D.H.J. (1975) *Social theory and the family*. London: Routledge and Kegan Paul.

Morgan, D.H.J. (1985) *The family: politics and social theory*. London: Routledge and Kegan Paul.

Morris, L. (1985) 'Local social networks and domestic organizations: a study of redundant steel workers and their wives', *Sociological Review* 33: 327-341.

Moss P. (1990) *Childcare in the European Community 1985-1990*. Brussels: European Community Childcare Network.

MRBI (1992) *Mná na hÉireann inniu: an MRBI perspective on women in Irish society today*. Dublin: Market Research Bureau of Ireland.

MRBI (1998) *Attitudes towards the Catholic Church*. Dublin: MRBI.

Mulkeen, M. (1994) *Evaluation report on women in management training programme*. Dublin: National Youth Council of Ireland and Women's Participation Working Group.

Mulligan, A. (1989) 'Women, family commitments and community work', *Co-options: Journal of the Community Workers Co-Op*, Dublin: 18-19.

Mullin, M. (1991) 'Representations of history, Irish feminism, and the politics of difference', *Feminist Studies* 17, 1: 29-50.

Mulvey, C. (1991) *Assessment of women's community group funding*. Dublin: Combat Poverty.

Mulvey, A. (1992) 'Irish women's studies and community activism: reflections and exemplars', *Women's Studies International Forum* 15, 4: 507-516.

Murray, P. and Wickham, J. (1983) 'Technocratic ideology and the reproduction of inequality: the case of the electronics industry in the Republic of Ireland', in G. Day and D. Robbins (eds) *Diversity and decomposition in the labour market*. London: Gower.

Muratroyd, L. (1984) 'Women, men, and the social grading of occupations', *British Journal of Sociology* 35: 473-497.

Murphy, C. (1994) *Christian feminism*. Dublin: Dominican Publications.

Murphy Lawless, J. (1992) *The adequacy of income and family expenditure*. Dublin: Combat Poverty.

Murphy Lawless, J. (1993) 'The silencing of women in childbirth or let's hear it for Bartholomew and the boys', in A. Smyth (ed) *Irish women's studies reader*. Dublin: Attic Press.

Murphy, M. and Whelan, B.J. (1995) *The economic status of school leavers 1992*. Dublin: ESRI and Department of Enterprise and Employment.

N

National Economic and Social Forum (1996) *Job potential of work sharing forum. Report no. 9*. Dublin: Government Publications.

National Youth Policy Committee (1984) *Final report*. Dublin: Government Publications.

NCCA (1994) *The leaving certificate examination: a review of results*, by B. Hickey and M. Martin. Dublin: NCCA.

NESC (1991) *The economic and social implications of emigration.* Dublin: NESC.

NHS Management Executive (1992) *Women in the NHS: an implementation guide to opportunity 2000.* UK Department of Health.

Ní Chárthaigh, D. and Hanafin, J. (1993) *Women's studies courses in Ireland.* Unpublished ms.

Ní Chárthaigh, D. and Mahon, E. (1987) *A world of difference: women's studies.* Dublin: RTÉ Department.

Ní Chárthaigh, D. (1986) 'Options for the future of women's studies', *Women's Studies Bulletin,* Spring 1-3.

Nic Giolla Phádraig, M. and Clancy, P. (1995) 'Marital fertility and family planning', in I. Colgan McCarthy (ed) *Irish family studies: selected papers.* Dublin: UCD, Family studies Centre.

Nic Giolla Phádraig, M. (1991) *Childhood as a social phenomenon.* European Centre for Social Welfare Policy and Research, Eurosocial Report vol. 36.

Nic Giolla Phádraig, M. (1995) 'The power of the catholic church in the Republic of Ireland', in P. Clancy *et al* (eds) *Irish society: sociological perspectives.* Dublin: IPA.

Nolan, B. (1991) 'Low pay in Ireland: report on a study commissioned by the Department of Labour', referred to in *Report of the Second Commission on the Status of Women,* Dublin: Government Publications: 103.

Noonan, J. (1993) *The Durex report: Ireland.* Dublin: Durex.

Norris, P. (1987) *Politics and sexual equality: the comparative position of women in western democracies.* Brighton: Wheatsheaf.

NYCI (1990) *Report on the position of women in the youth service.* Dublin: Women's Participation Working Group and NYCI.

NYCI (1998) *Get your facts right.* Dublin: National Youth Council of Ireland.

O

Oakley, A. (1972) *Sex, gender and society.* London: Temple Smith.

Oakley, A. (1974) *The sociology of housework.* Oxford: Martin Robertson.

O'Brien, M. (ed) (1995) *Divorce? Facing the issues of marital breakdown.* Dublin: Attic Press.

O'Broin, N. and Farren, G. (1978) *The working and living conditions of civil service typists.* Dublin: ESRI Paper No. 94.

O'Carroll, P. (1991) 'Bishops, knights and pawns? Traditional thought and the Irish abortion referendum debate of 1983', *Irish Political Studies* 6:53-71.

O'Carroll, I. (1994) 'Queers in the quad: lesbian and gay students and staff in third level institutions', in O. Egan (ed) *Equality of opportunity in Irish third level institutions.* Proceedings of a Forum, Cork: UCC.

O'Connell, P. and Rottman, J. (1992) 'The welfare state', in J. Goldthorpe and C.T. Whelan (eds) *The development of industrial society in Ireland.* New York: Oxford University Press

O'Connell, P. (1996) 'Sick man or tigress? The labour market in the Republic of Ireland'. Paper presented at the British Academy Symposium: *Ireland: North and South.* Nuffield College Oxford, December.

O'Connor, J. (1987) *Women in enterprise*. Dublin: Industrial Development Authority.

O'Connor, J. and Daly, M. (1983) *The West Limerick study: a baseline study of transition and change*. Limerick: Social Research Unit.

O'Connor, J. and Ruddle, H. (1988) *Caring for the elderly, part 2: The caring process: a study of carers in the home*. National Council for the Aged.

O'Connor, P. (1990) 'The adult mother-daughter relationship: a uniquely and universally close relationship?', *Sociological Review* 38, 2: 293-323.

O'Connor, P. (1991) 'Women's experience of power within marriage: an inexplicable phenomenon?', *Sociological Review* 39, 4: 823-842.

O'Connor, P. (1992a) 'Child care policy in Ireland: a provocative analysis and a research agenda', *Administration* 40, 3: 200-219.

O'Connor, P. (1992b) 'The professionalisation of child care work in Ireland: an unlikely development?' *Children and Society* 6, 3: 250-266.

O'Connor, P. (1992c) *Friendships between women: a critical review*. New York and London: Harvester/Wheatsheaf and Guildford.

O'Connor, P. (1993) 'Women's experience of the mother role', *Sociological Review* 41, 2: 347-360.

O'Connor, P. (1994a) 'Family rights project: an evaluation', Limerick: Paul. Unpublished Report.

O'Connor, P. (1994b) 'Very close parent/child relationships: the perspectives of the elderly person', *Journal of Cross Cultural Gerontology* 9, 1: 53-76.

O'Connor, P. (1995a) 'Tourism and development: women's business?' *Economic and Social Review* 26, 4: 369-401.

O'Connor, P. (1995b) *The barriers to women's promotion in the Midland and Mid-Western Health Board*, Limerick: Mid-Western Health Board.

O'Connor, P. (1995c) 'Defining Irish women: dominant discourses and sites of resistance', *Éire-Ireland* 30, 3: 177-187.

O'Connor, P. (1995d) 'Understanding variation in marital sexual pleasure: an impossible task?' *Sociological Review*, May: 342-362.

O'Connor, P. (1995e) 'Understanding continuities and changes in Irish marriage: putting women centre stage', *Irish Journal of Sociology* 5: 135-168.

O'Connor, P. (1996a) 'Organisational culture as a barrier to women's promotion', *Economic and Social Review* 27, 3:187-216.

O'Connor, P. (1996b) *Invisible players? women, tourism and development in Ballyhoura*. Limerick: University of Limerick Press.

O'Connor, P and Shortall, S. (1998) 'Does the border make the difference?', in R. Breen, A. Heath and C. T. Whelan (eds) *Ireland: North and South*. Oxford University Press for the British Academy. Forthcoming.

O'Connor, P. (1998) 'Women in the academy: the ultimate challenge?', in A.B. Ryan and B. Connolly (eds) *Women and education*. Maynooth. Forthcoming.

O'Donohue, M. (1995) 'The gender dynamics of career choice in engineering', in R. Lentin (ed) *In From the Shadows,* Vol 1. Limerick: University of Limerick Press.

O'Donovan, O. and Curtin, C. (1991) 'Industrial development and rural women in Ireland', in T. Varley, T.A. Boylan and M.P. Cuddy (eds) *Rural crisis: perspectives on Irish rural development.* Galway: Galway University Press.

O'Dowd, L. (1987) 'Church, state and women: the aftermath of partition', in C. Curtin, P. Jackson and B. O'Connor (eds) *Gender and society.* Galway: University Press.

O'Dowd, L. (1991) 'The states of Ireland: some reflections on research', *Irish Journal of Sociology,* 1: 96-106.

O'Dowd, L. (1992) 'State legitimacy and nationalism in Ireland', in P. Clancy, M. Kelly, J. Wiatr and R. Zoltaniecki (eds) *Ireland and Poland: comparative perspectives.* Dublin: UCD.

OECD (1991) *Ireland: reviews of national policies on education.* Paris.

Official Publications of the European Communities (1992) *Women in the European Community.* Brussels and Luxembourg: E SCC-EEC-EAEC.

Office for Health Management (1997) 'Leadership in the Health Services', 3 August, 1-4.

Offe, C. (1984) *Contradictions of the Welfare State,* J. Keane (ed) London: Hutchinson.

O'Hara, P. (1987) Article in C. Curtin, P. Jackson, B. O'Connor (eds) 'What became of them? Women in the west of Ireland labour force'. Galway: University Press.

O'Hara, P. (1993) 'Out of the shadows: women on family farms and their contribution to agriculture and rural development'. Paper presented at Wageningen, The Netherlands, 15-17 March.

O'Hara, P. (1994a) 'Women family farm community in Ireland'. Unpublished Ph.D. thesis submitted to Trinity College, Dublin.

O'Hara, P. (1994b) 'Constructing the future: co-operation and resistance among farm women in Ireland', in S. Whatmore, T. Marsden and P. Lowe (eds) *Gender and rurality.* London: Fulton Publishers.

O'Hara, P. (1994c) 'Out of the shadows: women on family farms and their contribution to agriculture and rural development', in L. Van der Plus and M. Fonte (eds) *Rural gender studies in Europe.* The Netherlands: Van Gorcum.

O'Hare, A., Whelan, C. and Commins, P. (1991) 'The development of an Irish census based social class scale', *Economic and Social Review* 22: 135-156.

O'Hare, A. and O'Connor, A. (1987) 'Gender differences in treated mental illness in the Republic of Ireland', in C. Curtin, P. Jackson and B. O'Connor (eds) *Gender in Irish society.* Galway: University Press.

Oliker, S.J. (1989) *Best friends and marriage: exchange among women.* CA: University of California Press.

O'Malley, E. (1992) *The pilot programme for integrated rural development 1988-1990,* Paper No. 27: Broadsheet Series. Dublin: ESRI.

O'Neill, C. (1992) *Telling it like it is.* Dublin: Combat Poverty.

O'Reilly, E. (1992) *Masterminds of the right*. Dublin: Attic Press.

Ó Riagáin, F. (1995) 'Reasons for marital instability and separation', in M. O'Brien (ed) *Divorce? Facing the issues of marital breakdown*. Dublin: Basement Press.

P

Pahl, R.E. (1984) *Divisions of labour*. Oxford: Blackwell.

Pahl, J. (1989) *Money and marriage*. London: Macmillan.

Pahl, J. (1991) 'Money and power in marriage', in P. Abbott and C. Wallace (eds) *Gender, power and sexuality*. London: Macmillan.

Parker, R. (1981) 'Tending and social policy', in E.M. Goldberg and S. Hatch (eds) *A look at the personal social services*. Discussion Paper No. 4. London: Policy Studies Institute.

Paukert, L. (1984) *The employment and unemployment of women in OECD countries*. Paris: OECD.

Peillon, M. (1984) 'The structure of Irish ideology revisited', in C. Curtin, M. Kelly and L. O'Dowd (eds) *Culture and ideology in Ireland*. Galway: Galway University Press.

Peillon, M. (1982) *Contemporary Irish society: an introduction*. Dublin: Gill and Macmillan.

Peillon, M. (1988) 'State and society in the Republic of Ireland: a comparative study', *Administration* 35, 2:190-207.

Peillon, M. (1992) 'State and society in the Republic of Ireland', in P. Clancy *et al.* (eds) *Ireland and Poland: comparative perspectives*. Dublin: UCD.

Peillon, M. (1995) 'Interest groups and the state', in P. Clancy *et al* (eds) *Irish society: sociological perspectives*. Dublin: IPA.

Phillips, A. and Moss, P. (1988) *Who cares for Europe's children? The Short Report of the European Childcare Network*. Brussels: CEC.

Pillinger, J. (1992) *Feminizing the market: women's pay and employment in the European Community*. London: Macmillan.

Pollert, A. (1996) 'Gender and class revisited: or the poverty of patriarchy', *Sociology* 30, 4:639-659.

Porter, E. (1996) 'Culture, community and responsibilities: abortion in Ireland', *Sociology* 30, 2:279-298.

Potter, P. (1991) *The paths of young people towards autonomy*. First Report of seminar held on 'Growing up and leaving home: facilitating participation and combating exclusion'. Dublin: European Foundation for the Improvement of Living and Working Conditions.

Povall, M. (1982) 'Banking on women managers', *Management Today,* February: 50-54.

Powell, G. N. (1990) 'One more time: do female and male managers differ?, *Academy of Management Executive,* vol. 3: 68-75.

Prendiville, P. (1988) 'Divorce in Ireland: an analysis of the referendum to amend the constitution', *Women's Studies Int Forum*, vol. 11, no. 4:355-363.

Prendiville, P. and Von Mohlmann, S. (1993) *Sugar and spice: a resource book for working with young women.* Dublin: Women's Participation Working Group NYCI.

Proctor, J. and Jackson, C. (1992) *Women managers in the NHS: a celebration of success.* Women's Unit, Department of Health, NHS Management Executive.

Pyle, J.C.L. (1990) *The state and women in the economy.* Albany: State University of New York Press.

R

Radway, J. (1987) *Reading the romance: women, patriarchy and popular literature.* London: Verso.

Randall, V. and Smyth, A. (1987) 'Bishops and baliwicks: obstacles to women's political participation in Ireland', *Economic and Social Review* 18, 3: 189-214.

Rapid Reports (1993) 'Women in the European Community', *Population and Social Conditions,* 10. Brussels: EC.

Reilly, B. (1995) 'Union and gender wage gap: estimates for young workers in Ireland: a note', *The Economic and Social Review* 26, 2: 221-231.

Reuter, R.R. (1983) *Sexism and God talk: toward a feminist theology.* Boston: Beacon Press.

Restivo, S. (1991) *The sociological world view.* Oxford: Blackwell

Reynolds, B. and Healy, S. (eds) *New frontiers for full citizenship.* Dublin: CMRS.

Rich, A. (1980) 'Compulsory heterosexuality and lesbian existence', *Signs: Women in Culture and Society* 5, 4: 631-660.

Richardson, D. (1996) 'Heterosexuality and social theory', in D. Richardson (ed) *Theorising heterosexuality.* Buckingham: OUP.

Richardson, D. (1997) 'Sexuality and feminism', in V. Robinson and D. Richardson (eds) *Introducing women's studies.* Second edition. London: Macmillan.

Riddick, R. (1990) *The right to choose.* Dublin: Attic Press.

Riddick, R. (1993) 'Abortion and the law in the Republic of Ireland, an overview 1861-1993'. An address to the New Boston School of Law, Boston Massachusetts.

Ringelheim, J. (1985) 'Women and the holocaust: a reconsideration of research', *Signs: Journal of Women in Culture and Society* 10, 4: 741-759.

Robinson, M. (1996) 'Equality and democracy: utopia or challenge?' *Irish Journal of Feminist Studies* 1, 1:1-6.

Robinson, V. (1996) 'Heterosexuality and masculinity: theorising male power or the male wounded psyche', in D. Richardson (ed) *Theorising heterosexuality.* Buckingham: OUP.

Roche, R. (1982) 'The high cost of complaining Irish style', *Journal of Irish Business and Administrative Research* 4/2: 98-108.

Roche, W.B. (1992) 'Modelling trade union growth and decline in the Republic of Ireland', *Irish Business and Administration Research,* 13:86-102.

Ronayne, T. (1987) *The social and economic situation of young people in Ireland: their position in the labour and housing markets and the implications for social cohesion.* A Report to the School for Advanced Urban Studies. Dublin: The Irish Foundation for Human Development.

Ronayne, T. (1992) *Participation in youth service provision during the transition from school to the labour market: gaps in provision and the policy issues arising.* Summary Report. Dublin WRC Social and Economic Consultants.

Rose, S.M. (1985) 'Same and cross-sex friendships and the psychology of homosociality', *Sex Roles* 12, 1/2: 63-74.

Rose, S. and Serafica, F.C. (1986) 'Keeping and ending casual, close and best friendships', *Journal of Social and Personal Relationships* 3: 275-288.

Roseneil, S. (1995) 'The coming of age of feminist sociology', *British Journal of Sociology* 46(2): 191-205.

Rosenberg, J., Perlstat, H. and Phillips, W.F. (1993) 'Now that we are here: discrimination, disparagement and harassment at work and the experience of women lawyers', *Gender and Society* 7, 3: 415-433.

Rossi, A. (1980) 'Life span theories and women's lives', *Signs: Women in Culture and Society* 6, 1:4-32.

Rottman, D. (1994a) 'Allocating resources within households: better off poorer?', in B. Nolan and T. Callan (eds) *Poverty and policy in Ireland.* Dublin: Gill and Macmillan.

Rottman, D. (1994b) *Income distribution within Irish households.* Dublin: Combat Poverty.

Rowley, R. (1989) 'Women and the constitution', *Administration* 37, 1: 42-62.

Ruane, F. and Dobson, E. (1990) 'Academic salary differentials: some evidence from an Irish study', *The Economic and Social Review* 21, 209-226.

Ruane, F. (1997) 'What has the celtic tigress done for Irish women?' Paper presented at EEA 1977-1997 Anniversary Conference Programme, *Look beyond 2000.* Royal Hospital Kilmainham, Dublin.

Rubery, J. and Fagan, C. (1993) *Occupational segregation of men and women in the European Community,* Social Europe Series. EC and Manchester.

Rubery, J. *et al* (1995) *Changing patterns of work and working time in the European Union and the impact on gender divisions.* Brussels: EC DG: V.

Rubery, J., Smith, M. and Fagan, C. (1996) *Trends and prospects for women's employment in the 1990s.* Brussels: EC, Equal Opportunities Unit.

Rubin, G. (1984) 'Thinking sex: notes for a radical theory of the politics of sexuality', in C.S. Vance (ed) *Pleasure and danger: exploring female sexuality.* Boston and London: Routledge and Kegan Paul.

Rubin, L. (1985) *Just friends: the role of friendship in our lives.* New York: Harper and Row.

Rudd, J. (1982) 'On the margins of the power elite: women in the upper echelons', in M. Kelly, L. O'Dowd and J. Wickham (eds) *Power, conflict and inequality.* Dublin: Turoe Press.

Ruddle, H. and O'Connor, J. (1992) *'Breaking the silence', violence in the home: the woman's perspective.* Limerick: Mid-Western Health Board and Adapt Refuge.

S

Savage, M. (1992) 'Women's expertise, men's authority: gendered organization and the contemporary middle class', in M. Savage and A. Witz (eds) *Gender and bureaucracy*. Oxford: Blackwell/Sociological Review.

Scheper-Hughes, N. (1979a) *Saints, scholars and schitzophrenics*. Berkeley: University of California Press.

Scheper-Hughes, N. (1979b) 'Breeding breaks out in the eye of the cat: sex roles, birth order and the Irish double bind', *Journal of Comparative Family Studies: Special Issues* 10, 2: 207-226.

Scannell, Y. (1988) 'The constitution and role of women' in B. Farrell (ed) *De Valera's constitution and ours*. Dublin: Gill and Macmillan.

Schwartz, P. (1994) *Peer marriage: how love between equals really works*. New York: Free Press.

Scott, J. (1985) *Weapons of the weak: everyday forms of resistance*. New Haven: Yale University Press.

Seager, J. and Olson, A. (1986) *Women in the world*. London: Pluto Press.

Second Commission on the Status of Women (1993) *Report to the Government*. Dublin: Government Publications.

Second Monitoring Committee (1996) *Second progress report of the monitoring committee on the implementation of the recommendations of the Second Commission on the Status of Women*. Dublin: Stationery Office.

Second Co-ordinated Report (1992) *The development of equal opportunities, October 1988-February 1992*. Dublin: Government Publications.

Second Report of the Third Joint Oireachtas Committee on Women's Rights (1992) *Gender equality in the Republic of Ireland 1984-1991*. Dublin: Stationery Office.

Sexton, J.J., Walsh, B.N., Hannan, D.F. and McMahon, D. (1991) *The economic and social implications of emigration*, Report No. 90. Dublin: National Economic and Social Council.

Sexton, J.J. and O'Connell, P.J. (eds) (1997) *Labour market studies Ireland: Series no. 1*. Luxembourg: EOC.

Shanahan, K. (1992) *Crimes worse than death*. Dublin: Attic Press.

Shortall, S. (1991) 'The dearth of data on Irish farm wives: a critical review of the literature', *Economic and Social Review* 22, 4: 311-332.

Simonds, W. (1992) *Women and self-help culture: reading between the lines*. New Brunswick, New Jersey: Rutgers University Press.

Sixth annual report on the implementation of the Equal Opportunity Policy and Guidelines for the Civil Service (1994) *Equality of opportunity in the civil service, 1992*. Dublin: Government Publications.

Slowey, M. (1989) 'Women in continuing education and training', in D. O'Sullivan (ed) *Social commitment and adult education*. Cork: Cork University Press.

Slater, E. and McDonough, T. (1994) 'Bulwark of landlordism and capitalism: the dynamics of feudalism in nineteenth-century Ireland', *Research in Political Economy* 14: 63-118.

Smart, B.(1995/1985) *Michel Foucault*. London: Routledge.

Smith Rosenberg, C. (1975) 'The female world of love and ritual: relations between women in 19th century America', *Signs: Journal of Women in Culture and Society*, 1: 1-29.

Smyth, A. (1984) *Breaking the circle: the position of women academics in third level education in Ireland*. Dublin

Smyth, A. (1986) 'Nice women like us in a place like that: the position of women academics in Ireland', *Women's Studies Bulletin*, Spring 9-15.

Smyth, A. (1987) *Women academics in Ireland*. Dublin: Government Publications Office.

Smyth, A. (1988) 'The contemporary women's movement in the Republic of Ireland', *Women's Studies International Forum* 11, 4:331-341.

Smyth, A. (1991) 'The floozie in the jacuzzi', *Feminist Studies* 17, 1:7-28.

Smyth, A. (1992a) 'A sadistic farce: women and abortion in the Republic of Ireland, 1992, in A. Smyth (ed) *The abortion papers, Ireland*. Dublin: Attic Press.

Smyth, A. (1992b) 'The politics of abortion in a police state', in A. Smyth (ed) *The abortion papers, Ireland*. Dublin: Attic Press.

Smyth, A. (1993) 'The women's movement in the Republic of Ireland 1970-1990', in A. Smyth (ed) *Irish women's studies reader*. Dublin: Attic Press.

Smyth, E. (1997) 'Labour market structures and women's employment in the Republic of Ireland', in A. Byrne and M. Leonard (eds) *Women and Irish society: a sociological reader*. Belfast: Beyond the Pale Publications.

South Eastern Health Board (1993) *Kilkenny incest report*. Dublin: Government Publications.

Spender, D. (1980) *Man made language*. London: Routledge and Kegan Paul.

Speed, A. (1992) 'The struggle for reproductive rights: a brief history in its political context', in A. Smyth (ed) *The abortion papers, Ireland*. Dublin: Attic Press.

Stack, C. (1974) *All our kin*. New York: Harper and Row.

Stacey, J. (1986) 'Are feminists afraid to leave home? The challenge of conservative pro-family feminism', in J. Mitchell and A. Oakley (eds) *What is feminism?*. Oxford: Blackwell.

Staggenborg, S. (1991) *The pro choice movement: organisation and activism in the abortion conflict*. Oxford: Oxford University Press.

Steinem, G. (1993/1983) 'Outrageous acts and everyday rebellions' in J. A. Kourany, J.P. Sterba and R. Tong (eds) *Feminist philosophies*. New York/London: Harvester/Wheatsheaf,

Sterne, J. (1984) 'Technology, ideology and the office worker', in C. Curtin, M. Kelly, L. O'Dowd (eds) *Culture and ideology in Ireland*. Galway: University Press.

Stiver Lie, S. and O'Leary, V. (eds) (1990) *Storming the tower*. London: Kogan Page.

T

Tansey, J. (1985) *Women in Ireland: a compilation of relevant data*. Dublin: Council for the Status of Women.

Tancred, P. (1995) 'Women's work: a challenge to the sociology of work', *Gender, Work and Organisation* 2, 1:1-20.

The Women's Studies Association of Ireland (1985) *Towards a new curriculum: gender and schooling*. Submission to the Curriculum and Examinations Board. Limerick: University of Limerick.

Thompson, L. (1991) 'Family work: women's sense of fairness', *Journal of Family Issues* 12 (2): 181-196.

Tong, R. (1992) *Feminist thought*. London: Routledge.

Tovey, H. (1992) 'Rural sociology in Ireland: a review', *The Irish Journal of Sociology* 2: 96-121.

Treiman, D. and Hartmann, H. (eds) (1981) *Women, work and wages: equal pay for jobs of equal value*. Washington DC: National Academy Press.

TUI (1990) *Equality of opportunity in teaching*. Dublin: TUI.

Tweedy, H. (1992) *A link in the chain*. Dublin: Attic Press.

U

Ungerson, C. (1983) 'Why do women care?' in J. Finch and D. Groves (eds) *A labour of love: women, work and caring*. London: Routledge and Kegan Paul.

Ungerson, C. (1987) *Policy is personal: sex, gender and informal care*. London: Tavistock.

United Nations (1995) *Human development report*. Oxford: Oxford University Press.

US Merit Protection Board (1992) *A question of equality: women and the glass ceiling and the federal government*. Washington: Report to the President and Congress of the United States.

V

Vance, C. (1984) 'Pleasure and danger: toward a politics of sexuality', in C.S. Vance (ed) *Pleasure and danger: exploring female sexuality*. Boston and London: Routledge and Kegan Paul.

Vance, C.S. (1989) 'Social construction theory: problems in the history of sexuality', in D. Altman, C. Vance, M.Vicinus, J. Weeks *et al* (eds) *Homosexuality, which homosexuality?*. London and Amsterdam: GMP Publishers.

Viney, E. (1989) *Ancient wars: sex and sexuality*. Dublin: Attic Press.

W

Walby, S. (1986) *Patriarchy at work*. Cambridge: Polity.

Walby, S. (1989) 'Theorizing patriarchy', *Sociology* 23, 2: 213-234.

Walby, S. (1990) *Theorizing patriarchy*. Oxford: Blackwell.

Walby, S. (1992) 'Post-post modernism: theorizing social complexity', in M. Barrett and A. Phillips (eds) *Destabilising theory*. Cambridge: Polity Press.

Walby, S. (1996) 'Women and citizenship: towards a comparative analysis, in R. Lentin (ed) *In From the Shadows.* Vol 2. Limerick: University of Limerick Press.

Wallace, C. (1986) 'From girls and boys to women and men: the social reproduction of gender roles in the transition from school to (un) employment', in S. Walker and L. Barton (eds) *Youth, unemployment and schooling.* Milton Keynes: OUP.

Wallace, C. (1987a) *For richer, for poorer: growing up in and out of work.* London: Tavistock.

Wallace, C. (1987b) 'Between the family and the state: young people in transition', in M. White and S. Hutson (eds) *The social world of the young unemployed.* London: Polity Press.

Walsh, B.M. (1993) 'Labour force participation and the growth in women's employment, Ireland, 1971-1991', *Economic and Social Review* 24, 4: 369-400.

Walters, P.P. (1987) 'Servants of the crown', in A. Spencer and D. Podmore (eds) *In a man's world.* London: Tavistack Publications.

Ward, P. (1993) *The financial consequences of marital breakdown.* Cork: Cork University Press.

Ward, E. and O'Donovan, O. (1996) 'Networks of women's groups and what (some) women think', in *UCG Women's Studies Centre Review*, Vol. 4:1-20.

Weber, M. (1947) *The theory of social and economic organisation.* New York: Oxford University Press.

Weber, M. (1968) *Economy and society.* Berkeley: University of California Press.

Weeks, G. (1989) *Sexuality.* London and New York: Routledge.

Whelan, C. (1994a) 'Poverty, social class, education and intergenerational mobility', in B. Nolan and T. Callan (eds) *Poverty and policy in Ireland.* Dublin: Gill and Macmillan.

Whelan, C. (1994b) 'Poverty, unemployment and psychological distress', in B. Nolan and T. Callan (eds) *Poverty and policy in Ireland.* Dublin: Gill and Macmillan.

Whelan, C. (1994c) 'Work values', in C. Whelan (ed) *Values and social change in Ireland.* Dublin: Gill and Macmillan.

Whelan, C. (1994d) 'Values and psyschological well-being', in C. T. Whelan (ed) *Values and social change in Ireland.* Dublin: Gill and Macmillan.

Whelan, C.J. (1992) *Stability and change in values and attitudes relevant to women's participation in the labour force and wider role in society: an analysis of the European values study.* Dublin: ESRI.

Whelan, C.J. and Fahey, T. (1994) 'Marriage and the family', in C.T. Whelan (ed) *Values and social change in Ireland.* Dublin: Gill and Macmillan.

Whelan, C.T., Hannan, D.F. and Creighton, S. (1991) *Unemployment, poverty and psychological distress.* Dublin: ESRI.

Whelan, C.T., Breen, R. and Whelan, B.J. (1992) 'Industrialisation, class formation and social mobility in Ireland', in J. Goldthorpe and C.T. Whelan (eds) *The development of industrial society in Ireland.* New York: Oxford University Press.

Whelan, C.T. (ed) (1994) *Values and social change in Ireland*. Dublin: Gill and Macmillan.

Whelan, C., Hannan, D. and Smyth, E. (1996) 'Education in the South'. Paper presented at the British Academy Symposium: *Ireland: North and South*. Nuffield College, Oxford. December.

Whyte, J.H. (1980) *Church and state in modern Ireland 1923-1979* Second edition. Dublin: Gill and Macmillan.

Whitehouse, G. (1992) 'Legislation and labour market gender inequality: an analysis of OECD countries', *Work, Employment and Society* 6,1:65-86.

Wickham, A. (1982) 'Women, industrial transition and training policy in the Republic of Ireland', in M. Kelly, L. O'Dowd and J. Wickham (eds) *Power, conflict and inequality*. Dublin: Turoe Press.

Wickham, J. and Murray, P. (1987) *Women in the Irish electronics industry*. Dublin: EEA.

Wiley, M.M. and Merriman, B. (1996) *Women and health care in Ireland*. Dublin: Oak Tree Press.

Witz, A. (1990) 'Patriarchy and the professions: the gendered politics of occupational closure', *Sociology* 24, 4: 675-690.

Witz, A. (1992a) *Professions and patriarchy*. London: Routledge.

Witz, A. and Savage, M. (1992b) 'Theoretical introduction', in M. Savage and A. Witz (eds) *Gender and bureaucracy*. Oxford: Blackwell/Sociological Review.

Willmott, P. (1987) *Friendship networks and social support*. London: Policy Studies Institute.

Women's Participation Working Group – NYCI (1989) *New options in youth work: seminar on working with young women*. Dublin: NYCI.

Wood, K. as told to him (1993) *The Kilkenny incest case*. Dublin: Poolbeg Press.

Working Party on Childcare Facilities for Working Parents (1983) *Report to the Minister for Labour*. Dublin: Stationary Office.

Working Party on Childcare Facilities for Working Parents (1994) *Report to the Minister for Equality and Law Reform*. Dublin: Stationary Office.

Woolf, N. (1993) *Fighting fire with fire*. London: Chatto and Windus.

Wynne, R., Clarkin, N. and McNieve, A. (1993) *The experience of stress amongst Irish nurses – a survey of Irish Nurses Organization Members*. Dublin: INO.

Y

Young, I. (1981) 'Beyond the unhappy marriage: a critique of dual systems theory', in L. Sargent (ed) *Women and revolution*. London: Pluto Press.

Young, M. and Willmott, P. (1962) *Family and kinship in East London*. Revised edition. Harmondsworth: Pelican.

Index